The Professional Recruiter's Handbook

SECOND EDITION

The Professional Recruiter's Handbook

Delivering excellence in recruitment practice

Jane Newell Brown and Ann Swain

KoganPage

LONDON PHILADELPHIA NEW DELHI

First published in Great Britain and the United States in 2009 by Kogan Page Limited
Second edition 2012
Reprinted 2013, 2014

2nd Floor, 45 Gee Street
London EC1V 3RS
United Kingdom
www.koganpage.com

1518 Walnut Street, Suite 1100
Philadelphia PA 19102
USA

4737/23 Ansari Road
Daryaganj
New Delhi 110002
India

© Jane Newell Brown and Ann Swain, 2009, 2012

The right of Ann Swain and Jane Newell Brown to be identified as the author of this work has been asserted by them in accordance with the Copyright, Designs and Patents Act 1988.

ISBN   978 0 7494 6541 4
E-ISBN   978 0 7494 6542 1

British Library Cataloguing-in-Publication Data

A CIP record for this book is available from the British Library.

Library of Congress Cataloging-in-Publication Data

Brown, Jane Newell.
  The professional recruiter's handbook : delivering excellence in recruitment practice / Jane Newell Brown, Ann Swain. – 2nd ed.
     p. cm.
  Includes bibliographical references and index.
  ISBN 978-0-7494-6541-4 – ISBN 978-0-7494-6542-1   1. Employees–Recruiting.   2. Employment agencies.   3. Business consultants.   I. Swain, Ann, 1960-   II. Title.
  HF5549.5.R44B698 2012
  658.3'111–dc23
                                                                    2012012304

Typeset by Graphicraft Limited, Hong Kong
Print production managed by Jellyfish
Printed and bound by CPI Group (UK) Ltd, Croydon, CR0 4YY

CONTENTS

ACKNOWLEDGEMENTS

Many people have helped in writing this book. Some have supported both the project and us in general and others have offered their views and stories of good recruiting practice, many of whose names appear below.

First, however, thanks must go to our families who have put up with us writing at weekends and through the night around already busy working lives. Special thanks to Jane's husband Andrew for creating, painstakingly, all the tables and figures in the book and to Ed for giving his mum the 'time off' to get the book done, to Ann's husband Agapios for his full support and regular foot rubs and their daughters, Genevieve, Melpo, Eloise, Constance, Michaela, Ariana and Olympia for giving her the space and time to write in a pretty busy household!

Second there are those who contributed indirectly through having been either an inspiration to work for, or with, over a lifetime in the industry and finally all those generous enough to give up their time and share their stories with us, not forgetting our publishers and their support.

Specific thanks go to:

Angela Masters; Ann Jamieson; Anita Baglee; Alex Snelling; Becky Gleyne; Bill Bottriell; Brian Wilkinson; Chris Hermannsen; Chris Sale; Christian Mansfield-Osbourne; Dan Hyde; Dan McGuire; Danielle Asano; Dave Pye; David Hay; David Head; David Higgins; David Hurst; David Mason; David Treacher; Debbie Loveridge; Dee Dee Doke; Denise Morris; the late Dennis Linscott; Diane Martyn; Dom Martinez; Dorian Webb; Doug Woodward; Eddie Austin; Fiona Lander; Francesca Peters; Gavin Gaskin; Godfrey Morrell; Ian Pearson; Jack Gratton; James Caan; Jerry Wright; Jon Irvine; Jonathan Barber; Jonathan Beavis; John Bissell; Kate Bleasdale; Keith Evans; Keith Robinson; Laurence Simons; Louise Triance; Lucy Simpson; Marilyn Davidson; Mark Bull; Martin Rush; Matt Hobson; Matthew Eames; Michael Hollobon; Miles Hunt; Mohamed Ali; Neil Clements; Niki Shu; Paul Hanikene; Penny Davis; Peter Bennett; Peter Flaherty; the late Peter Lloyd; Peter Tanner; Rachel Riddington; Radu Manulescu; Raymond Pennie; Richard Fisher; Richard Herring; Rick Bacon; Romney Rawes; Russell Clements; Sally Scutt; Samantha Hurley; Shirley Pruden; the late Stephen Hill; Steve Crabb; Steve Walker; Sue Evans; Tara Ricks; Tracy Ashton; Tony Reeves; Tracey Richardson; Val Abl; Vicky Rogers; Warwick Bergin; Zena Everett.

ACRONYMS

AESC	Association of Executive Search Consultants
APSCo	Association of Professional Staffing Companies
ASA	American Staffing Association
Ciett	International Confederation of Employment Agencies
CIPD	Chartered Institute of Personnel and Development
CRM	customer relationship management
CSR	corporate social responsibility
CV	curriculum vitae
HRO	Human Resource outsourcing
ITT	invitation to tender
KPI	key performance indicator
KSP	key selling point
MSC	managed service company
MSP	managed service provider
MV	master vendor
NHS	National Health Service
PDP	personal development plan
PESTLEC	Political, Economic, Sociological, Technological, Legal, Environmental, Cultural
PSL	preferred supplier list
REC	Recruitment and Employment Confederation
REQ candidate	one who matches requirements from an existing client (cf SPEQ)
RPO	recruitment process outsourcing
SLA	service level agreement
SMART(ER)	Specific, Measurable, Agreed, Realistic, Time Bound (Enjoyable, Recorded)
SPEQ candidate	likely to be attractive to clients, but without a specific requested role (cf REQ)
SWOT	Strengths, Weaknesses, Opportunities, Threats
TAWD	Temporary Agency Workers Directive
USP	unique selling point

Introduction

Real success is finding your lifework in the work that you love. DAVID McCULLOUGH, US BIOGRAPHER AND HISTORIAN

This is a book for professional recruiters. Recruiters who love the job they do. Recruiters may get frustrated with their job, stressed by it, need a break from it at times, but ultimately are fascinated and driven by it and its rewards and want to keep on getting better and learning more from it.

Since the first edition of this book was published recruitment has undergone enormous change; perhaps more change has taken place in the last five-plus years than took place in the preceding 25. This has been coupled with a shift in the economic power bases in the global economy, the rise of emerging markets and the reach for talent becoming more global.

Changes in recruitment have therefore taken several forms but perhaps one of the most notable is the continued growth of internal recruitment expertise residing within organizations, rather than being supplied in externally. This is true both of UK markets especially but also in emerging markets. The shift has enabled organizations to drive down some costs of recruitment, which has been a benefit in turbulent economic times – although the need for strong specialist suppliers into those teams is unlikely ever to disappear, as no internal recruiter will have the expertise to cover all business-critical hires in their organization. The continued rise of the RPO (Recruitment Process Outsourcing) and MSP (Managed Service Provider) business models are also prevalent although it seemingly proves difficult to get the service right as the same number of agreements are procured each year as they are returned to an in-house model.

The other dramatic change has been the rise in use of social networking, which was in its infancy when the first edition of this book was written. It is now gaining pace as a key strategy in the attraction of top talent. Relatively speaking it is still in its infancy as whilst there is an awareness of how it might help in engaging future employees it's currently being used by most at a very basic level. Few businesses have developed strategies around it as a tool in their attraction plans and herein lies a real opportunity. Despite the backdrop of global economic challenges this top talent still remains an elusive animal.

Fifteen years ago McKinsey conducted a survey throughout 56 companies in the US and identified 'The War for Talent'. In 2000 this was updated and it was found that, despite the economic slowdowns, the war for talent was simply intensifying.

The success of any organization in a knowledge-based economy is increasingly dependent upon the quality of the people they are able to attract, recruit and retain. Yet, it is still only recently that the crucial role the recruiting industry plays in enabling businesses to secure this important competitive advantage is becoming recognized and the management of talent being seen as an important professional discipline.

'Any organization that does not take recruitment seriously is cutting its own throat. It must be a top priority for any business,' says Steve Crabb, ex-Managing Editor of *Personnel Today* magazine and now an independent consultant. Some organizations are beginning to develop recruitment strategies and the rise of the role of Talent Directors in major organizations shows that businesses are beginning to take the business of hiring and retaining top talent seriously. This is great news both for organizations and professional recruiters.

For many recruiters in-house or in external recruitment consultancies, there is still little practical help available on how to do a great job. Many recruiting organizations provide initial training on the recruitment process but there is rarely anything more detailed to refer to after the training event. Tips and advice can be picked up from more experienced consultants 'on the job' but there has been to date no reference handbook, no guide and no structured 'how-to' book available. Furthermore, there has been no resource for managers to use with recruiters, new or experienced, to help them support a guided learning process of continued professional development.

This book provides practical guidance, best practice and the underpinning theory of best-practice recruitment. Each chapter is packed with case studies from a top recruiter or human resource professional in the recruitment industry so you can learn what works for both recruiters and their clients. Alongside both of these are suggested tasks you complete to support your own learning as you work your way through the book. You'll learn how to attract and approach new candidates and clients, along with how to manage the recruitment process from start to finish to ensure success.

As recruitment remains a key tool for a business to achieve its corporate objectives, recruiters must continue to raise their game, delivering new and innovative solutions, but also just doing their job really well and professionally and achieving the results needed for their clients.

Who is this book for?

Potential recruiters interested in entering the industry or existing recruiters working in-house, as corporate recruiters, in a recruitment agency, a search consultancy or an MSP or RPO. One of the objectives of this book is to bring the debate amongst professional recruiters, regardless of role, closer together to continue to develop and improve this great industry.

Rarely do internal and external recruiters see each other as symbiotic, although in fact the reverse is true. The authors hope that this book can show that both can learn from each other and help each other as, ultimately, both have the same aim: to recruit great people for their organizations and clients.

Recruitment managers can use the book to help their new recruits develop and understand the core skills to make them successful; recruitment trainers may want to use it to support their training and learning programmes; potential industry entrants may want to read it to give them a flavour of their possible new role; and we'd like to think that all new recruits to the profession would be given a copy as a reference book to become well-thumbed and dog-eared on their desk as they become more and more successful in this exciting industry, which can have its highs and lows but is never, ever dull!

How to use this book

The book has not been written for everyone to read from cover to cover as you might a novel – although it is also perfectly possible to read it that way. Its three parts each have a different purpose. The first part is an introduction into the profession. It puts the industry in context as well as looking at some future trends. This part deals with the ethical and legal aspects of the recruitment industry and, whilst it is not a guide to staying on the right side of the law, it does cover the legislation impacting the industry and considers the ethics that surrounds it.

The second part will be of interest if you are already in the industry and want to improve your strategic approach to business delivery, consider how to expand your market or improve the way you work with your clients. It sets the scene for success, considering what type of recruiter you are, offering two possibilities and some thoughts as to how to make the most of your strengths. It outlines a new model of the recruitment process and uses a classic marketing-led approach to recruitment consultancy as a service. Working through the exercises in this chapter will enable you to take a strategic review of where you are in your recruitment business, where you want to be, and how to get there. Recruiters thinking of starting their own business, or business owners interested in developing their existing or new teams will also find this section valuable.

Part Three is an intensely practical 'how-to' section, detailing everything from how to win a tender to how to open a headhunting call, from how to interview to how to take and qualify a job brief. This is the section you'll have open at your desk when you make a call, the one you'll turn to when you have to prepare a pitch and the one that you can either read straight through or dip into when you need it. It looks in detail at each of the four aspects of the recruitment process as we have defined it. We have chosen not to go into great detail on basic telesales technique, which is covered in so many general sales books.

This book takes the view that a good recruiter is always looking ahead to the next economic cycle and the way the market shifts, in order to deliver the best possible service to their candidates and clients and achieve the best possible results for themselves. If you follow the advice and guidance in this book and overlay it with your own talents and personality, focusing on your strengths, a career in recruitment offers much.

PART ONE
The recruitment industry

The development of the recruitment industry

01

The Americans may claim that they invented the recruitment industry. After extensive research, however, we believe that the UK founded the earliest recruitment consultancy.

The Industrial Revolution during the late 18th and early 19th centuries saw major changes in the need to recruit relatively large numbers of employees to work in mechanized agriculture, manufacturing and transportation. The manual labour-based economy of Great Britain began to be replaced by one dominated by industry and machine-based manufacture. Over a period of around 70 years the effects spread across Western Europe and then to North America. With this demand for skilled employees a 'gang master' approach of recruitment provision was emerging. As the British economy grew, with it came the emergence of a 'middle class' and, with childhood mortality dropping dramatically, a desire for education.

In 1873 Mr John Gabbitas and his business partner Mr Thring formed Gabbitas, the first recorded recruitment company. Launched to provide teaching staff, and still thriving today as Gabbitas Educational Consultants, it included Evelyn Waugh, W H Auden, H G Wells, Sir Edward Elgar and Sir John Betjeman amongst its candidates. Other recruitment companies followed, providing domestic as well as factory workers, with Alfred Marks forming his iconic recruitment brand in 1919. Europe was slow to follow suit but the American staffing sector pushed ahead, with Fred Winslow opening his Engineering Agency in 1893 and Katharine Felton responding to the construction industry's problems in staffing building projects after the San Francisco earthquake in 1906. The end of the Second World War provided an opportunity for entrepreneurs to seek out the limited number of highly skilled, mainly male, individuals and match them with the huge demand for growth in both infrastructure and, of course, business. An industry was launched.

FIGURE 1.1 Number of private employment agencies

Greece	9
Macedonia	27
Slovenia	59
Italy	85
Argentina	92
Romania	129
Belgium	140
Chile	179
Czech Republic	215
Portugal	265
Turkey	283
Slovakia	355
Spain*	363
Norway	400
Finland	450
Mexico	500
Sweden	500
Colombia	610
Hungary	667
Peru	722
Canada	945
Poland	1,086
Austria	1,200
France	1,200
Denmark	1,347
South Korea	1,419
Brazil	1,611
South Africa	3,000
Australia	3,500
Netherlands	3,640
USA	6,000
Germany	9,078
UK	11,500
Japan	20,000

*figures for 2008; **ILO-Private employment agencies, temporary agency workers and their contribution to the labour market | 2009
SOURCE Ciett, 2011 report

The value of the recruitment industry

The global recruitment market is huge. In their 2011 report Ciett suggest that there are around 72,000 private recruitment companies, 169,000 individual branches employing 741,000 internal staff worldwide (see Figure 1.1). In 2009 the total global annual sales of the top 10 companies equated to 29 per cent of the world market (see Figure 1.2).

FIGURE 1.2 Top 10 staffing companies in billions of $

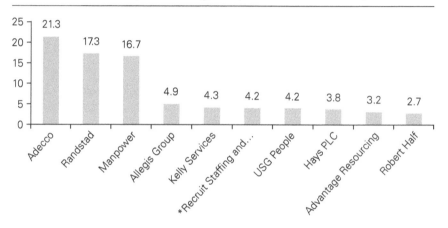

SOURCE Staffing Industry Analysts 2009 – www.staffingindustry.com
*Consolidated figures for Recruit Staffing and Staff Service

In 2009 Ciett found that there were 9 million full-time (or equivalent) temporary agency workers – a rise of over 3.8 million since 1999. Figures 1.3 and 1.4 respectively show the sales revenue splits per country and penetration rates outside Europe (2009) for agency work, while Figure 1.5 shows the penetration rates for agency work in Europe in 2009.

Although the recessionary period has slowed the uptake of temporary workers in many countries, relaxing of restrictive legislation in many has created the platform for growth. And indeed, why not?

- Temporary agency work broadens the range of work solutions available to candidates, facilitating transitions in the labour market. It creates opportunities for workers to match lifestyle changes or indeed, personal constraints.
- The use of temporary agency work has been shown to contribute to reducing unemployment by creating a stepping stone to the labour market. According to Ciett 2010, 3 per cent of temporary workers registered as 'unemployed' before embarking on their temporary role compared to 15 per cent, 12 months afterwards.

FIGURE 1.3   Agency work sales revenues split per country

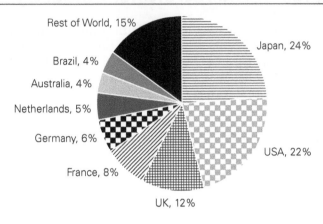

SOURCE Ciett national

FIGURE 1.4   Agency work penetration rates outside Europe in 2009*

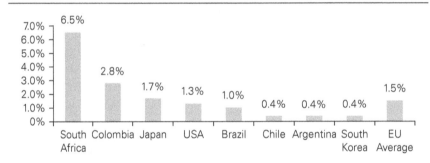

*Defined as the number of full-time equivalents – as supplied by Ciett National Federations – divided by the total active working populations – as published by the ILO
SOURCE Ciett, 2011 report

- Higher temporary worker penetration has shown to reduce the level of undeclared (and therefore untaxed) work within a country.
- Recruitment firms often provide training to their temporary workers, which add to the work experience gained and upgrades the national skill set.
- Recruitment companies have been shown to pursue a diversity agenda ahead of the government. When employers have a narrow view of their ideal candidate, it has been recruiters that have widened the person specification beyond age, creed or gender, changing the client's perspective of 'square pegs' and 'round holes'. Temporary

FIGURE 1.5 Agency work penetration rates in Europe in 2009*

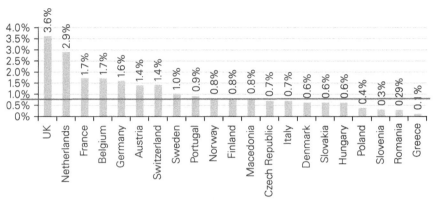

*Defined as the number of full-time eqivalents – as supplied by Ciett National Federations – divided by the total active working population – as published by the ILO
SOURCE Ciett, 2011 report
European average penetration rate: 1.5%

agency work also provides an opportunity to enter the labour market for potentially vulnerable groups, eg migrant workers, female returners or disabled candidates.

- Unions often worry that temporary work is a substitute for permanent job creation and therefore have a negative view of the concept. Yet research has shown (continual Research Capitation) that 80 per cent would not have existed if no agency solution were available.

- Generally temporary roles are created to meet peaks in demand or to fill in for absent permanent employees.

- Ciett found that the average profile of a temporary agency worker is:
  - less than 30 years old (but ageing);
  - working within service, manufacturing or public sector;
  - motivated to temporary agency work by gaining work experience, to find a job or flexibility;
  - satisfied with their position;
  - do not want a permanent job.

- Recruiters have an extensive knowledge of local labour markets of special niche sectors.

- They advise on salaries, career paths or availability.

- They have access to extensive pools of both available workers and those passive candidates that do not apply to advertisements on job boards, are not turning up at job fairs and are not looking at corporate websites.

- They match the requirements of the client company to the needs of an individual and manage both expectations on each side of the recruitment process from start to completion.
- Recruiters select 'the one' from the thousands available and ensure that 'the one' recognizes the benefits of the opportunity.

The European recruitment market

Apart from the worldwide search companies, the majority of non-UK European recruitment businesses specialize in providing flexible workers. Around 2 per cent of the European workforce is temporary, with fairly mature markets found in Belgium, France, the Netherlands and, of course, the United Kingdom. Germany, Spain and Italy are consolidating and, with recent entrants into the EU, new geographical markets are emerging. As it did within the United Kingdom, the European market is developing from providing low-skilled, mainly young males towards office-based, mainly young and female staff. It is easy to predict that the market will evolve further up the value chain over time, as the UK market has.

Highly restrictive legislation has stunted the market growth potential of some countries, and it is certainly fair to suggest that there is a level of distrust about the motivation for organizations to utilize flexible workers; indeed, there is a view that everyone would really rather be in a secure permanent job. The recruitment industry is increasingly becoming recognized as a legitimate player in the flexibility/security debate ('flexicurity' is a hot topic in Brussels) and there is an overall trend for labour market deregulation. However there are still too many misconceptions about our industry, with severe image problems particularly in the Southern European countries.

The UK recruitment industry

The UK recruitment sector has a combined turnover of around £27 billion. The largest 100 UK businesses in the market turn over around £16 billion. Providing an exact figure of the number of UK recruitment companies is difficult, due to lack of licensing, low barriers to entry and substantial labour movement, especially amongst single-operator businesses. However evidence suggests that there are around 10,500 recruitment businesses in the UK. There are approximately 120,500 recruitment industry professionals with over 8,100 owners and senior directors working in around 19,000 offices. Approximately 1.6 million temporary workers are on assignment each day, with over 750,000 candidates being placed in permanent jobs by recruitment consultants, each year (Recruitment International, 2011).

The structure of the industry

As with any service-driven market, the UK recruitment industry has developed a structure around the business opportunities. Figure 1.6 gives an overview of the UK workforce and the types of recruitment business that supplies to each area, from both a permanent and a temporary perspective.

FIGURE 1.6 Data on the UK recruitment industry

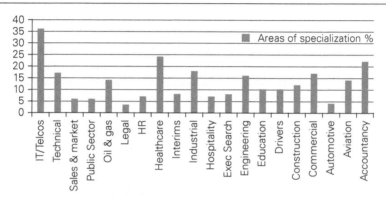

SOURCE Recruitment International 2011

Executive-level recruitment

Senior executives and company directors are a very small but important percentage of the workforce. There is often a shortage of good candidates at this level and as the role of such people within any business is key to its success, organizations do resort to recruiting individuals from direct competitors or 'like' companies. Although these high-calibre candidates may have valuable experience they are likely to be content in their current roles and therefore potentially difficult to find, interest, and motivate toward a new challenge, especially on terms acceptable to the potential employer. Executive search practices provide senior-level expertise, often on a global basis, for employers to acquire such high-level talent. Executive search practitioners specialize in recruiting the most senior individuals across a full range of private and public sector environments; search is the most proactive form of recruitment.

A flexible solution at this level is provided by 'interim' executives, placed on relatively medium-term assignments by interim management companies. A smaller or medium-sized business might need, for instance, to develop a detailed long-term marketing strategy, but then need a more junior and therefore more affordable marketing person to put the strategy into practice. An interim executive can be engaged for six months to create the strategy and the implementation can be undertaken by a permanent manager. Interim management is different from using external management consultants in that the interim executive is part of the team and assumes the responsibilities for delivery of a well-specified project. Interim management companies often specialize in niche sectors such as the public sector, marketing and finance. They may be joined to an executive search practice, but rarely operate on such a global basis as the executive search companies.

Middle to senior management

Middle to senior managers are generally recruited on a permanent basis rather than as flexible workers. The relationships with staff and the company-specific knowledge required to perform senior roles lend themselves toward long-term, internal employees. Historically, the method used to recruit these individuals was advertised selection. This is where a selection-based recruitment company, usually with a high profile in *The Sunday Times, Telegraph* or some more industry specific journal, such as *Computer Weekly* or *Accountancy Age*, would be retained to design, write and place an advertisement. Responses would be received, acknowledged and assessed by the recruitment company and a shortlist created. Interviews and sometimes assessment centres would be undertaken on behalf of the client, who would then be presented with three or four pre-screened candidates for second interview.

With the advent of online advertising this form of recruitment has diminished substantially although there is talk of a renaissance using the World Wide Web as an advertising medium, replacing paper-based journals.

Knowledge-based specialist and professional staff

Recruitment businesses in this area were quite generalist in nature until the salary levels of knowledge-based specialists in fields such as engineering, banking and IT, and the professions such as lawyers, doctors and teachers, along with roles such as marketing, finance and sales matched and overtook management ones. Specialist recruitment consultancies dominate this space, with the high-street chains often acquiring smaller niche players to get a 'foot in the door' of a new market.

Contractors take up the flexible-working aspect of the knowledge-based specialist market. They often have their own limited company or work through an umbrella company, maintaining a 'professional' distance from the end client and enabling taxation requirements to be managed. Contract recruitment businesses have shown huge growth over the past 10 years as more client organizations use a strategic approach to staffing. Bringing in specialist knowledge or skill sets on an 'as and when' basis creates superb staffing flexibility to cover peaks and troughs or development prospects and, although contractor rates are often twice that of a permanent individual, can be a very cost-effective option for the company.

'Workers'

This sector covers most general office workers, as well as more junior candidates in the professions such as nursing and healthcare workers, higher-end catering professionals, salespeople and so on. These individuals are provided to potential employers on either a permanent or temporary basis by a mix of multi-branch recruitment businesses, often with niche divisions or smaller specialist recruitment companies, sometimes based around a clear geographical hub. Most of these companies provide a mix of permanent and temporary candidates, either with individual recruitment consultants covering all types of labour requirements for their clients or, in larger companies, with separate departments specializing in either temporary or permanent.

Unskilled labour

Generally the least well-paid end of the workforce is that of the unskilled worker. Here we can include entry-level jobs in a range of areas such as kitchen and waiting staff, care workers, retail staff, construction labourers, farm hands or fruit pickers and sanitation staff. Because of the potential seasonal nature of some work and the general lack of transferable knowledge needed, large numbers of temps have often been used. When more permanent members of staff are required the employer will often advertise directly to attract large numbers of available labour. The temp side of this sector is covered by the high-street agencies, while gang masters tend to recruit for and provide labour to agricultural organizations; specialist event recruiters are emerging who provide staffing for major events.

See Figure 1.7 for an illustration of the breakdown of the labour market.

A career in recruitment

Choosing a career in recruitment offers a range of superb career development opportunities. Entering the industry can be achieved in a variety of ways by a wide range of people and success is directly related to your core competences. Entry requirements can be low; you can start in the sector from a background in a specialist market sector (eg as an engineer) or from human resources or sales, or indeed straight from academia.

Full training is generally provided by your employer. Obviously some companies will provide more training than others, but it is universally accepted that the industry must develop the potential of 'right stuff' recruiters.

Success is entirely in your own hands. Very few careers provide the level of self-determination that recruitment has to offer. The choices that you make, how many hours you put in, how many calls you make and to what quality, how organized you are, all have a direct impact on your success and immediate earning potential.

FIGURE 1.7   Labour market breakdown

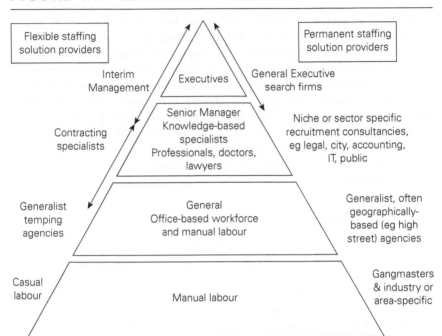

In the recruitment industry we have the opportunity to affect the careers, and therefore, the lives of individuals, in an amazingly positive way. It is not uncommon to receive thank you notes or even gifts from grateful candidates!

As a quality recruiter you will gain unique access to your client base, which often provides you with a clear insight into corporate or public sector culture and even business methodologies, which can be a rewarding aspect for people interested in organizational development.

Industry suppliers

Service providers who can offer both flexible and permanent staffing resources can provide maybe three or four staffing solutions to one vacancy. They may offer an immediate short-term temp whilst they recruit a longer-term interim candidate followed by a longer-term more permanent hire, for whom they may also offer a comprehensive assessment service.

Flexible staffing

As discussed earlier the senior end of this sector is the interim staffing market, providing executive-level through to mid-range candidates. Interim candidates will either fill a gap left by short to mid-term absence through sickness or maternity leave perhaps, or a gap during a re-structure or whilst conducting a search for a permanent hire. In the middle of the market this can be a contractor service, the bulk of which is serviced by the IT and financial services sectors, followed by low to mid-range roles serviced by the temp markets. Below this is the casual labour market, which may vary from an organization with a large number of students on its books to service a large catering event, to the construction trade. All of these sectors make up the flexible workforce in any country. Flexible working is becoming more and more a question of choice as flexible workers are often chosen for their interim career experiences of turn-around, and workers themselves are choosing a better work–life balance rather than a permanent nine-to-five job, perhaps working hard for six months then travelling for three.

All part-time workers are now protected by developments in law ensuring they receive the same employment rights and protection as comparable permanent and full-time employees. Recruitment consultancies often operate as employers with their temporary and contractor workforces, ensuring their clients do not need to worry about this aspect of employment and so adding further value as a supplier. Part of the casual labour market is now governed by the GLA (Gangmaster Licensing Authority), which was set up to curb the exploitation of workers in the agriculture, horticulture, shellfish gathering and associated processing and packaging industries.

Permanent staffing solutions

The permanent sector is made up of specialist and generalist providers. As the industry has evolved, suppliers have developed a core competence from senior candidates to localized resource provision. At the top end there are the top executive search firms, all of whom operate across a range of sectors globally in order to ensure a business that is immune to sector recession, but also to offer a wide set of expertise in moving candidates from sector to sector at 'C' level and above. Many search providers are now offering an interim service to complement their full search service. Attempts to offer a wider range of assessment and coaching (executive on-boarding [settling-in period] and then ongoing) services have met with mixed success in this sector. In the next tier down providers are niche or sector specific, offering mid-range executives across a specialist sector, backed up with excellent knowledge and expertise in their chosen field. Sectors such as the City, law, accountancy, IT, HR and marketing are represented in this way. Interestingly only 10 per cent of the UK population earn more than £46,000 (BBC, 2008) so the market for senior sector-specific staff is relatively small but rewarding. At the bottom of this sector, and where most of the candidates are (following the pyramid in Figure 1.7), is the generalist sector, often the high-street providers or local agencies providing local firms with local staff on both a temporary or permanent basis.

The choice of provider, then, is based on a relationship between volume and fees (the lower the salary as a rule the lower the fee for recruiting) and specialization and sector knowledge.

Recruitment procurement

As recruitment becomes more important to organizations, and takes up more time, businesses are often taking advantage of the option to outsource all of their staffing provision to a specialist RPO (recruitment process outsourcing) provider.

An MSC (managed service company) or RPO aims to outsource the responsibility of the full recruitment process from one client. This puts the administrative responsibility firmly in the lap of the MSC and it is important, for the success of the relationship, that this is seen as a partnership rather than a pure supplier relationship on both sides. Typically the MSC will have recruiters on site and the client and contracts will be negotiated for three or more years with a six-month option to terminate. Some MSCs will be vendor neutral and others will be the RPO arm of a larger recruitment consultancy.

If one consultancy supplier has been very successful supplying staff across the organization, that business may consider a master vendor (MV) arrangement where the agency contracts to supply the vast majority of the staff at some cost benefit to the business, and fill the rest of the role through some specialist arrangement it makes itself with other suppliers. This leaves the administrative burden with the business and can leave it vulnerable if the MV cannot deliver, as it will have severed all other relationships. However it will dramatically reduce the amount of contacts the business has to deal with, and if it predominantly recruits a particular type of individual this can be a good choice.

Many organizations will run recruitment in-house and develop a PSL (preferred supplier list) to support the recruitment process. PSLs are usually a collection of agencies, often through a tiered or niche system, which are the sole suppliers of staffing into that organization or MSC. PSLs are usually created by a tender process and reviewed on an annual basis; selecting such an arrangement involves checking that a consultancy can supply the required staff, has ethics and values congruent with the organization, and has the right financial backing to enable them to deliver.

Temporary labour can be procured via e-auctions as it can be seen as a more commoditized service and therefore comparable to buying the supply of stationery or cars, for example. However, for organizations who place some value on the quality of their workforce, by necessity the e-auction route means that recruiters will be paring margins to the bone resulting in an inevitable reduction in service, often not to generate greater profit but so that the operation may be commercially viable. The added value that a recruiter offers may then be reduced, so whilst e-auctioning is a method of securing labour supply it rarely attracts bidding from quality service providers.

Industry governance

Recruitment itself is becoming increasingly constrained by legal developments. Here we can also include customs, ethics, norms and best practice. Figure 1.8 shows a timeline of legal developments that affect the recruitment industry. This should not be treated as an exhaustive list, but rather as a guideline to show the increased development of law affecting the industry – although others not shown here may also have considerable impacts.

Here we can also look briefly at how each of these Acts may affect the industry (see also Figure 1.8).

Legislation affecting the recruitment sector

This list contains details of most of the legislation directly affecting this sector. Naturally, nearly all legislation has some effect or other on any company and so this is not, and could not be, an exhaustive list.

1 *Employment Agencies Act 1973.* The key matter dealt with in this Act is the general prohibition (to which there are a few exceptions) on charging work seekers a fee for finding them work.

2 *Conduct of Employment Agencies and Employment Business Regulations 2003.* These 'Conduct Regulations' are notoriously complex. Key provisions include Regulation 10, which limits the ability of employment businesses to charge hirers 'temp to perm' and 'temp to temp' fees.

3 *Transfer of Undertakings (Protection of Employment) Regulations 2006* ('TUPE'). The TUPE regulations preserve employees' terms and conditions when a business or undertaking, or part of one (including an appointment as preferred supplier), is transferred to a new employer.

4 *Asylum and Immigration Act 1996 and Immigration Act 1971.* Recruiters must obviously not employ illegal workers themselves. Many recruiters are also expected to check the status of temps and contractors. Facilitating illegal working is a serious criminal offence.

5 *Working Time Regulations 1998.* These regulate the organization of working time, oblige employers to give temps paid holiday and also contain measures relating to the employment of children and young persons, affecting recruiters' employment of their own employees and their supply of agency workers to clients.

6 *Data Protection Act 1998.* This Act is intended to ensure that personal information is handled properly. The Act gives individuals

FIGURE 1.8   Timeline of legal developments affecting the recruitment industry

2010	Equality Act 2010
	Bribery Act 2010
	Agency Workers Regulations 2010
2008	Pensions Act 2008
	Proposed pension bill
	Proposed temporary agency workers directive
	Corporate manslaughter and corporate homicide act
2007	Finance act 'managed services companies'
	Money laundering regulations
2006	Employment equality (age) regulations
	Transfer of undertakings (protection of employment) regulations 'TUPE'
2003	Employment equality (sexual orientation) regulations
	Conduct of employment agencies and employment business regulations
	Employment equality (religion or belief) regulations
	Income Tax (earnings and pensions) Act 2003
2002	The fixed-term Employees (Prevention of Less Favourable Treatment) Regulations 2002
2000	
1999	National minimum wage regulations
	Sex discrimination (gender reassignment) regulations
	Contracts (rights of third parties) act
1998	Competition Act 1998
	Data protection act
	Working time regulations
1995	Disability discrimination act
1990	
1980	
1976	Race relations act
1975	Sex discrimination act
1973	Employment agencies act
1971	Asylum and immigration act
1970	Equal pay act

the right to know what information is held about them and imposes criminal penalties on recruiters who use the information unlawfully.

7 *National Minimum Wage Regulations 1999.* These Regulations are designed to provide workers with minimum levels of pay, setting hourly rates below which pay must not be allowed to fall. Breach can be a criminal offence.

8 *Contracts (Rights of Third Parties) Act 1999.* This Act enables a person not party to a contract (a 'third party') to (in his or her own right) enforce a term of the contract under certain circumstances. This could have effect where, for example, pursuant to a contract between an agency and an end user, a worker is provided by the agency to the end user.

9 *Income Tax (Earnings and Pensions) Act 2003* (s44–47 – agency tax provisions) (formerly ICTA 1988 s34). Essentially the Act enables HMRC to collect the equivalent of PAYE and NIC from employment businesses in respect of workers who would not otherwise be 'employees' under the PAYE regime.

10 *Income Tax (Earnings and Pensions) Act 2003* ('IR35' – now part of ITEPA ss48–61). This 'IR35' legislation was designed to eliminate avoidance of income tax and National Insurance Contributions (NICs) through the use by contractors of intermediaries, such as personal service companies or partnerships, to avoid liability under the PAYE regime or ss44–47 ITEPA.

11 *Finance Act 2007 SCHEDULE 3 'Managed Service Companies'* (ss61A–I ITEPA). The legislation deems all payments received by a worker working through an MSC to be employment income. This means PAYE and, Class 1 National Insurance Contributions must be applied to all income received by individuals in MSCs for the services provided via the MSC. Most staffing companies are now familiar with the new regime and should have risk mitigation procedures in place with checklists and other measures. HMRC's latest guidelines confirm this.

12 *Money Laundering Regulations 2007.* These regulations impose on certain recruiters a strict obligation to carry out checks of their clients and adopt other procedures in order to help combat the criminal activity of money laundering.

13 *Criminal Records Bureau Regime.* Recruiters supplying workers to work with vulnerable people are expected to check with the Criminal Records Bureau (CRB) that they are suitable and do not have relevant criminal records.

14 *Proposed Pensions Bill 2008.* This bill is intended to allow moderate-to-low earners to save more for retirement. Providers of

agency workers will be required to make minimum contributions. There may be exceptions.

15 *Equality Legislation* [1970–2007]. There are several pieces of equality legislation that affect the employment and recruitment sector. This is not an exhaustive list and their application is self-explanatory.

   – Disability Discrimination Act 1995;
   – Employment Equality (Age) Regulation 2006;
   – Employment Equality (Religion or Belief) Regulation 2003;
   – The Employment Equality (Sex Discrimination) Regulations 2005;
   – Employment Equality (Sexual Orientation) Regulation 2003;
   – Equal Pay Act 1970 (Amended);
   – Equality Act 2006, Race Relations Act 1976;
   – Sex Discrimination Act 1975;
   – The Sex Discrimination (Gender Reassignment) Regulations 1999.

16 *Corporate Manslaughter and Corporate Homicide Act.* Came into force in April 2008 and imposes on staffing companies an obligation to take certain steps to ensure that their employees and workers supplied by them are not in danger of death or serious injury.

17 *Special VAT arrangements affecting staffing 1995–2004.* There are a number of ways in which staffing companies can legitimately supply temps to end users without charging VAT on the full cost of supply. The latest HMRC guidance on this is set out in HMRC Business Brief 10/04 of 2004.

18 *Equality Act 2010.* The purpose of this legislation was to replace the various anti-discrimination laws previously in place with one act, which provided a simpler and more consistent approach. The act strengthens some areas of discrimination allowing for direct, and indirect discrimination, victimization and harassment, and now provides for nine protected characteristics.

19 *Agency Workers Regulations 2010 ('AWR').* The aim of the AWR is to give agency workers the same basic working and employment conditions they would have received if they were recruited directly by the end-user client. The comparison may be made to standard contractual documentation or to the relevant terms provided to a comparable permanent employee. The law requires that an agency worker complete a 12-week qualifying period in the same role with the same client before being entitled to these equal treatment rights. From day one of an assignment an agency worker will also be

entitled to access to the end-user client's collective facilities and internal vacancy information.

20 *Competition Act 1998.* This act came into force in 2000, it prohibits any behaviour aimed at limiting, preventing, or distorting trade in the UK, including anti-competitive agreements/arrangements and cartels. It also prohibits any abuse of a dominant market position to restrict trade.

21 *Bribery Act 2010.* The act came into force in July 2011. The act makes it an offence to actively or passively bribe another person or a foreign public official and it also introduces an offence which can be committed by commercial organizations that fail to put in place procedures to stop persons associated with them from committing acts of bribery on their behalf.

22 *Pensions Act 2008.* This encompasses significant work-based pensions reforms. Dependent upon the size of the business, the implementation of these reforms will be staggered over four years starting in October 2012. All eligible jobholders must be automatically enrolled into a qualifying pension scheme, which requires a contribution from the employer. Eligible jobholders will include all employees and agency workers aged over 22 and earning more than £7,475 per annum in 2011/12. Limited Company contractors may be outside of scope due to the lack of personal service contract.

23 *The Fixed-term Employees (Prevention of Less Favourable Treatment) Regulations 2002.* This legislation provides that fixed-term employees must be treated the same as permanent employees in relation to pay and conditions, benefits, pensions, and opportunities to apply for permanent roles with the client.

24 *Special VAT arrangements affecting staffing.* HMRC withdrew the VAT staff hire concession from April 2009, which allowed companies to exclude the wages element of their supplies and charge VAT on the margin element of the supply only. This withdrawal was challenged by a tax tribunal decision in April 2011, which HMRC decided not to appeal. This does not, however, leave a clear and open path for recruitment firms to stop charging VAT on the whole supply.

25 *Income Tax (Earnings and Pensions) Act 2003 ('IR35' – now part of ITEPA ss48–61).* An update on what this clause currently says: The 2011 budget made it clear that IR35 would not be repealed or changed, however, HMRC were tasked with setting up an IR35 Forum to review and improve IR35 administration.

(Information provided by Kevin Barrow, Partner at Osborne Clarke and Samantha Hurley APSCo.)

Agency Workers Regulations 2010

The Agency Workers Regulations 2010 ('AWR') came into force on 1st October 2011, a fact that no one in the recruitment industry could have missed completely unless they were locked in a cupboard or out of the country in the preceding year.

The AWR has been the most anticipated piece of legislation to affect the recruitment industry. It originated out of Europe and was much debated and campaigned for and against for ten years from inception of the original European directive until its final enactment in the UK. Leading business and recruitment industry bodies lobbied for the Regulations not to be applied to all levels and sectors of recruitment, but like many other laws pertinent to our industry the final outcome was a one-size-fits-all set of Regulations.

The Agency Workers Directive – the EU directive from which the AWR is derived came about because the rest of Europe has a fundamentally different approach to the UK when it comes to temporary recruitment. In most European countries using temporary staff is seen as a vehicle for clients to avoid giving staff employment rights. In the UK, however, we have a very different situation: we have a thriving flexible recruitment industry where workers often make the life choice to become temporary workers, and clients see this flexible resource as a necessary tool to enhancing growth.

Clearly there are sectors of industry in which temporary workers are not always treated appropriately, and there obviously is a need for some regulation regarding potentially vulnerable workers. However, unfortunately the AWR also applies to highly paid business consultants who are not, in any sense of the word, vulnerable.

The AWR broadly provides three new sets of rights to agency workers: day one rights, equal treatment rights, and pregnancy and maternity rights.

The AWR provides that from the first day of an assignment an agency worker is entitled to access to the collective facilities provided at a client's site, and access to information about any relevant internal vacancies of the client.

The AWR provides that the same basic working and employment conditions are applied to an agency worker as if they had been directly engaged by the client. In other words, they are entitled to treatment equal to their permanent comparable workers. These equal treatment rights apply after an agency worker has worked in the same role for the same client for 12 weeks – known as the qualifying period.

The AWR provides certain enhanced rights for agency workers who are pregnant or new mothers. These are the provision of paid time off for antenatal appointments, and where the agency worker is unable to continue in the assignment for health and safety reasons relating to her pregnancy/ maternity the recruitment firm providing her services has an obligation to find her alternative work on the same or better terms, or to continue to pay her for the duration or likely duration of the terminated assignment.

One area of the AWR, which has had most publicity and attention, particularly from the unions is Regulation 10, which allows for a 'Pay Between Assignment' employment contract to be used. In this situation, the recruitment firm (or other intermediary) may employ a worker under an employment contract which allows for the worker to be paid at a certain rate when they are between assignments. When such an employment contract is in place, then the worker is exempt from the equal treatment provisions contained within the AWR to the extent that they relate to pay. Unfortunately Regulations 10 and 11 regarding this Pay Between Assignment ('PBA') model are ambiguous at best, and have left various aspects open to interpretation. Partly because of this the unions are extremely unhappy with this PBA model (otherwise known as the 'Swedish Derogation'), and openly call it an avoidance mechanism. It does appear likely that the first claims, which appear at employment tribunal will be concerning PBA models, and it is likely to be some time before it is clear what a compliant PBA model will look like.

Although there is no opt out available to workers regarding the AWR, the legislation does give one opportunity to workers who are genuinely in business on their own account to be outside of scope. This has been generally interpreted by the industry as meaning that workers who provide services via their own limited companies, and who do not work under the supervision and direction of the client will be outside of scope. The industry has also made the link (although this does not exist in law) between the AWR and IR35, because the employment status and tax status tests are very similar, and hence limited company contractors outside IR35 are, generally speaking, being treated, by both the workers and the recruitment firms as being outside of scope.

This legislation is difficult for recruitment firms to deal with mainly because there are few certainties, and most decisions made are based on a level of risk. So businesses must make risk-based decisions based on the probability of workers making claims.

Ethics

Like any other profession the staffing industry has a broad range of ethical guidelines and considerations. The REC (Recruitment and Employment Confederation) has a code of professional practice, as does APSCo (Association of Professional Staffing Companies), the AESC (Association of Executive Search Consultants), and as do, internationally, Ciett (the International Confederation of Employment Agencies), and the ASA (American Staffing Association). Examples of each of these can be found on the relevant websites.

Taking APSCo as an example the ethical code covers:

- general points relating to members acting in accordance with the code of conduct and offering the code as reassurance to APSCo clients that all members promote excellence within the staffing solutions sector;

- members' understanding of and compliance with relevant legislation;
- that members will champion equality and diversity;
- members' responsibility for training all staff to enable compliance with the code;
- the recruitment process, its documentation and placement of candidates;
- the way in which members work with clients;
- the way in which members will work with candidates, including pay and contractual obligations;
- miscellaneous points like the environment;
- Code for Managed Service providers and how they will behave as APSCo members.

One of the key holdings of any of the codes is to uphold confidentiality of both candidates and clients and not to act without the agreement of either party. This confirms the essential role of the recruiter as an intermediary between the client and the candidate and a facilitator to both in providing work and staffing opportunities.

There may well be future developments in both law and ethics as the industry continues to develop.

Other future trends

Business can generally be driven by one of two main factors:

- a vision for the future;
- external factors and competition.

Whilst most industries combine factors in varying degrees it might be suggested that, historically, the recruitment industry has evolved mainly through input from external factors and competition. This has also meant therefore that as an industry we have been 'catching up' rather than trying brave new approaches on our quest for survival and growth. Therefore one could argue that to predict future trends we must look to external factors to evolve and adapt.

Generally the industry's future will be shaped by a number of socio-economic, political and technological forces, the interplay of which will create the recruitment landscape.

Demographics

For some years now the ageing population of the western world, caused by longer lifespan and lower birth-rates, has been producing an effect on the recruitment industry. Although skills shortages are generally a boon for recruiters, demographic predictions for the future are worrying. In the 1960s there were 6–8 working adults to every post-65 year old; in 2010, around 4 : 1. Predictions are that by 2020 there will be 3 : 1 and by 2030 there may only be 2.5 : 1. Demand for those of working age is set to increase dramatically and staffing issues will resonate across boardroom agendas. Also with the increase in retirement age many older workers will add an extra 7–10 years on to their careers – which could be an opportunity for recruitment companies that are geared up to attract mature candidates.

Legislation

As you will notice from the section on legislative advances, in the recent past the employment and recruitment legislative landscape has changed dramatically over the past 15 years across Europe, a trend that we might surmise is set to continue. New legislation has created an increase in the requirement for employers and users of flexible workers to capture, analyse and store more data about the recruitment process and indeed the applicant experiences. This has already affected the expectations of client organizations, and altered the relationship between customer and supplier. Often the recruiter has taken much of the administrative and cost burden and it is likely that the demand for management information as part of a service offering will continue to increase.

Sophistication of buyers

With the spend on recruitment increasing, the buying process was always going to become scrutinized. The tender process for large scale staffing process takes months and even years, with a huge proportion of buying decisions driven by procurement professionals; criteria for inclusion include a range of compliance proof and delivery bench marketing, but are focused very heavily on price – or indeed margins. Staffing Industry Analysts found that in 2005 37 per cent of supplier selection was diversity by procurement departments, compared to 69 per cent in 2010.

Supplier Management Strategy for 2011

82% – Approved supplied list
70% – Consolidation of suppliers
63% – Supplier tiering list
50% – Master suppliers
44% – Domestic outsourcing
36% – MSP
30% – RPO
30% – HRO

(Source: Staffing Industry Analysts)

Professionalism of the temporary market

Historically, most temporary markets will open from a fairly low base, such as agriculture or factory labour. The use of temporary workers will then increase and start to encompass more senior roles within industrial and then service sectors. In some established markets eg the UK and US, the use of the Professional Temporary worker is commonplace, and the largest growth sector (albeit from a low base) is interim. This trend is set to spread and indeed figures from Adecco's 2011 annual report show that revenues as a percentage of overall turnover derived from 'Professionals Temporary Workers' (not office or industrial) were:

Europe – 12%
US – 53%
Australia and New Zealand – 57%
UK and Ireland – 68%

UK research from October 2011 shows that 79 per cent of interim executives were paid over £500 per day and 13 per cent were paid over £1,000 per day. When asked why they engaged with an interim executive 69 per cent of clients said that they were results oriented, 68 per cent quoted that they were 'hands on', 66 per cent said their flexibility made a difference, and an interesting 59 per cent valued their apolitical stance.

Measuring global markets will increase the use of flexible profession resources and we, as recruiters must be geared up to supply. It also suggests those in professional markets differentiating themselves from the industrial and office sectors will become a focus. Often the senior end of the recruiter's spectrum can become collateral damage from a legislation and pricing perspective and the creation of specific trade associations such as APSCo, highlighting the specifics of the professional, niche recruitment market, is likely to continue around the world.

Globalization

With the global staffing market calculated to be worth around US $1–7 trillion and the European market around €91 trillion in 2011 (S.I.A.), the industry is both large and spread. The emergence of new markets, both from the economic power houses of China and India and indeed the growth of the recruitment hotspots such as Brazil, Singapore etc provide us with opportunities both to capitalize on back office off-shoring and to expand the geographical recruit of our business, spreading revenue potential and mitigating risk. When our market slumps there is always another booming and the best-run staffing businesses have maintained profits during recessionary times through their global portfolio. (See Figure 1.9.) SThree is a leading player in the field of specialist recruitment, with revenues in 2011 of over £540 million. Founded in 1986 with a team of four focusing on the UK IT market, it launched its first international office in Brussels in 1998.

FIGURE 1.9   Globalizing SThree

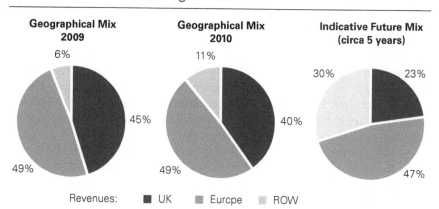

As in most business evolution, the biggest catalyst for change within the recruitment sector has been technology. There is no question that the use of databases and indeed personal computers streamlined the saving and storage of information about available candidates and client relationship management, which is captured, and retained, at the touch of a button. E-mail has, without question, made life easier for recruiters, with near-instant access to candidate details, and clear postal routes to contacts and applicants alike. However, the over-reliance on e-mail as an actual communication – or even sales – tool has negatively affected both the success and perceived value of recruitment consultancy. No written format, particularly one with abbreviated or poor use of English, can persuade of the benefits of a particular candidate or specific role, or indeed why your company's service should be considered at all. Professional recruiters communicate by telephone or on a face-to-face basis.

The process of candidate attraction has seen a huge change in recent years and has affected nearly every facet of the industry. From junior or low-skilled applicants to top level executives, the internet has provided access to active job seekers and is set, over the next few years, to create opportunities to find and contact the recruiter's 'elixir', passive candidates.

The decline of the 'old' way of attracting applicants by placing expensive and relatively slow-acting advertisements in national, trade or local paper-based media started, unsurprisingly, within the information technology sector. The first job board in the world was Jobserve. Launched in 1983, it provided the temporary IT recruitment sector with an audience of skilled IT professionals and IT contractors with real-time access to consultants' vacant positions. The immediate success of Jobserve heralded massive growth in the job-board market and a major decline in revenues within the paper-based advertising market – and huge cost savings to the recruitment industry.

There are now huge numbers of job boards in the UK with many more worldwide. Some are large generalist players such as Monster, Jobsite and Totaljobs. Others specialize in particular niche areas. There has always been a certain fear by recruitment companies of the advent of job boards, in that the low cost and ease of use would lead to 'disintermediation' (ie the clients recruiting for themselves). In fact only around 10.5 per cent of advertisements on job boards are placed directly by client organizations. This is actually less than the percentage placed directly in the paper-based media. Employers are rarely interested in looking through large numbers of non-qualified applicants to find the few interesting candidates.

As the internet makes it easier for organizations to find potential candidates for roles, the perceived value of this aspect of an external recruiter's role diminishes. Recruiters therefore need to provide a fuller service and added-value portfolio to boost the depth of the in-demand parts of what they do. Such services include:

- *Candidate qualification.* This involves identifying key competencies or skill sets from a potential applicant population.

- *Selection.* Here recruiters offer a full range of selection procedures beyond usual interviewing, to provide clients with not only first-tier, but also second or even third-tier selection: psychometric testing, competency-based interview techniques, assessment centres, role play scenarios, detailed reference and background checking, qualification validation and so on.

- *Offer management.* This entails taking further control of the offer management, and even induction processes, to ensure lower levels of fall-out.

- *Managed service provision.* Many organizations are attracted to the idea of outsourcing the responsibility of the full recruitment project life cycle to a recruitment company. Whether this service is provided by one company creating a formal alliance between client company and supplier, a specific MSP with no actual recruitment agent, or a small number of recruitment businesses – often in niche markets – grouping together to provide an onsite presence, it is a growing market.

The recruitment market has been intrigued by the emergence of interactive, social media and indeed virtual technologies but has looked on while marketers have embraced their potential for product sales, branding and sales. The reality is that the growth of the use of social networks in recruitment proves inevitable. Most of our clients have a social media presence and leverage it to improve their employment brand as well as to source passive candidates. Recruitment businesses need to embrace social media from a strategy perspective rather than continuing to acknowledge it with tactical usage.

- 65 per cent of online adults use social networking sites (double that of 2008) (*PEW Research Center, August 2011*).
- 73 per cent of 18–34 year olds used online social networks to find their most recent job.
- Jobseekers who use social networks and job boards found jobs through SN (*Jobseeker Nation, 2010*).
- Social media will soon take over e-mail usage (*Comscore, December 2010*).
- Social Networking is global (*Nielsen, September 2011*).
  - **Australia** 7 hours and 17 minutes spent online per person.
  - **Brazil** 30.3 million are active on Orkut, the number 1 social networking site in Brazil.
  - **France** Nearly 25 per cent of French internet users visited the number 2 social networking site, Overblog.
  - **Germany** Internet users spent more time on social networks than anywhere else, a total of 12.7 billion minutes in May 2011.
  - **Italy** Internet users spent 31 per cent of their internet time on social networks.
  - **Japan** Over half of active Japanese internet users visited the top social networking site, FC2 Blog, in May 2011.
  - **Spain** Internet users average 4 hours, 42 minutes per person on the number 4 social site, Tuenti.
  - **Switzerland** 60 per cent of active internet users are on social networks and blogs.
  - **US** Blogger is now the number 2 social networking and blog site.
  - **UK** Internet users viewed Facebook 20.2 billion times.

LinkedIn

- Nearly 2 billion people searches.
- More than 120 million users and growing.
- Business only.
- Used to find passive candidates, pre-check their knowledge or experience set and prepare for dialogue with both candidates and client contacts.
- Fortune 500 companies are on LinkedIn.

Youtube

- Used to learn from client or candidate posted videos.
- Used to create branding for specific client campaigns on recruitment businesses.

Twitter

- 400 million unique users per month.
- 50 million users log in every day.
- More than 200 million users 'tweet' in 140 characters or less.
- Allows quick, easy thought-leadership or more mundane subjects to be communicated across a community.
- Marketing opportunities for recruitment and also employment brands.

Branchout

- Facebook application allowing differentiation of personal and business life.
- Allows targeted employer job posts.
- Allows endorsements and shows connections.
- Tool to find passive candidates.

Beknown

- A master.com product launched as Facebook application.
- Merges Facebook and LinkedIn connections, whilst harnessing the fewer users of Master.com.

Google +

- Currently individuals only but plans to offer businesses and school pages in 2012.
- Access to everything on Google.
- Can categorize social connections through 'circles' ie trends, colleagues or family.
- Streams information based on a user's pre-selected interests.
- Allows video conferencing for up to 10 people at a time – one could hold small career fairs (!).

(Source: Shelly Gorman, UNC Executive Development 2011)

Mobile recruitment – The smartphone was tailor-made for the recruitment market. Predictions suggest that by 2013, the usage of mobile internet will overtake the traditional desktop web. The Apple iPhone has driven Smartphone adoption with Google's Android catching up, and mobile jobseekers are already accessing jobs from their smartphones.

- 2.8 million UK jobseekers a month view job listings on a mobile phone device. 67 per cent of those look daily (*ComScore*).
- 88 per cent of jobseekers are or would search for jobs via mobile internet.

- The biggest current activity is to 'search for jobs', followed by 'looking for career related information'.
- The second largest desire is to be alerted to jobs.
- When asked why use mobile, jobseekers state that the ability to engage anywhere, anytime maximizes time (*Potentialpark*).

Pretty obviously, as recruiters, we cannot afford to miss this shift towards mobile internet, which has gone way beyond that of early adopters. Yet can many recruitment businesses go beyond creating a mobile application to ensure that your company's website supports mobile? A recent report by KPCP Meeker suggests that 33 per cent of all Facebook traffic is mobile internet and 53 per cent of Twitter is from a mobile device. They also found that over 40 million recruitment-related mobile searches were made in the UK per month. Today's mobile internet users are comfortable with completing transactions via their mobile and are ready to apply for a job that way. The recruitment market needs to create a simple process to push specific opportunities to applicants, and a low-friction process to receive details and pre-screen candidates.

Simulations and virtual worlds – Simulations replicate job-related tasks to allow employers to assess a candidate's skills. They can give realistic job previews and cut bias and subjectivity. Virtual worlds allow participants to interact with each other through avatars. This technology can be particularly useful in creating virtual jobs fairs, where participants can interact with different employers and jobseekers. Recruiters must not only engage with new tools as they emerge, but look ahead to predict the impact of technological developments in their business.

PART TWO
The successful recruiter

Introduction

If you're reading this part, you have an interest in becoming successful, or more successful, in recruitment. This section looks at some recruiter success stories, what recruitment is about; the recruitment cycle and your own personal strengths and development areas. It will help you explore whether you are doing enough of the right activities to be successful, and lead you, step by step through writing your own business plan. Before you start that journey it's worth spending some time considering what that success may look like or what might encapsulate success in your business. Try the following exercise:

might you live, how might people perceive you, what sort of car might you drive, how much travelling might you be able to do? What career plans might you make, how much will you be earning? How might you feel about yourself and how might you inspire others? Picture all of this.

Then relax.

Once you know what it might feel like to be there and you know that is what you want, you'll need to do three things:

- Hang on to that feeling by closing your eyes when you need to and taking yourself back to your mental picture.

- Act like you are already there.

- Plan how to get there.

By suggesting you should act like you are already there, by the way, this is not advocating a swagger round the office and a large overdraft; this is about taking a mental leap to being a success and all that that entails. This is behaving like a successful person and having the confidence in yourself that you can make that happen. Most successful people will say that their achievement is about having faith and sticking to dreams.

What makes a recruiter successful?

The job of recruitment is all about marrying sales skills with psychological skills. That is to say, in order to be good at the job you need to have an innate ability (developed on with good training) to present things in a good light, the tenacity to keep going when you think something is of value, a genuine interest in people that really helps you understand them and the capacity to build strong, sustainable relationships. Sales and good service could be two key words to describe a great recruiter. Add to that a huge amount of hard work in speaking to candidates and clients and following a process to make placements, and you have the essence of recruitment. Here's what four different, but all successful people in recruitment have to say about success.

CASE STUDY

Deb Loveridge, Managing Director, Asia Pacific Ranstad Pte Ltd, is clear that success in recruitment is about developing and maximizing relationships with both candidates and clients. She feels consultants need to be out meeting clients face to face (even though that can be challenging with today's often technologically based systems), as that is where real value-add lies. As a new recruiter she was taught always to bear in mind what it can be like to be a job seeker; trying to chase applications, wondering what is happening and feeling concerned about this big step they are about to make. Maintaining an empathetic approach to candidates, as well as developing relationships with clients, is a recipe for success in recruitment.

CASE STUDY

Chris Herrmannsen, CEO of Ochre House Ltd, a recruitment services firm with a range of well-known and innovative brands, is not concerned with previous experience of recruiting when he hires. Instead, he is more interested in the personal attributes or competencies inherent in a prospective employee. 'Training can develop specific skills,' he says, 'but it is more difficult to fundamentally change the way a person thinks and behaves.' Typically, Ochre House look for a strong drive to succeed, coupled with a clear focus on results. The best people in the business are well organized, and comfortable with leading, influencing and working together to delight the customer. 'Solutions rather than product experts have been most successful for us across our business,' says Hermannsen. Many of their best people have never worked in recruitment before joining the business and would have acquired their capabilities in an unrelated role or industry.

CASE STUDY

Laurence Simons, of the eponymous international legal recruitment group that he founded after a short period practising as a lawyer and then setting up the legal practice for Michael Page, is clear there are four qualities for a successful recruiter: determination, tenacity, commitment and focus. He says the legal market is highly consultative. Recruiters in this market need to operate with integrity and professionalism. Many of his recruiters are also ex-lawyers, helping them towards a strong knowledge and understanding of their marketplace, which he also considers to be critical. The capacity to work across global boundaries is also important, because 55 per cent of his business is now done overseas.

CASE STUDY

Dorian Webb, interim resourcing and talent specialist set up the recruitment division for the new mobile telecommunications company '3'. He had a clear view of the skills and expertise he looked for when recruiting his new team. His brief was to set up, from scratch, a centralized function and recruit 2,500 new staff, across all disciplines, from a standing start in 12–15 months.

He says what he looked for in an internal recruiter, to carry off this huge undertaking, was a recruitment consultancy background, ideally with some in-house experience as well, and a strong commercial task-orientation, as delivery was critical. He also looked for recruiters who could source candidates directly as well as manage suppliers.

His management team came from a blend of in-house and external, perfect for the brief. The combination of recruitment expertise and skills inherent in the team he brought in, which at its height numbered 25 or so people, meant that not only did they hit all their targets but also that their acceptance rate for jobs was as high as 98 per cent.

These are four different views from across the world and very different sectors yet with some common themes. Although none of the people profiled, all indisputably very successful people in the industry, have mentioned sales per se, it is clear great recruiters do need the power of persuasion and the capacity to give great service. What does it take to be a successful salesperson? Let's take a look at the definition of sales. Many recruiters will be deterred immediately from the idea that they are in a sales role. Many others will not see it as debateable. Whichever group you fall into, let's explore this concept for a moment.

For many people 'sales' is pushing people into things they do not want to do or buy. Some people sell like this. Sometimes it works. For others sales is about identifying things that people want and making people aware of them so they can buy them. The latter might be more of a marketing perspective. Let us suppose that sales and marketing are about:

- finding a product, service or solution that a market might want;
- providing it on time;
- at a price that provides value to the market;
- in a way that makes it easily accessible (ie you know where to find it).

In that case there are some clear similarities here to a model for recruiters. In such a model, recruitment is about providing a candidate or a recruitment service that clients might want to buy, at a price that they perceive as value for money and making them aware of what is available. This can be as simple as ringing a client up, or it can involve developing a sophisticated marketing programme to reach clients to communicate your brand. Either way it is about matching the needs and expectations of the market – ie clients and candidates – to your service or product (broadly your clients and candidates) along with the methodologies you employ to match them together.

The next chapters look at what recruitment is about, what needs to be done to make it successful and how to build a recruitment business for your desk or your in-house recruitment function.

The recruitment cycle

02

Before making decisions about developing your desk or your business it is important to be clear about the recruitment framework needed to ensure success. This chapter focuses on developing a clear picture of recruitment as an activity and role, and explores both a framework and its component parts.

The recruitment cycle, as a framework, illustrates the essence of recruitment. It works a little like the learning cycle (Kolb and Fry, 1975). You can start working anywhere within the cycle but there are four key activities. Paying attention to each of them at different times, and with varying emphasis, will enable any determined person to be successful in recruitment.

Sometimes one of the hardest things to do as a recruiter is to decide where to start working the recruitment process. For an in-house recruiter it can be straightforward – you are likely to have a signed-off role spec and a budget to fill the role. External recruiters may be in the same situation, but one of the challenges, and freedoms, of the role of a professional recruiter is that recruiters often make their own choices about how to write business and deliver placements or revenue.

Figure 2.1 outlines each of four cornerstones of the recruitment process: what recruiters need to do to achieve their goals and be successful. Within each of these cornerstones there are a range of activities. Sometimes these activities are broken down into steps (such as the 30 steps proposed by recruitment trainer Tony Byrne in the 1980s), shown as a wheel or described as 'the placement process' (as in the training courses of leading industry training company Learning Curve in the 1990s). It is important to recognize each of the stages of the process and ensure they are completed. Before going into the detail of each of these stages you need to take a macro look at the recruitment cycle as it will help you organize your business strategy and therefore your time. Some people might describe this as taking a 'helicopter' view. When you are closely involved day to day in a project or a piece of work, it is important to be able to look down from above and see the bigger picture. This is where the cycle can help. At the end of each week, for example, you could use the cycle to evaluate how much work within each cornerstone you have done that week or that month.

FIGURE 2.1   The recruitment cycle

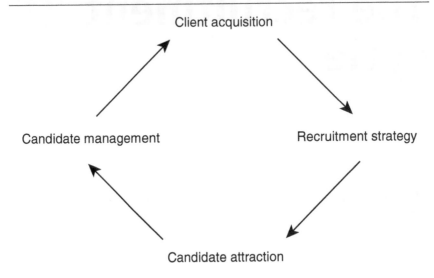

Client acquisition

Candidate management

Recruitment strategy

Candidate attraction

The cycle indicates the way in which placements happen. A consultant may start the process at any point within the cycle but must then always continue through the four points in a clockwise manner. Jumping a section will mean that the placement is much less likely to succeed and you are less likely to deliver the expectations of the candidate or client.

So, for example, if you start with a great candidate you need to manage that person effectively in order to find a client to place them with. If you miss out 'candidate management' the chances are you will mismanage the client expectations and the placement will not work. Once you have 'managed' the candidate, which includes interviewing and qualifying them, you then need to identify a range of clients (or you may only have one if you are in-house) to market the candidate to. At this point you move into 'client acquisition'. Once you have successfully acquired the client you then need to develop the strategy for that client (which includes managing the candidate for the client) through to successful placement.

Alternatively you may start with a requirement or a vacancy or a brief. This places you in the start of 'client strategy', as you have already acquired a client with a role you need to deliver on. You need to work out how to fill it (in-house recruiters do not need to acquire clients in the same way). It might be that you have acquired a client with 250 vacancies (for example, you have taken a role as Director of Talent in-house) and you need to manage the whole process. Whether you have 250 roles or one to fill the client strategy determines your plan of action for your recruitment programme. Once you have decided on this you move into 'candidate attraction' and through 'candidate management' until the candidate is placed, or a long-term solution to managing the 250 vacancies is implemented and is pulling through candidates to placements.

You may have a candidate that someone else has attracted and managed. In this case you start with candidate management but you may not need to complete all of the tasks within candidate management, just those needed to move you towards client acquisition. You may already have a client for them, so again you may not need to complete all the tasks in client acquisition. Client strategy could be your starting point when an existing client calls you to discuss a new type of role or brief they want you to hire. Each of the cornerstones has a set of activities that, put together, form the complete recruitment cycle. You may not need to undertake all the activities personally every time, but they all need completing by someone to make a successful placement.

You can start anywhere in the cycle but you always need to move in a clockwise direction and follow the circle round 360 degrees to be effective. It may be that your own role only covers one or two of those areas. So long as you can see the whole picture and are clear how your section fits into another section and with whom, this can also work well. Indeed some consultants work effectively when they are only doing one aspect of the cycle, acquiring clients for example, after which other consultants are introduced who can develop the client strategy and devise an attraction plan that is then implemented by someone else who also manages the candidates. In an executive search assignment, the researcher often completes the candidate attraction, at the first stage. The implementation of the cycle can be developed in a myriad different ways. What's important is that you need to ensure the whole cycle is being proactively managed to make recruitment successful.

We will now take each option in turn and explore its component parts in order to help choose where to start working in the cycle.

Candidate management

All candidates need managing in one way or another. Sometimes this is an area of the cycle that receives scant attention, yet this lack of attention can mean a high risk to the business.

For an in-house consultant or manager the importance of talent-banking and developing a long-term relationship with candidates is becoming crucial in the war for talent. For a recruitment consultant to build a great relationship with a candidate can mean access to a huge range of other excellent candidates from that candidate's network, it can mean that candidate turns into a client, it can be another step to building a great brand and it can be the difference between acquiring your candidate for your client, or not.

CASE STUDY

A successful US company called 'Entre' came over to Europe to set up in business, and hired really strong talent. The European arm of the business did poorly and eventually Entre pulled out of Europe leaving all of this great talent (some 40 people) looking for work. One of the marketing team went to see a recruitment agent in London who seemed to have several good opportunities for her and came back into the office to tell everyone. This recruitment consultant ended up placing about 10 of the candidate's colleagues over a month to six weeks through the recommendation of the first candidate.

Candidate management works in a linear way. The success of the whole depends enormously on the success at the start. The tasks therefore are described here in order. There is much more detail on this linear relationship in the detailed chapter on candidate management, where you can find out 'how' as well as 'what' to do. The step-by-step approach of managing your candidate is based on the core of managing expectations and as Steven Covey (1989) advises in his book *The Seven Habits of Highly Effective People*, you should 'begin with the end in mind'. The 'end in mind' is likely to be that:

- The candidates take a job or a contract they have secured through you or in your company.
- They are part of your short-list as a qualified and motivated applicant for your client's role.
- You have built a good relationship with them for a future placement.
- They help you by sourcing other candidates.
- They refer you to other candidates and clients.
- Your relationship with them has enhanced your consultancy or company brand.
- They become clients.

Candidate management is not just about you, the consultant; it is about the whole candidate experience. It may not be within your direct control to manage or change each of the activities but we mention them as we feel that they are an integral part of this part of the recruitment cycle, and you can do your best to lobby for excellence and change in these areas that you do not directly control. The vast majority of activities however will be your responsibility.

Candidate management activities include:

- You, reception or colleagues answering the phone in your office, demonstrating the knowledge base of the rest of the business by getting the candidate through to the right person quickly and effectively. A great candidate might only suffer one or two wrong people before putting the phone down.
- How CVs, e-mails and letters are acknowledged and replied to.
- Rejection letters, phone calls and e-mails.
- Advertisement copy. If the attraction strategy has been advertising and what you have written is an inflated view of a role or cites a top-end salary, you already have an expectation management problem. The candidate will be expecting more than can be realistically offered.
- First-stage evaluation of the candidate; does the candidate have the skills and experience matching the needs of your clients? Will this candidate build your database, and therefore your business?
- Starting and managing a short, medium or long-term conversation with the candidate that impacts their view of you as an employer and your brand leading to an offer of employment or a contract now or in the future; an increasingly important element in any organizational attraction strategy.
- Qualifying the candidate in or out of a role – identifying at an early stage whether candidates might have some of the qualities required to be progressed for a role or a client, and whether they meet your qualification criteria – a step further on than evaluation. This might mean reading a CV or it might be having a conversation or even taking up an informal reference.
- The candidate interview: the cornerstone of candidate management. This can be a formal in-depth interview for a senior role you are retained to search for, or part of a resourcing call for a contract you have two hours to submit a shortlist for. Clearly these two activities will differ hugely in their depth and length. They have a common theme, however, of setting the scene for the professional relationship where both parties will agree how they expect to operate and what they can expect from each other.
- Preparing the candidate for a first client interview and for subsequent interviews or assessment procedures. A search candidate briefing will have an entirely different flavour from a graduate interview.
- De-briefing post-interview.
- Trial closing the candidate against a potential offer. The objective of course is to create a win–win situation where clients feel they have achieved value and parity in their business and candidates feel they have what they want or need and that the move is a good plan.

- Asking the candidate for referrals or sources for roles you are working on.
- Re-directing candidates you cannot help to other sources.
- Handling candidate objections about a role they are interviewing for.
- Deciding how to market a strong candidate whom you think your client, or new clients, will be interested in. This is a great way of acquiring new clients and there is more detail on exactly how to go about this in the candidate acquisition section, but for a plan on how to work with your candidate, look in the chapter on candidate management.
- Managing the offer and resignation process.
- Managing the candidate through to start date.

CASE STUDY

Sue Evans, Head of Resourcing at HSC, a recruitment process outsourcing firm that bases much of its success in recruiting for high-growth, fast-moving firms on smart direct sourcing, but also on great relationships with agencies who really deliver for it, says: 'Nothing opens a door for me like a great CV for a requirement where candidates are in short supply.' Sue has accountability to her client for delivering each role against a set of clear key performance indicators (KPIs). Occasionally, she allows, it is simply through the CV from a new agency not on her preferred supplier list (PSL) that she has recruited for a 'hard-to-fill' role.

The advent of PSLs (Preferred Suppplier Lists) has meant this way of working can be more challenging for external recruiters than it has been in the past. For some clients this has also meant that they have missed out on great talent by only using one supplier although their recruiting costs will also have decreased. Organizations should really take a balanced approach for best value; limit the bulk of candidates supplied to key suppliers with a strong track record with your business but always keep an open mind towards a well-targeted thought through approach from a new recruiter.

For consultants it's worth spending the time researching the right person to send the candidate through to so that the candidate does stand a chance of being considered. Make sure you have a strong candidate who will be attractive to a particular client, ideally ring them up and present your candidate and this may enable you to begin working with the client.

This leads us on to the next element area of the recruitment process – that of acquiring a client to work for.

Client acquisition

This section deals with ways of finding clients to work with. This may not seem directly relevant to the in-house recruiter but there are some common themes, like ensuring you have strong relationships with all of your clients so you can achieve both your and their goals.

Client acquisition includes both first-time acquisition and then the continuous acquisition of that client into a stronger and more loyal relationship until they become an advocate of your service both internally and externally.

Candidate acquisition activities include:

- Researching clients and your market; gaining knowledge so you can service your market most effectively (see case study opposite).
- Getting past gatekeepers to speak to the client.
- New business development. This can be as simple as phoning potential clients or may involve planning a business development campaign involving corporate sales, tender writers and senior managers.
- Account management and development:
  - You work with one section of the business but don't work across the board.
  - You have placed a couple of people there but they don't always call you first when they have a requirement.
  - You are not on the PSL and want to be.
  - You have no relationship with the recruiter to whom you are a tier-two supplier.
  - You have a great relationship and want to develop it further and extend your recruiting for the client.
  - Building a relationship with the decision-making team.
  - You need to respond to an ITT.
  - An invitation has been extended to the beauty parade of the PSL and you need to prepare a presentation.
- Qualifying your clients and assessing business potential:
  - Do they recruit many staff?
  - What recruitment strategy do they normally employ?
  - How much of a problem is recruitment to them?
  - How much does recruiting great talent impact on their bottom line or capacity to deliver?
- Making speculative approaches with great candidates.
- Handling client objections.
- Securing and managing client meetings.

- Networking through candidates and existing client relationships.
- Working at a range of levels within a business – corporate sales, securing PSL status across a large business with recruiters in a consultancy, developing relationships at hiring manager or in-house recruiter level.
- As an in-house recruiter, ensuring you have strong relationships with both hiring managers and recruitment strategy developers within the business. The way to retain in-house outsourced accounts or stay in place as an in-house team is to become a knowledge base for the business that adds value over and above the normal process of recruitment.

CASE STUDY

An ex-telecoms salesperson set up as a recruitment consultant. When she was briefed on a particular role she sourced four candidates for the client to see. She then told the client that she would be attending on the day he was interviewing, and worked out of the client's offices managing the candidates before and after each interview. This meant that at the end of the day she had obtained feedback from all the candidates, found out what their offer needed to be and whether they would take the job. She was then able to meet directly with the client, agree two offers (instead of the original one) out of four candidates, ensure they were good offers, and tie up the whole piece of recruitment in terms of verbal offers, acceptances and rejections by 7 o'clock that evening. The candidates were pleased not to have to wait too long for feedback, and the two who had been offered posts were pleased with their conditions and accepted the jobs. The client was thrilled that simply taking a day out of his diary solved his recruitment problem and that he had had such fantastic service. He organized for her to deliver all the recruitment for the entire company on an exclusive basis from then on, and she had launched a career in recruitment consultancy.

Client strategy

Client strategy involves finding the best possible recruitment solution for each recruitment need and adding value in a consultancy capacity, which might be advising on salaries or rates, offering an unrivalled service both in terms of sourced candidates and service levels of managing those candidates, developing a recruitment strategy and a process that is fit for purpose, and ensuring you can fill the role(s) you take on.

For an in-house recruiter or recruitment director, this might start with a high-level strategy around being an employer of choice in your labour market, dropping down into the detail on candidate sourcing and process management.

For a recruitment consultant it needs to involve being clear what services you are great at offering, those you excel in and those you don't. This forms part of any client recommendation strategy.

Client strategy activities will include:

- Developing a recruitment or service strategy for the role(s). This may include the following:
  - retained search and selection, including competency-based or behavioural interviewing with detailed reporting to accompany short-lists;
  - combination of targeted search, advertising and selection, run either in-house or by an agency/consultancy/search firm;
  - operational research to build up a talent bank and recruit middle management or specialist technical resource, either run in-house or by a research specialist agency or a combination of both;
  - internal direct applicant model supplemented by an agency management scheme;
  - internal recruitment referral scheme;
  - agency contingency service, including using the agency database and perhaps an informal networking/referral approach;
  - retained agency approach;
  - added value services such as preferential rates on trade press advertising, ad agency briefing and sourcing, advertisement design, online assessment services, assessment centre design and implementation, outsourced graduate recruitment service and a range of other services;
  - a fully outsourced recruitment service;
  - exclusive agency supplier agreements;
  - using metrics to evaluate the effectiveness of current recruitment methods employed; eg explore the CV received to interview ratio to explore the understanding of your business needs from your supplier base. For a recruitment consultancy use this to explore how effective you are as a consultant at understanding your client's needs.
- Evaluating a job role.
- Developing a role and person specification.
- Offering benchmarking of salaries.
- Taking a requirement including advising on the necessity for flexibility.

- Selling a retained piece of work.
- Helping the client develop a sales proposition for prospective candidates.
- Developing a compelling role proposition.
- Developing a candidate briefing pack.
- Writing a service proposal – both internal or external to the client.
- Developing and agreeing a media campaign.
- Developing and agreeing an initial search list.
- Developing a search pitch.
- Laying out a search or advertisement response report.

Candidate attraction

This is one of the key ways to add value to your client. Attracting and presenting candidates with scarce skills, ideally ones who are also exclusive to you, will gain you real competitive advantage as a recruiter.

The activities include the following:

- Working for a brand leader consultancy or in-house and receiving a great unsolicited CV.
- Building a strong brand profile for your company through actively being an employer of choice; communicating you are a leader in your field, developing a talent strategy, having a strong graduate programme, great career opportunities, above average working conditions, opportunities for learning and development; driving traffic to the web to generate direct candidates. Companies like Vodafone, Procter & Gamble, Unilever, Marks & Spencer, Deutsche Bank, Freshfields, Accenture and Oracle, for example, are all aspirational organizations that generate a passport to another good role.
- Building a strong brand profile for your recruitment consultancy through press and online advertising (either client-paid or from your own budget) in the key markets where you aim to achieve best results for candidates and clients, with CVs and role specifications that are supplied through your consultancy. How much business development on a role-to-role basis do the 'names' in recruitment have to do? Michael Page is a good example.
- Directly resourcing a range of candidates through ringing candidates on your in-house database.
- Networking for more candidates in a range of ways.
- Writing and placing advertisements for the candidates you want, whether this be part of a brand-building exercise, a corporate identity

piece or simply a few effective lines written for Jobsite
(**www.jobsite.com**), one of the internet job boards.

- Formally headhunting candidates and conducting a search including research tools and mapping your market.
- Developing a social networking strategy using a range of tools to develop candidate interest and drive conversations about your organization to gain valuable feedback.
- Setting up a virtual recruitment fair on the internet.
- Developing relationships with talent pools to generate candidates; this could be a relationship with a professional body like CIMA (Chartered Institute of Management, Accountants), a supply of ex-service personnel candidates through a specialist consultancy such as Forces Recruitment Services, or relationships with the careers offices of key universities you want to target.
- Developing a candidate referral scheme. This might be an internal scheme such as 'Talented Friends', where employees are rewarded financially or in other ways for recommending a friend to a particular role, or a consultancy-based scheme where candidates are rewarded for recommending their friends and are offered a gift or money if those candidates are successfully placed.
- Networking with other consultants in your company.
- Job board CV searching.
- Internet tracking of names.
- Directly headhunting a person who has been recommended – sometimes by a client who is interested in talking to that person.
- Using clever search strings on Google to uncover the CVs of passive candidates.

The end of the candidate attraction phase can mean that you have developed a constant inflow of candidates from a range of sources that will continually, with management, enable you to submit candidates for suitable roles. It could mean you have one candidate, whom you are going to place and offer to a range of clients, or it could mean that you have generated enough candidates from your search to begin to evaluate them and manage them.

Where to start in the recruitment cycle

If you have a choice about where to start the general rule of thumb is to consider whether you are in a candidate-short or candidate-rich environment:

- Is it easier to pick up roles to work on than it is candidates?
- Do clients call you with jobs to fill?

- Do your candidates typically have several job offers?
- Are counter-offers prevalent?

If you answer yes to these, it is likely you are in a candidate-short market so finding great candidates and then managing them through to successful placement is a good strategy. Now consider the opposite scenario:

- Do you have a large response to each of your advertisements?
- Do you have to contact a lot of clients before you find a brief needing filling?
- Have there been recent redundancies in your sector?
- Do you spend a lot of time talking to candidates who call in looking for work?

If you answer yes to these, it is likely you are in a candidate-rich market so finding a great role to work on and managing it through to successful placement is a good strategy.

If neither of the above apply then it matters less where you start and you might work opportunistically on both candidates and roles, or decide to take a strategic approach depending upon your market. To help you think more strategically about how to develop your desk, market or business area, the next chapter offers some tools for developing your desk.

Working to your strengths

03

Developing and improving in anything, career, sport or relationships takes some self-awareness and practise. This chapter will enable you to improve what you do and how you do it. There are some tasks to carry out and some ideas to get you thinking, as well as pointers to additional reading. It's an important precursor to developing your business plan.

A great book is Buckingham and Coffman's *First, Break All the Rules* (2001) written as a result of market research conducted by Gallup. They come up with a list of 12 questions a good manager should ensure their staff can answer to positively. One of the questions is whether people are able to do things they are good at every day, as part of their job. This is not just work around 'being nice' to employees but is proven to contribute to the business's bottom line and has a clear impact on employee engagement.

Often training is requested for someone who is 'good at account management but not so good at opening doors', or someone who is 'great at getting new candidates in but not so good at developing the long-term relationship'. Of course we all need to be able to perform all of our role and not just part of it. Good recruiters need to be able to manage all four parts of the consulting process.

However, maximizing on what you are good at and what you enjoy doing is really important. Recognizing your strengths is the first step to being able to identify how best to work. You may work in an organization with clear guidelines about what you have to do each day to be successful, or you may work in one where you determine your own workload each day. It does not really matter as the principle is the same. Ask yourself, using the tools coming up:

- What do I do best?
- What is important to me?
- What do I really enjoy?
- How can I organize myself to ensure I make the most of my strengths?

We have already explored the essence of being a good recruiter and the importance of marrying psychological and persuasive skills. But there is always more than one way of accomplishing a job. It is possible to be successful in recruitment in different ways so long as you have the core competences.

Artistic and scientific recruiters

In the same way that people are generally either owls or larks (best late at night or best early in the morning), it's likely that recruiters fall into two broad categories in how they work. Figure 3.1 shows how each type can prefer to work with both their candidates and clients.

Artistic recruiters

Artistic recruiters tend to be driven by relationships and enthusiastic about people. They can be 'scatty' and poor at forecasting. Their managers will worry each month whether they will hit target. Invariably however the artistic recruiters pull a couple of great placements out of the bag at the last moment to overshoot their target. For a manager with a scientific bent they can be a real challenge to manage. For artistic recruiters with a scientific manager who does not appreciate and work with their differences, this can be a real headache and preclude success.

FIGURE 3.1   Scientific and artistic recruiters

	Candidates	**Clients**
Scientific	Work through structured list	Analyse your client base. REQ driven
Artistic	Network and SPEQ when inspired	Recruit for companies you'd love to work for

If artistic recruiters are forced into a corner and made to work in a structured way they are likely to feel stifled and become unsuccessful. If they are given more of a free rein however they will fly. They may tend to do less actual work but their ratios (success rates) are high. They will still work hard but tend to take longer over things and may not be the best time managers. Clients love them and they probably spend too long on their client relationships, until they get bored with that set of clients and then move on. New business will be gained by inspiration and networking rather than an organized plan (although they may well write one to start with). They do need a hard enough edge however to be certain of what they are trying to achieve and to have the will to achieve it or they will not be successful.

Scientific recruiters

Scientific recruiters are successful because they are brilliant at following process and good enough at what they do to be successful. They tend to be highly organized, and once trained will be painstaking about making sure they do the right things at exactly the right times. They can be very business-like but are not always warm. Their client and candidate relationships are built out of good businesslike behaviours, professionalism and delivery capability. They set themselves meaningful goals and make sure they achieve them and are very operationally focused. Never worry about the scientific recruiter as far as making sure the files are in the right place and the database is updated.

If scientific recruiters are not given enough direction, guidance and clarity when they do not know their job well, however, this can create problems and they may not be successful, but give them the tools, techniques and structure of how to do the job well and they can fly, so long as they have the raw inter-personal skills to manage people in and around the role. However, again, if they are managed by an artistic recruiter, who may feel their need for structure is unnecessary, they will struggle, especially if they are new to the role.

People don't always fall completely squarely into one box or another but try this quiz to see where you sit. Recruitment organizations themselves often work in one way or another themselves (and that aspect of the culture can be driven by the original orientation of the founder of the business) although many have room for both types. Try our fun quiz to give you an indication of where you sit in the artistic and scientific spectrum.

Are you an artistic or scientific recruiter?

1 Did you read the previous section and think:

   A This is really helpful, I will diarize a time to write my plan.

   B This really makes sense to me – I must try and get round to giving it some thought but I've just spotted an article in the trade press about a candidate I knew a few years back and must call her.

   C I didn't really read it in detail; I skipped to the bit about playing to your strengths.

2 At school or university did you:

   A Take an arts degree/study arty subjects.

   B Take a science degree/study science subjects.

   C Take a combined degree/studied both arts and sciences.

3 With your friends and acquaintances do you:

   A Make sure you keep in touch with everyone regularly (every few months at least) and always remember birthdays and anniversaries because you have them in your Blackberry or on your calendar. Arrange your friends into groups for weekends away and parties.

   B Make sure you see your friends often and remember birthdays – often buying a card or present but you don't always get it there on the right day.

   C Think about your friends regularly. Although you have a wide circle of friends you change them frequently. However whenever you meet an old friend (which you are often moved to do), it's like you have never been apart and your friendship just slots back in as normal.

4 At work or whilst studying have you:

   A Developed a clear method of time management from reading a range of books on the subject and sticking to a plan of action that you review regularly. David Allen is your favourite time-management guru.

   B Read David Allen (2001) and Mark Forster (2000) as you know you need to be more organized, and have often implemented a new system but it only lasts for about three weeks.

   C Thought it's clever how some have earned a fortune from time management like some gurus – everyone knows it doesn't work and stifles creativity.

5 If you are a recruiter do you tend to:
   (for this question, ring *all* answers that apply to you, ignore those that don't)

   A Write a clear list of candidates and clients you are actively working on and work out where you can match them or which clients and candidates you can introduce them to. Then work though your list.

   B Interview a candidate and be reminded of a few clients you have met recently whom you know will love this candidate and hop on the phone to them.

C Work through your brought-forward calls for the day in accordance with both a series of call-backs you have identified and clients you have not spoken to for a while.

D Divide your day into sections so you work on a part of the recruitment process every day.

E Work reactively to your candidates and clients and do what you feel like on a day-to-day basis so long as it all leads to potential placements.

F Be driven by the SLAs in your company, either internal or external, so if you pick up a requirement you then process it within two hours and ensure you send the required number of CVs.

G Follow the methodology as laid down by your employer and find this helpful.

H Have a rule where you work on the elements closest to the results. Manage your time around prioritizing your offers first, then concentrate on the next step down – the second interviews – then first interviews, CV send-outs, and so on down the line.

I Work in a different way on different days depending upon what you have on and what energy level you have at the time.

Scoring key

To find out which you are more inclined towards, code your answers as follows:

Follow the key and give yourself an 'S', 'AS' or 'A' tick for each answer that correlates to yours. In Question Five score only those you have ticked.

Collate your points here:
S
AS
A

Key

Question 1
  A S
  B AS
  C A

Question 2
  A A
  B S
  C AS

Question 3
  A S
  B SA
  C A

Question 4
  A S
  B SA
  C A

Question 5

- **A** S
- **B** A
- **C** S
- **D** S
- **E** A
- **F** AS
- **G** S
- **H** AS
- **I** AS

Now count up your As, Ss and ASs.

Mostly As

You are mostly an artistic recruiter and need to be able to work creatively and autonomously. Make sure you play to your strengths both where and how you work in recruitment. If you have a few ASs in there somewhere, you'll like to use measures after the event to explore your KPIs (key performance indicators). This will help you work out how to develop more.

Mostly ASs

You sit between the two and have great flexibility. Remember to use both sides of your talent to make the most of recruitment. If you have ASs with a few As, then let your creative side out often, particularly when coming up with creative ways of resourcing or developing recruitment strategies or matching candidates to clients.

Mostly Ss

You are mostly a scientific recruiter and need to work to a process and a routine. Make sure you play to your strengths both where and how you work in recruitment. If you have a few ASs in there somewhere you'll like to match candidates on cultural fit as well as skills and experience and this will help you in your interview-to-placement ratios.

How to use this information

To give you the best chance of success you should try to adopt some of the behaviours that are less natural for you. Playing to your strengths is not about ignoring the parts of the role you don't like, but it is about making sure you have the opportunity to do work you are good at every day. So, if you are an artistic recruiter make sure you have some creative working activity for a good part of your time every day. If you are scientific, try to see the value in your artistic colleagues' creative way of working and see if you can also adopt some of these traits.

Whether you are artistic or scientific, the more you can tolerate the opposite way of working the more choices you have. This does not mean you cannot work in an environment that does not match your strengths, but you may find it more stressful and have to develop strategies to overcome it.

In today's recruitment environment there is less opportunity for artistic recruiters to survive outside small businesses; organizations demand far greater compliance with procedure than ever before. The legal demands from Data Protection, Right to Work (RTW), referencing and the relatively new Agency Workers Regulations (AWR) coupled with most recruiting firms, and direct organizational recruiters, placing strong value on their candidates databases as a critical element of intellectual property mean that there is a heavy burden of administration and compliance on individual recruiters. Some agencies work round this by separating out administration from recruitment sales thereby enabling both scientific and agency recruiters to do well but others see the administration as part and parcel of a good recruiter's role. Whichever organizational strategy you adopt or work for the important thing to check is that it works for you and you are not forever fighting or swimming in a different direction as this is unlikely to make you successful.

Motivation and values

The next aspect to explore is what is important to you in terms of your motivation and values. Many organizations see values as an integral part of the business, and with good reason. We all have particular values that are personal to us. Many will have been shaped by our upbringing and others will have been self-determined. Some of these values may be around morality, some around political leanings, some around what is important to us. Values often change over time – the things that are important to us at 18 are not, in most cases, the ones that we care most about at 40, for example. At 18 we will perhaps be interested in our friends, exam grades and how we look. At 20 to 30 perhaps we'll be interested in developing a career, travelling the world and considering buying a place of our own to live in. At 40 we might be interested in paying off the mortgage, getting our children into good schools, making sure the family is well and supported and we're really enjoying our work. Although this is quite a stereotypical list, and certainly won't apply to everyone, a value is what is important to you now, regardless of others.

It is important for employers to understand their employees' values and motivations so they can provide an environment in which people can fulfil their motivations and aspirations. This means the quality of work is higher as they are more motivated. This is no different from paying attention to your candidates' motivations and aspirations at interview. Satisfying these when placing them is key to the acceptance of the jobs they are offered.

It is also important to understand our own values and motivations so we can take charge of them for ourselves. Figure 3.2 will help you work out your values so as to see what is important to you at work.

FIGURE 3.2　Values builder

Most important outcomes:		A	B	C	D	E	F	G	H	I	J	K	L	M	N	O
Develop myself and learn more	A															
Earn a significant income	B															
Get promoted regularly	C															
Be in charge of my own destiny	D															
Be cared for at work	E															
Have a good work-life balance	F															
Feel all is fair at work	G															
Play hard	H															
Work hard	I															
Work as part of a good team	J															
Have and implement my own ideas	K															
Recognized for good performance	L															
Work in the way I want	M															
Compete with others	N															
Work in a friendly environment	O															

Complete the table by comparing each outcome with each other by comparing outcome A with outcome B. For example, in box AB, compare 'develop myself and learn more with 'earn a significant income'. Decide which is most important to you and note the most important factor in the box eg A. Continue down the table until all the boxes are complete. Then add your totals in the totals box at the bottom and note your top three outcomes.

Totals															
	A	B	C	D	E	F	G	H	I	J	K	L	M	N	O

Once you have worked out what your core values are this will help you make decisions about the right work environment for you, but also to share this information with your managers, so they can help you achieve what you need to at work. If you are happy and well motivated, it is likely you will achieve more.

Now you have worked through what you want, it's time to consider how you might develop your business.

Developing a business strategy

04

This chapter takes you through a step-by-step plan for developing your desk strategy. It will be of most help if you are a more experienced recruitment consultant who wants to start choosing which sectors and clients to work on, a team leader perhaps or head of a division who is interested in thinking about how to extend your own business through developing clients and candidates strategically. As an in-house recruiter you can also use some of this section to consider your candidate attraction strategy and the business proposition you make to your client. The principles and challenges, for both in-house and external clients remain the same.

You will find tools to help you identify different elements of your existing business and think through options for extending it. This chapter is less about how to do the job well and more about planning which clients and candidates to focus on to give you the greatest chance of success. Some of the choices may not be wholly open to you, as you may already work for an agency or consultancy that has a clear focus, and you may also have a desk with a certain sector focus. Recruitment consultancies and agencies themselves have become much smarter and more strategic about focusing their business in an area where they can develop expertise and therefore offer an outstanding service to their clients. Equally, there will always be some choices in developing a desk or extending a business area; working proactively in this way will make you feel much more in control of your own destiny.

This approach may be most appealing to you if you are a 'scientist' rather than an 'artist' where your focus is likely to be more on developing an environment for yourself where you can be creative. However, if the idea of planning everything down to the 'nth' degree is unappealing to you, you may like some of the creative thinking that can emanate from the tools given.

Often starting a plan is the hardest part. You don't know where to start or what you need to consider. A great place to start is to think about where you are now, and where you want to be. This sets the goals of your plan and you will then be able to address how you might get there. You'll have some thoughts on this already from the exercise in the earlier part of the book.

Examples of where you are/want to be might include:

- I have eight contractors running currently and I want to get to 15 out by the end of this year.
- I work on an average of 60 temps a week out and I want to increase that to 75 to afford my holiday next year.
- We place 15 per cent of our candidates from direct in-house sources currently. I want to move that to 25 per cent by the end of this year.
- I billed £450,000 last year and want to hit that magic £1 million figure within three years.
- 42 per cent of possible recruits perceive our brand positively. I want to lift that to 65 per cent this year.
- I placed three 'heads of service' roles this year through search. I want to move towards 'C' suite level roles this year.

Often this is the hardest part, but once you have done it you'll have completed the first part of your business planning process.

Business planning process objectives

- setting goals;
- gap analysis;
- assessing the internal environment – SWOT analysis;
- assessing the external environment – PESTLEC analysis;
- business strategy development;
- tactical options;
- programme development;
- measurement and review.

Setting goals

What do you want to achieve? This could have a whole range of answers. In general if you are not clear what you want to achieve you are unlikely to achieve it – not least because you won't know whether you have been successful or not!

If you are working for a company your goals must 'fit' with the corporate objectives. So, if your company has an objective to increase its market share in its chosen sectors by 5 per cent while you want to start a new sector, this may not be in line with the corporate plan. So you first need to find out what your company's objectives are.

Task

If you don't know what your company's strategy and objectives are, ask your manager or director before thinking about the next stage. When you know what the strategy and objectives are, or if you are choosing your own, you can move on to the next stage.

We have already looked at some possible scenarios but here are some more goals:

- an increase in revenue from last year of 50 per cent;
- an increase in graduate applications from top 20 universities this year by 25 per cent;
- 15 per cent more briefs filled than last year;
- 500 more qualified candidates on the database;
- a reduction in agency costs (if you are working in-house) by 15 per cent;
- my target of 220k permanent revenue;
- two deals a month each month above 15 per cent margin;
- three retained assignments with fees above 30k per month.

'SMARTER' objectives

What do you notice about each of these? They are, as you may have noticed, all SMARTER objectives. If you do not make your objectives at least SMART then you will not know if you have achieved them.

S – Specific

M – Measurable

A – Agreed

R – Realistic

T – Time Bound

E – Enjoyable

R – Recorded

Let's look at those above and see what they look like when they are not SMART:

- more revenue than last year;
- an increase in graduate applications from top 20 universities this year;
- more briefs filled than last year;

- more qualified candidates on the database;
- a reduction in agency costs;
- bill well;
- improved margins on consistent number of deals;
- sell retained assignments.

How would you know if you had achieved those? How many more briefs? How many candidates? How many more applicants? Does success mean one or two or half a dozen? If it's not clear, the goals are pretty worthless.

So making your goals SMART is crucial to success, or at least to knowing when you have been successful. There is a story – which may be an urban myth – that in one year at Harvard all the graduates were invited to write down three goals they had. Some did and some did not. Several years later they all met at a reunion and found that the ones who had written their goals down had achieved them and more. Those who had not written down their goals had not achieved as much.

Equally we should not let goals constrain us – you'll get to know yourself quite well and you'll recognize what works for you. Some people are happiest when they have a goal set for them, some will hate that and want to set the goal for themselves. Others won't be keen on goals at all and feel constrained by them. They will need to have a minimum level that they know they need to achieve and then the freedom thereafter to achieve as much or as little as they want, or are able to.

If you find your SMART goals, when you have set them, don't inspire a sense of job satisfaction to come, a sense of excitement, a sense of reward or recognition to follow, then they may not be the right goals. If you personally are not motivated and enthused about achieving your goals, you need to ask yourself some long hard questions about whether this is what you really want.

Let's assume, however, that you are clear about what you want to achieve and that you are motivated to achieve it. After all, there are fantastic rewards to be had from working within the recruitment industry both agency- and client-side.

Task

Take some time out to write your goals now. You can be as short or long term as you like – you can focus on this week's goal or this quarter's, or use this as a planning tool for next year's business activity. You wouldn't want to complete this whole process each week of course but it will get you started.

Gap analysis

This is the second stage of the process. Let's take the first two SMARTER goals as an example.

- An increase in revenue by 50 per cent. This could apply to any discipline in recruitment; permanent revenue, contractor revenue written or search revenue.

- An increase in graduate applications by 15 per cent. More likely to apply to an in-house recruiter or someone outsourcing a graduate recruitment scheme. Of course you can still apply this to any group of candidates, so this can apply to anyone as a goal focusing on candidate attraction.

The first action is to establish what this involves in real terms. Whenever you identify an increase or uplift in anything you'll need to do a gap analysis to see what this really means. Figure 4.1 shows a gap analysis looking at the first objective: an increase in revenue by 50 per cent. Displaying it pictorially really helps us focus on what needs to be done.

FIGURE 4.1   Gap analysis for proposed increase in revenue

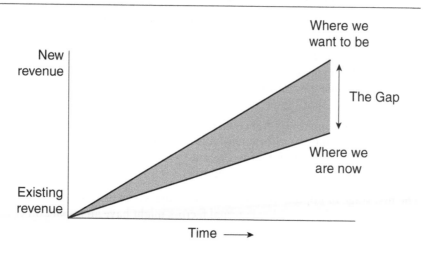

The shaded section is the gap you'll need to fill. The line showing where you are now is where you will be if you make no changes and keep working as hard and in the same way as you are now. This may be your existing target or number of placements. It may be that moving to the top line may just be a matter of working smarter, being in your sector longer or working three evenings a week, but either way the next stage is to do a more detailed examination of where you are. This means looking both internally and externally at your business or your desk or your department. Once you know where you are you can work on closing the 'gap'.

Assessing the internal environment – doing a 'SWOT' analysis

This is the first step in looking at your desk. It means taking an analytical view of you and your desk or your internal business in order to look for ways to fill your 'gap'. SWOT (SWOT analysis originated at Stanford Research Institute from 1960–70 and was developed from research funded by Fortune 500 companies as a way to discover why corporate planning failed) stands for:

S – Strengths

W – Weaknesses

O – Opportunities

T – Threats

- A *strength* is a particular skill or distinctive competence that you have in yourself or within your team or organization that will help you in your role. So the strengths you list must be relevant strengths to your work. These might be experience in particular client groups or abilities in certain aspects of the recruitment process.

- A *weakness* will be anything likely to stop you achieving – it could be a lack of knowledge, support, skills, experience or process.

- An *opportunity* is any aspect of the external environment that could help you achieve your business objectives. This might be a forthcoming event that could increase demand, like the Olympics or another sporting event.

- A *threat* is anything in the external environment that could hinder you achieving your objectives, this might be a competitor for example. Something that is a threat to one organization could of course be an opportunity for another.

The first stage of populating your SWOT analysis is to examine the external environment and assess what external factors might have an impact on your business. Once you have done this you can then complete the S/W elements.

Examining the external environment – PESTLEC analysis

This tool enables you to look outside your business into your market sector and beyond, to check out what influences might be around to adversely or otherwise affect your sector. Cyclical activity can impact on the recruitment industry and this is one way to stay on top of it.

PESTLEC stands for different areas of our world. Ask yourself how this element impacts your business in the future. Consider what impact might this have and how you can maximize its opportunity, or minimize its threat.

P – Political

E – Economic

S – Sociological

T – Technological

L – Legal

E – Environmental

C – Cultural

Some of these may be more relevant than others – it depends upon the business you are in. In our industry LEST might be, arguably, the key ones.

Political

This refers to the political landscape. This will be particularly relevant to organizations involved in recruiting overseas, search firms conducting global searches, or multinational corporations moving executives from one country to another. The impact on the process and IT industries of offshore working and of labour arriving from emerging markets occurred as a result of political actions. Labour shortages in some developed countries mean that labour has to be imported from overseas, and political immigration policies can affect that one way or another. Closer to home, any change in a political party may or may not impact on the business environment. Shifts in public sector spending are of particular relevance, as recruitment markets will shift up and down depending upon whether the public or private sectors are increasing their spending.

CASE STUDY

Radu Manulescu, who runs a search firm in Romania, says he can compare the Romanian economy with the situation in most of the countries in Western Europe 30 years ago. The major search consultancies, he says, are struggling to gain a market in the sector as firms do not understand the value of the search service. There has been little investment in talent in the country, which means that senior managers are often recruited externally. The demand for experienced people is very strong, leading to real challenges in the development of the economy and a saturated search market for the senior people with skills. This all affects Radu's market opportunity and is a classic example of selling into an immature market.

Economic

Arguably this is the strongest area of influence on the recruitment industry. Often the industry experiences a downturn earlier than anyone else, but it can also be early to recover out of a recession. Sometimes there is a selective downturn. In the lead up to 'Y2K', spending on IT systems to prevent a possible crash in the year 2000 was at an all-time high. This precipitated an immediate slump in IT immediately thereafter. It was 18–24 months before there was a reprieve. The industry as a whole was impacted by the most recent 2008/09 recession, the deepest cut the industry has ever seen where it saw a reduction by some 25 per cent, although this varied hugely globally and sectorally; the worst hit sectors unsurprisingly mirroring their economies with the US and Europe faring particularly poorly. As this edition goes to press the focus is on the challenges in the Eurozone and possibilities of a double-dip recession. It does not look likely that a fast-growth economic bounce similar to that of both the 1980s and the early 2000s will return as quickly as previously.

A study on *Working Futures from 2004 to 2014*, produced by the Warwick Institute for Employment Research, has some detailed predictions about the labour market (expected to remain largely steady with employment growing slightly), the pattern of that labour market, the sectors that are expected to grow, those expected to decline and the roles within sectors similarly. This is their prediction for occupational change:

- Faster growth is now indicated for:
  - managers, some professional and many associate professional occupations;
  - protective service occupations and culture /media/ sports occupations;
  - caring personal service and customer service occupations.
- More rapid declines have been observed for:
  - administrative, clerical and secretarial occupations;
  - skilled manual and electrical trades;
  - other skilled trades.

One of the current challenges is the almost unprecedented levels of youth unemployment in the UK, with one million young people unemployed. This will have a major impact upon talent flow and skills availability.

The business life cycle

Some markets may also need, in their planning, to consider how the economic business life cycle impacts on them. Sectors such as hotel and catering may experience an upsurge in temporary staffing needs during peak periods like Christmas and New Year. The weather may also affect demand for services; catering at Wimbledon is less busy during bad weather!

Sociological

The sociological aspect covers the way people live and work, and the shifts in a range of different areas of life have an influence on the recruitment industry in one way or another. Such changes include the move towards working more from home, portfolio careers instead of a job for life, the mobility of the labour market in general, the decline in extended families staying together, the increase in the number of single people, the lengthening of the working life, the return of women into the workplace and greater longevity. All these have effects on the workforce. B&Q, the home improvement retailer, is well known as an employer that recruited people aged over 50 to fulfil a range of roles in its business to wide acclaim and great success. We may not always live in the same way that we do now. The potential for change may also have impacts on your desk and make a difference about where you focus your business efforts. It may affect your candidate flow in a corporation as an in-house recruiter and should always be included as part of your external analysis.

The most recent recession has also spawned wider sociological change in that the loss of value of pension funds means that people will be working much longer than they ever did before. The previous generation of Baby Boomers are also likely to be the most economically wealthy retirees that the UK and other European countries has ever seen and will ever see again. The next generations, Generation X and Y will be working much later in life, partly because they cannot afford to retire, partly because they are staying fitter and living longer. This also creates a shift in the labour market make-up.

On top of this there is a shift taking place in the type of work being done and the skills needed to complete it.

CASE STUDY

Dr Ian Pearson, the futurologist from Futurizon GmbH, has an interesting perspective on the future of markets, age and gender on recruitment. He says that in spite of major changes over the last few decades, teaching, care work and most human skills jobs are all dominated by women and goes on to explain:

> The rapid development of artificial intelligence and robotics over the next two decades will automate a great deal of the intellectual, administrative, strategic and manufacturing work that exists today. What is left will include a much higher proportion of work that involves interpersonal contact and requires human skills. Perhaps the future of work therefore belongs to women.
>
> Machines will automate traditionally 'male' work, whereas 'female' work is harder to automate. Of course, it is not so simple. Many women also do intellectual, administrative and skilled manual jobs, and will be vulnerable to the same processes

of automation. Similarly, men involved in interpersonal jobs such as policing, teaching and personal coaching will be largely protected. Both men and women will have to adapt and retrain as appropriate to fit the jobs in this new 'care economy'. But women will certainly have the overall advantage since evolution has given them an inbuilt orientation towards people skills. The era where men's evolutionary advantages dominated will soon be over.

Gender is not the only factor here. Age is another. While today, companies prefer to recruit young energetic people with new ideas, in a human skills world, older people are better suited. Social skills gradually improve throughout adult life. Conveniently, as the pensions problem forces people to work longer, work will change to suit older people better.

If the future of work is oriented towards human interaction, the winners will be carers, those who are beautiful, with nice personalities, leadership and motivation skills, political and social skills, communication skills, the entertainers and sports heroes, and the celebrities. That these are not surprising reflects that the process is already under way.

So those organizations already positioned to deliver skills in the softer, people-oriented skills, and those taking care of their female and older candidate base will be well-placed to deal with the work challenges of the future.

Technological

Changes here are self-evident and include changes to home and work; the use of the internet was discussed in some detail in the first chapter. Technology has increased the pace of everything, not least recruitment. This is probably the biggest single revolution the world has seen. Generation Y (the c. 30-year-old labour market) expect to be online 24/7 and consider their Blackberry the norm, instant messaging and texting their candidates to keep in touch.

Generation Z, M, the Net Generation, nicknamed 'digital natives', have had life-long use of communications as they were born after the year 2000 when internet communications were very much a way of life. Many will have been brought up by parents working from home as a result of the new connectivity leading to their understanding of the 'norms' of work. This generation is already eschewing the corporate world of work for a more integrated work-life, running their own businesses and online consultancies.

As we said in the introduction one of the biggest changes for recruiters in this section has been the advent of social networking sites to identify and develop relationships with candidates and present a profile to your client and candidate base.

Recruitment consultants need to take care not to let the technology available rule the way they work. Systems are there to help get the work done, not to dictate how it should be done. Finding a way in which technology can help build a competitive advantage is the way forward. This is likely to become ever more critical as data becomes easily accessible and free to all. Knowing who a candidate is, how to find them, their background and on paper their suitability for a role will become common knowledge and accessible to all through sites like LinkedIn. This used to be a key selling point of recruitment consultancies and in particular search consultancies. Their database was seen as a competitive advantage. Now the database will only be of value in relation to the quality of the detail on the candidate on that database. It is not enough to know that Fred Bloggs works at X insurance company as an underwriter, they live in Gravesend and have ten years' experience. Everyone in that sector can find that out through social networking. What's really important is the quality of the information and the relationship of that person with the recruiter or the recruiter's organization or their perception of the recruiting organization's brand. Recruitment skills and employer branding come much more to the fore. The critical skill now for recruiters will be a combination of sales, relationship building and career counselling. For organizations it's about reputation management and the employee experience.

CASE STUDY

Whilst Dave Pye (now CEO at the JM Group, a leading IT recruiter) was with Highams Recruitment, a provider of IT talent for the insurance and financial markets, they developed their own social networking site 'bluefuse site', 'a business community for technology talent'. 'We want to provide a forum and a network for candidates and clients in our sector to share expertise and information on,' he said. 'Membership will be by invitation only and we aim to take up the spare five minutes in the day our clients and candidate have to update themselves on the latest industry information, find someone to share ideas with or a service provider that others rate.'

Legal

This includes not only the laws that have had impacts on the industry recently and the ones that are on the horizon, but also the ones that might affect our client and candidate base. A shift in immigration laws might have a major impact on the capacity for some firms to attract labour. Recruitment itself is becoming increasingly constrained by legal developments.

Laws will need to keep up with the changes in society so those changes we can see coming in relation to society are likely at some point to be reflected in new laws. As recruiters it is our responsibility, and that of the business leaders within our industry, to ensure we have a good understanding of the law so we comply with it in all areas of recruitment from interviewing through to reference taking and giving. However, it is unlikely to be a key factor in deciding where to focus your desk unless you are working in an area where working practices legislation is likely to have an adverse impact on your business.

CASE STUDY

Martin Rush and Paul Hanikene, founders of Square One Resources in the IT sector, always held in mind that there was always the potential that contracting would be made illegal. Although this might sound unlikely there has been a point at which employing contractors was looking potentially very difficult. Their perspective helped the business grow by focusing on an area of core competence and the development of highly transferable sales skills that could then apply to any industry.

Environmental

The environment is an increasingly important agenda for us as a society, as well as organizations. This will doubtless grow and affect everything from the paper we use – and whether we use it at all – to the vehicles we drive, the offices we design and work in, the amount of home-working done, the energy we burn and the way we travel to work. Responsible organizations will want to be conserving energy. The key here is to use the environmental analysis to consider your clients and also their clients – in other words your client's supply chain – and to understand the impact of potential environmental changes to their business and their clients' businesses and to see whether this will be of help to you or a threat.

Cultural

This affects a product or service in a range of ways. Culture can mean the dominant behaviour in a certain sector, which could be divided in a range of ways: gender, nationality, religion, regional base or social group. In rural areas, for example – where people have less internet access, more access to printed media and are more likely to look in recruitment consultants' 'shop windows' at the jobs on offer – the face-to-face recruitment model is still highly prevalent. For agencies working in a rural environment, although the internet as a recruitment tool must be part of their range of tools, it is much less applicable than it is in urban environments.

The reduction in global barriers to the movement of labour has meant a surge in different nationalities available to work in the UK. Some consultancies have a thriving business recruiting overseas staff to work in UK skill-short markets. It has also meant that searches for senior roles are invariably global. This cultural change has meant the global recruiters need to consider whom they are recruiting to be able to deal with a range of cultures.

CASE STUDY

Eddie Austin reports how ITN Mark Education has recognized the structured imbalance within the availability of UK teachers especially in the specialist subjects such as maths and science. ITN Mark has developed a competence as a market leader in the recruitment of international teachers. As a key part of the recruitment process their specialist education consultants, operating from several international branch locations, recruit both experienced and newly qualified overseas-trained teachers.

Teachers are recruited through relationships with international teacher training colleges and universities plus specific career fairs and open days. An important piece of the recruitment process consists of a face-to-face interview with UK head teachers. Prospective teachers are evaluated on their knowledge and understanding of the national school curriculum and their suitability for work in the UK.

International teachers are then supported by UK-based education consultants as part of their transition into the UK and education system. Schools and teachers recognize the ongoing support that ITN Mark delivers to each individual, and it is this level of support and innovation that creates competitive advantage and differentiation.

Task

Complete the appropriate aspects of your PESTLEC analysis and then use these elements to complete your SWOT for your desk. The strengths and weaknesses are about you as a recruiter or are internal to the company and the opportunities and threats are drawn from your PESTLEC analysis, include your competition and are external or independent of you or the company.

Figure 4.2 is a SWOT analysis for a fictitious consultant. As a sense check to your SWOT, you might want to get a colleague or your manager to do one on you as well and compare notes afterwards. This is important, as your own view of your own SWOT is only helpful if your clients and candidates would see things the same way and value the findings. That is to say, the fact that you are an ace team worker in the company is unlikely to matter to your client unless that means you are able to generate better candidates as a result of that. For an internal recruiter or department the same principles apply.

FIGURE 4.2   SWOT analysis

S	W
• Great candidate network, candidates often referred on • Good recruitment process and follow up • Closes well • High conversion rate from CV to placement • Can turn candidates into clients	• Slow to find new clients from cold
O	**T**
• Digital market is still evolving and getting bigger • Global markets increasing in importance	• Other agencies have a good digital offering • Marketing can be first to lose budget in a recession • No overseas operations

Once you are happy you have completed the SWOT you can then see at a glance what kind of shape you are in as a recruiter.

- Do you have more strengths than weaknesses?
- Do you have more opportunities than threats?
- How important are each of the strengths and weaknesses and opportunities and threats?
- Can you match any of the strengths to the opportunities?
- Can you convert any of the weaknesses to strengths?

You can see in the example SWOT this recruiter has more strengths than weaknesses and more opportunities than threats, so is on the face of it in good shape. Strengths are only useful however when they can be matched to an opportunity.

The SWOT analysis will not provide you with a strategy in itself but is a great framework for laying out all the information in order to decide upon a strategy.

CASE STUDY

A director worked with his senior managers on a SWOT analysis as part of a wider piece of work on defining their go-to-market proposition. After completing the SWOT it became clear that, in their market segment, they were the only team offering an executive search and selection service with a dedicated senior team. This important differentiator became one of the cornerstones of their client proposition.

At this point you have developed a really good picture of where you are and where you want to be. You will have identified some weaknesses in your own desk and area that you can develop, and some strengths that you can really build on to meet opportunities in the market to beat your competitors. You'll need to decide how to make the most of them.

Business strategy development

A *strategy* is a systematic plan of action stating how you are going to achieve your objectives – an action plan if you like. So this might be to develop your top three clients so as to double your revenue from them, and to open three new ones. It might be to develop excellent relationships with all of your internal clients and to advise and help them with interviews, so that you are adding value over and above just generating candidates for them.

To be effective the action plan must detail how to offer services and candidates that clients will want to adopt or hire. So any strategy has to be developed in the framework of the market knowledge developed in your SWOT and PESTLEC.

Tactics are the specific actions you take to fulfil the strategy. This might be mailing and then ringing six clients about a fantastic candidate, with a view to developing three of those new clients. It might be to invite those six new clients to a drinks evening where you have already invited good existing clients. It might be to gain a meeting with those clients. It might be to do all three, or anything else appropriate for your market. You are likely to have a range of tactics for any strategy. Your tactic for developing relationships in-house might be to walk the floors more and 'drop-in' on people more regularly, or wander round with CVs and present them personally rather than relying on the system. It might also be ensuring that you are seen as the fabric of the business by going to, and being invited to, social occasions from work and holding some yourself.

A useful tool in thinking about developing your strategy is Ansoff's Matrix (Kotler, 1980), which looks at the use of products (or services) along with markets (or clients) and how to combine the two in order to increase revenue. It is actually a very simple tool and offers four choices (strategy is all about making the right choices) as to how to develop in a broad sense (Figure 4.3).

FIGURE 4.3 Ansoff's matrix

		Product (Candidates)	
		Existing	New
Market (Clients)	Existing	Market penetration	Product development
	New	Market extension	Diversification

As an internal recruiter you may want to consider this tool as a strategy for developing more candidates and explore all the options in relation to your internal clients. As an external recruiter you'll be thinking about these options in relation to your client base:

- *Market penetration* is the least-risk strategy, and the one most likely to develop additional business quickly. This means offering or selling more of the same products (services or candidates) into the same clients. Kellogg's did this when its advertisers suggested we should eat two bowls of cornflakes a day, re-positioning the breakfast cereal as a snack as well.
- *Product development* is when you develop a new service or product and offer that to your existing clients. So when Mars developed Mars Ice Cream they asked you to buy two types of product from them, Mars bars as confectionery and also as an ice cream, thus extending their opportunity for you to buy from them. Various retailers have used this strategy by selling a wide range of new products into their client base, from financial services to furniture.

- *Market development* is when you market or sell an existing product to new clients. This can mean taking clients from competitors or finding new clients to that product or service. In the mobile phone industry, the monthly churn of contracts coming to an end is fought over by all competitors. The interest in winning new customers and locking them into an 18-month contract is high.

- *Diversification* is when you go into a new market with a new product. This does not have to be completely unaligned to your existing market. It could be a recruiter selling a range of new services (say, training) to a new client group. It might be, on the other hand, that as an investment company you invest in a range of products servicing new markets. Often diversification is done through acquisition. This is a higher-risk strategy as it generally means moving into a sector where you have no knowledge of the criteria for success.

Applying Ansoff to the recruitment industry

Consider the opportunities in your desk, or business area for each of these.

Market penetration

Selling more of the same candidates or services into an existing client. Clearly people are slightly different from products here as they do not roll off the production line and you cannot 'make more' to satisfy demand. However, part of the value you add to your clients is the capacity to deliver more good candidates into existing clients, and to penetrate that business so other competitors find it hard to get in at all. Here are some ideas on how to do this:

- Put forward two excellent candidates so the client creates a further opportunity or role for the second candidate as well as the first.

- Develop relationships with other decision-makers in the business as a result of your excellent relationship with your existing contacts.

- Identify a good source of candidates like the ones the client has hired in the past.

- Supply more than one type of candidate (not new to the business) to a client whom you are already working with. So, if you recruit for one area of technology you could also recruit an aligned one that is used by your client: horizontal supply increase.

- Supply more or less experienced staff to your existing client. So if you recruit secretarial staff you could also supply office managers. If you supply them with a range of specialist staff you could also supply them with a range of non-specialist staff: vertical supply increase.

- If you are operating a managed agency function, this is about ensuring you place as many staff as possible through your own agency sources and have to use external suppliers as little as possible. This will both drive through your own profit and ensure you are putting your delivery to your own clients first.

- As an internal recruiter recruiting staff directly and using agencies – find a great source of candidates untapped by competitors. Develop relationships with alumni groups through existing employees perhaps or by using an internal referral scheme. Actively re-recruit 'regretted leavers'.
- Develop a talent bank for a client externally or internally.

Whichever tactic you choose, market penetration is the least-risk option and also the least expensive to implement. The disadvantages are that you are potentially leaving yourself open to working with too few clients and not spreading your risk. On the other hand it is profit-heavy in the short-term, the cost of sale is low and time to market is short, and if you do a great job it leaves you with very happy clients.

Product development
Selling different candidates or services into existing clients. Your capacity to identify an additional need within your existing clients (or suggesting that you can help in a different area) is key to the success of this strategy. This is a great way to build a new product or service offering and get it moving. Selling something new, a very new type of candidate or a new service that differs from the normal one to a 'warm' client can mean you learn a great deal about how to develop the product or service so as to go on to work with other clients thereafter. Here are some ideas of how to do this:

- Sell a client-paid advertising campaign alongside your usual contingency service.
- Develop a new recruitment service and sell that to existing clients first.
- Agree an exclusive on a requirement or vacancy where you would normally compete against others.
- Offer a more direct model to your clients where you are a managed agency, recruiting a higher proportion of your candidates directly.
- Propose to deliver a research-only model with a daily rate set of fees rather than a percentage basis.
- Simply offer different candidates for aligned, but slightly different, types of roles.
- Speculatively offer candidates to clients where there is no role you are aware of. Show other capabilities to existing clients.
- Offer assessment or testing services alongside recruitment.

Market development
Selling existing candidates or services into new clients. Often a great way of being able to demonstrate capability to clients you have not worked with before by showing the calibre of candidates available to you. Great candidates are a terrific way of demonstrating the value you can add and can often lead to placements outside a preferred supplier list (PSL). Here are some ideas:

● Identify new clients you want to work with.

● Offer your best candidates into the new clients, widening the opportunities for your candidates and giving new clients access to a great candidate.

● Offer a client-paid advertising service for a harder-to-fill role instead of scouring the database, if you have the skills to implement it.

● Source a search company to work on your specialist technology role as an internal recruiter.

● As an employer, market your candidate proposition to a wider range of candidates. This might be where you educate a new group of candidates to the benefits of working for your business, recruiting from overseas perhaps.

Diversification

Selling new candidates into new clients. This may mean starting a recruitment business in a different sector with a different client base. You could diversify even further by starting a different business altogether. Even in recruitment this is a higher risk, but in a declining market where your desk is quiet this may be an option. Here are some ideas how to do this:

● Examine your market carefully and take the closest candidates or clients to that market and see if there is demand for them. So, if your market is providing physiotherapists to the NHS and the NHS has stopped hiring, see if you can place your candidates into the private sector of any large corporates, private hospitals or individual practices. If you are placing paralegals in the large law firms and they are only recruiting trainee solicitors, see if you can build up a network of trainee solicitors through your paralegals through networking and place them.

● If you are working in an agency supplying marketing staff to agencies, see if you can supply them in-house. A low-risk form of diversification.

● When analysing advertising, both online and in the press, notice what sectors and what roles are still in demand. In a recession there is always a need for public sector roles, accountants and professionals in general, and business development people with a track record.

● In-house, see if there are other areas of the wider business you could support. If the UK is quiet for example or has a head-count freeze, can you support a global or group function? If no one is hiring, diversify by offering other services and skills. Find out what roles are likely to be in demand in the next round of hiring and begin developing a talent bank of passive candidates perhaps (those not looking but who might be good for your client at some point). This is a good time to re-evaluate your preferred supplier list, and perhaps re-negotiate fees for a smaller list or some exclusivity on certain roles and higher volume if you know this is coming up in the near future. It's also a good time to overhaul things like interview guides, role specifications, systems and processes so when the recruiting starts again you are in good shape.

> **Task**
>
> Decide which of these four options might be best for you to achieve your goals. You may decide on one strategy to start with a second to follow through on. Clearly, constraints here will be the business you work in and what is possible. Share the results of this activity with your manager. Better still, get everyone in the team to undertake this process together.

Once you have some clarity about your strategy it is time to focus on the tactics you will employ to achieve your strategy. A useful way of categorizing your tactics is to use the marketing 'Four Ps' (Figure 4.4). Marketeers use the Four Ps to work out their tactics for launching a new product or developing a plan for an existing one. You can use them quite simply to order your options.

FIGURE 4.4   The four Ps

Price	Place
Product	Promotion

Tactical options

Price

For recruitment consultants this is about fees. For internal recruiters it is about setting fees for suppliers or setting salary bands for hires.

If you are a recruitment consultant you may have no control over terms and conditions that are offered to your business but you will always have control over whether you charge a full fee or not. Increasingly large clients are implementing their own terms and conditions which you'll negotiate with them on.

Reducing fees or margins brings a range of significant problems; it suggests a lack of confidence in your own ability to deliver; it sends a signal of desperation to the client, who may wonder why you are charging so little and worry that there is a problem with the temp or the service. It also devalues the industry as a whole.

There will, however, be times where negotiating terms in exchange for something else from the client may be advantageous to both of you. The opportunity to work exclusively on a vacancy may on occasion be worth a small fee reduction, depending upon the amount of work required to find the right person for the role. The inclusion on a good PSL may also be worth a reduction – of course in many circumstances you will be required to reduce your fees for this. You'll need to decide if this is worthwhile and whether the reduced 'cost of sale' justifies the reduction. If your business is specialist and you provide scarce talent you may feel that strategically it is not worthwhile taking a PSL approach as your margins will be much reduced.

In-house, you'll want to set the supplier fee level at a level low enough for you to feel you are gaining value for money, yet not so low that it becomes uneconomic for agencies to do business with you. You'll be aware how your salaries sit in relation to the rest of the market and know how you will position this.

Place

This relates to how you will distribute your service or product. It is relevant to a recruitment business owner or someone starting up in business, but recruitment consultants joining an organization will already have this decided for them. 'Place' is about whether you will set up a shop front on a busy high street or offer an internet service or whether you will network and work with other consultancies or stand alone. In-house it's about deciding how you will operate as an internal recruitment team but much of this will be to do with your approach to talent.

Product

This means the type of candidates and services you can offer to clients. To be successful here the candidates and services you offer must be in demand. (This may sound obvious but is easily overlooked.)

CASE STUDY

After Y2K, many recruitment consultants working in IT services continued to market expensive IT consultants when the demand for them had dropped off – it took six months for this to be fully recognized as fees gradually declined and contracts were not renewed. Tactically, from completing a regular PESTLEC analysis, these consultants could have switched quickly to other skills for which there was still a demand, albeit weaker. In any market, but especially one with candidate or client shortages, the recruiter's skills, both internal and external, become part of the product offering.

In a candidate-short market, services such as search, headhunting and selection are sought after as demand outstrips supply and really strong, focused recruiting methods are needed to deliver quality candidates. In a client-short market these services become less critical for mid-range recruiters, as demand outstrips supply and good people are much easier to find. The top search firms will always have a business that offers this service as there are always senior executives to place, but they too are not immune to recessionary times by any means.

Your product tactic is about which candidates or services you are offering, and the key to success is the capacity to be aware of market changes before or as they happen and the agility to switch your offering in response.

Promotion

The way you communicate with your clients and candidates is crucial. It will impact upon:

- Whether they have heard of you. If they do not hear of you or from you regularly you will not be in their mind as a possible supplier.
- How well you communicate with the clients and candidates. If you are writing e-mails and letters to introduce yourself, make sure you are good at doing this.
- The messages you are giving about you and your business to your clients and candidates.

- The profitability of your business.
- How you are perceived by your candidates and clients.

If you are working in-house, this aspect is no less critical. Your delivery to your clients is as important as your suppliers' service to you. It is just as important to manage the relationships in this service role to the business as it is in an external consultancy role. It is equally important to manage your supplier relationships. For an in-house recruiter to imagine that they will fulfil all hiring transactions to time and budget with no external support and help is both naïve and serving their business poorly. In-house recruiters need to recognize the value of external recruiters both as a source of rich market intelligence, which they won't get elsewhere, and as a source of excellent specialist candidates motivated to join their organization.

Promotional activity could include a wide range of options as shown in Figure 4.5.

FIGURE 4.5   Promotional activity

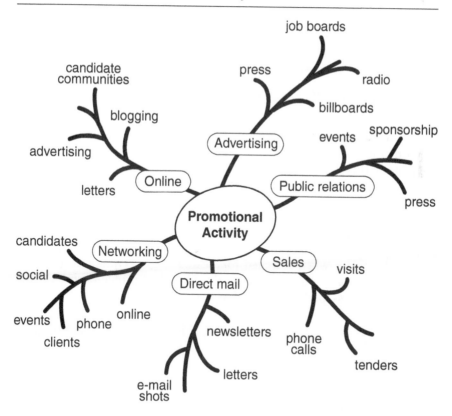

In the 1990s the *Sunday Times'* Appointments section was a recognized showcase for the mid-range search and selection recruiters. Many had targets of how many front-page ads they could run for their clients and how many inside pages. They would keep a tally on how many ads each week. Most recruitment buyers would check out the *Sunday Times* to see who the prolific recruiters were and would ask them in to pitch for their advertised selection roles as a result. Harvey Nash has been a leader in this with its distinctive red logo appearing on most pages more than once every week. With the reduction in print advertising however this particular aspect is declining and recruiters have to find new ways of appearing to be top of their sector.

CASE STUDY

Jerry Wright, latterly MD of search firm Prism Executive Recruitment and Grosvenor Wright, made it a stated objective, when he started Prism in the late 1990s, to appear each week in the *Sunday Times* as a brand-building exercise that showcased both the firm and its clients as leaders in their individual fields. The strategy was highly effective as it established both them and their clients firmly in the minds of the *Sunday Times* readers as key players in their respective markets.

Clearly the major shift most recently has been from print to online. It is no secret that most advertisers, whilst not abandoning their offline advertising are pouring their budgets into online strategies including social networking again. No recruitment business starting up today would consider a print-only strategy and any promotional strategy will include a large proportion of online activity. Research shows that job-seekers are looking online for jobs and that their searches are job-led rather than employer or agency-led so perhaps the most important element is to ensure that jobs appear easily on search engines when searched for. Search Engine Optimization (SEO) replaces *The Sunday Times* as a critical tool as does profile-raising of your service or business, perhaps using blogging.

CASE STUDY

Louise Triance (**www.ukrecruiter.com**), an early adopter of the genre, has developed a wide community of recruitment consultants and has demonstrated how to build a brand through blogging. She has been followed by a wide range of others and there are now blogs on any element of recruitment you might care to think of.

Louise suggests that creating a recruitment blog can bring great rewards. For an external/agency recruiter, it allows you to 'touch base' with a large number of candidates and clients regularly without the effort of producing a weekly/monthly newsletter. If you are an in-house recruiter it can help you engage further with current or future candidates, as well as keeping other functions within the organization updated on your activities. However, you do need to ensure that you have something to post worth sharing and that you can post regularly enough to keep clients/candidates coming back.

Task

Work out your tactics on price, place, product and then promotion on the basis of the market opportunities and threats you have determined. Then do an analysis to see whether your skill set (verbal and written communication, knowledge and understanding of market issues) matches the tactics you are proposing to use. Do you need any additional training to be really effective? If you have 10 clients and only one chance at them, it pays to be really planned and skilled up before your chosen approach. If you have 1,000 and are still developing your skills, the odd mistake is normal, desirable (because it helps you learn) and not a problem.

Measurement and review

The last thing to do with your business plan is to put in some measures and review points so you don't just fold it up in a drawer and never look at it again. You might want to think about reviewing every month or so and if you are slipping your targets, then shift your activity measurements to weekly.

The next thing to explore is how much activity you need to do to achieve your aims, and how to manage your time to achieve your activity goals. You've already considered how best to plan your day, when to do what. Next you'll need to work on what to do and how often, and how to get it all done! The next chapter focuses on just that.

05 Developing key performance indicators

This chapter helps you develop some measurement of your activities. This will help you work out what you do well and where you could develop further, as well as enabling you to plan to take enough action and actually 'do enough work' to achieve your goals or targets. It then offers some tips on how to manage your time well.

First we look at your work levels and then how to plan your day so as to fit all the activity in – time being the one commodity you cannot increase!

We have already referred to Stephen Covey and his book *The Seven Habits of Highly Effective People* (1989). Again, start with the end in mind.

If you have followed Chapter 4, on developing your business strategy, you will have established your goals and strategic approaches. You will have learned how to play to your strengths, and Chapter 2 on the recruitment cycle will have delivered some clear information to develop your plan of action. Now you need to consider exactly how much activity you need to do to reach your goals, which means developing some KPIs to help you:

- how much to do;
- planning your time.

Activity levels

In the recruitment industry activity – actions you are actually taking – can be seen as a key predictor of success. That is not to say raw activity without talent is all it takes to deliver success, but talent alone is not a sufficient criterion. You need to put both together. It's no accident in this industry that people who spend most time on the phone or in front of clients and candidates are the most successful. It is also no accident that when asked for a key piece of advice for recruiters some of our profiled industry gurus said: 'make more "calls" than anyone else.' Activity is really important.

If you have a target to achieve, it is important to develop a plan to achieve the number of placements needed to reach the target. For external recruiters the drive is likely to be revenue or margin-based, with measures on the pipeline-building activity needed to reach those revenue targets. For internal recruiters the emphasis may be on placements made, cost per hire and time from 'requisition raised' to 'job filled'.

These are the sorts of questions you might ask about your performance to explore where it might be improved:

- Can I generate more candidates?
- Can I generate more clients?
- Am I getting the best quality candidates?
- Can I improve my process?
- What opportunities for development are there in my recruitment process?
- Am I getting as much work done as I can in a day?
- What are my conversion ratios and drop-out rates like?

These can all become KPIs to drive up your delivery capability. We would encourage you to develop and use your own KPIs to support your drive for improved overall performance or maybe even your ability to get better results with less effort. If you fail to measure how you do your job, or to look at what you are really good at and what needs support or further development, then you are not taking responsibility for your own work.

If you know what you do well, and what it takes to meet your targets you are immediately in control of what you are doing and can predict your own business results. When you are having a difficult patch you can trace what needs to happen to change, and when things are going really well you won't miss the opportunity to explore why and what it is that underlies this success.

Artistic or scientific recruiters may have different feelings about KPIs. The true artistics are unlikely to pay much attention to these indicators and may also find them constraining. The artistic recruiters will prefer to do as much as they can, relying on their natural drive and creativity to achieve their goals. The artistic scientists will perhaps collate their KPIs weekly, retrospectively, to admire their strengths, especially if they are doing well! Those with more of a leaning towards the scientific artist style may use them to write a PDP (personal development plan) as well. A scientist will review them a couple of times a day and live by them to help achieve his or her target.

Either way, even extreme artists can, we hope, see some value in understanding how the recruitment process works, and how well we manage it, in order to improve on what we do.

Measures to take

Below we set out some of the measures, or activity targets, which you may find helpful in developing an analysis of your work (Table 5.1). Our general advice would be to keep it relatively simple. It's better to measure three things each week than to measure 40 occasionally when you get round to it, as those three things will build up a better picture of trends than the occasional 40. Ratios are generally expressed thus 20 : 2.

TABLE 5.1   Key performance indicators

Measure	What you can learn	Part of the recruitment process	Ratio derived
Time spent on the phone each day	Your office may have the software that enables you to measure how long you spend on the phone each day. This is a hugely rough guide and depends enormously on what business you are in. But it does give you a guideline. If you are not doing two hours plus then this might be a cause for concern.	All	Time spent to monthly billings. There will be a correlation.
New client contacts made	This will measure not the number of calls you put in or messages left, but conversations you had with clients who are decision-makers. This is less relevant for RPO or internal recruiters if they already have developed relationships with all the hiring managers in their company. Suggest you measure on a weekly basis (some organizations and business may find daily measurement appropriate) as few recruitment businesses will be sustained in the long term without acquiring new clients on a weekly or monthly basis.	Client acquisition	You can then measure this against the number of jobs picked up from new clients.

TABLE 5.1 *Continued*

Measure	What you can learn	Part of the recruitment process	Ratio derived
Existing client contacts made	As above, except with existing clients. These calls are about furthering and developing the relationship you have with clients or progressing placements, including briefing and de-briefing interviews, but not including two minutes confirming an interview with someone's PA! This can, for internal recruiters, be about chatting over coffee with internal hiring managers who are not hiring currently but whose area has plans for development in the medium term, so relationships need to be built.	Client acquisition	Again, measure this against the number of new jobs picked up from existing clients.
New candidates generated proactively	This is candidates you have registered, or for whom you have a CV or have booked an interview, that you have generated through your own proactive work of individual advertising or referrals, not general candidates who approach the agency or employer on spec.	Candidate attraction	Measure this against the number of first interviews arranged.
SPEQing out candidates	This will measure the number of candidates you SPEQ out on a daily basis. You'll need to divide these into new and existing clients.	Candidate management/ client acquisition	Candidates SPEQ'd out : interviews arranged. In either category this will tell you how well you have matched your candidates to your knowledge of your clients, or prospective clients.

Continued overleaf

TABLE 5.1 *Continued*

Measure	What you can learn	Part of the recruitment process	Ratio derived
Jobs/ vacancies registered/ requirements taken	The number of new, qualified roles that you take on to work on each week.	Client strategy	Number of decision-maker calls made : number of jobs taken. This will vary from market to market and with the economic health of your market, but if some people in your team need to make 10 calls to pick up a requirement and others only four, then this is a developmental area for you.
Candidates resourced against a role	The number of candidates that you contact about a particular role.	Candidate management	Candidates resourced: candidates submitted. This can give some useful information on either how you are choosing which candidates to resource and how successful your matching is, or how successful your pitch is.
Candidates submitted to client against a role	The number of candidates that you submit as a shortlist for a particular role.	Candidate management	Candidates submitted: first interviews requested. Shows your capacity to match.
Number of tenders or proposals written	The number of formal proposals or beauty parades you attend or write over a period.	Client acquisition	Shows activity only.
Retained assignments won	Number of assignments, whether advertised selection or search, that you win over the same period.	Client acquisition	Tenders written : tenders won.
First interviews arranged	Every first interview you arrange. This is arguably one of the most useful measures. If you measure nothing else, measure this, as it is the beginning of the placement pipeline. Without a first interview you are unlikely to make a placement unless you are running a temp desk.		First interviews : second interviews; or simply, first interviews : candidates placed.

TABLE 5.1 *Continued*

Measure	What you can learn	Part of the recruitment process	Ratio derived
Second interviews arranged	Every second interview you arrange.	Candidate management	First interviews : second interviews. Drop-outs could be for a range of reasons and need investigating – note whether the candidate dropped out or the client. Both need exploring further if rates are unnaturally high. Sometimes this will always be 6 : 2 as this is the objective of the hiring manager. Again we are looking for 'against the norm' here.
Offers received	Firm offers you make to your candidates.	Candidate management	Second interviews : offers received. Depends upon number of second-interview candidates but should not be above a reasonable rate.
Placements made	How many placements have you confirmed this month with a full acceptance and a start date?	Whole recruitment cycle	Jobs taken : placements made. The ratio of jobs you have picked up versus the number of placements you have made, eg 7 : 2. In a candidate-short market this will be higher than in a client-short market. First interviews: placements. The number of first interviews you have arranged versus the number of placements you have made, eg 11 : 2. When a recruiter starts his or her career, this ratio will be higher. As a recruiter becomes more successful the aim is to reduce this right down. Some contingency recruiters will make 2 : 1 or less. Retained recruiters with a prescribed shortlist of four candidates at first interview will only ever get to 4 : 1.

Continued overleaf

TABLE 5.1   *Continued*

Measure	What you can learn	Part of the recruitment process	Ratio derived
Retained assignments completed	Number of assignments resulting in placements.	Whole recruitment cycle	Looking for 75% plus. Some niche firms aim for 90% plus.
Temps or contractors or locums running each week/month	How many temps have you out working for you at any point?	Whole recruitment cycle	Look for an average number and not to fall below that. Varies from industry to industry.

CASE STUDY

A leading high-street recruiter, in a recessionary time, measured how many vacancies were being filled out of those registered. It found that a mere 37 per cent of vacancies coming in from clients were being filled. This was at a time when jobs were incredibly hard to find. The business set a simple target of one measure only: to increase this target to 60 per cent. If this target was achieved the business would increase its turnover by a phenomenal amount, simply working with the roles they already had.

Make the KPIs relevant

It's equally important of course to tailor what you measure to what you are measured on in your role. There is little point in measuring things that you are not measured on yourself. So if you work internally and you are measured on candidate attraction only, this is the key measure for you. There is little point in your measuring conversion rates, as although they are interesting from the business perspective they will not help you improve your results.

Task

Complete your own performance measurements and design your own table to measure them on. Make sure they are aligned to what you will be measured on. Measure yourself for the next four weeks and see where there is an opportunity to develop your skills.

Managing your time

This is not a book on time management and if you want to read more about that there are a wide range of books available. Here are some basic guidelines that work.

Four key rules

The first thing, which you have already done, is to start at the right place. Work out what you are measured on and what you therefore should spend your time on. The key rules are:

- Work on what you are measured on.
- Allocate time to measured activities and be ruthless, keeping to it.
- Work nearest to the placement.
- Work all of the recruitment cycle each week.

Divide up your day

Be ruthless about your day. Often working out what you are being paid an hour can help you focus on whether you want to spend that amount of money on that activity. Taking the view that each hour is an investment of £50, what will you happily spend that much money on? It may be a good investment to spend £50 going out for lunch or to the gym at lunchtime, as it will leave you recharged for the afternoon. Spending an hour desultorily surfing the net and the job boards for inspiration (almost every recruiter must do that from time to time) may not be such good value, as you feel no better afterwards, have sat at your screen too long and still have the afternoon to contend with. If you are not feeling inspired, go and get some fresh air and let the afternoon incubate away in your mind. That is to say, ask yourself what you should do this afternoon to best effect (this may appeal to the artistic!) and instead of trying to answer it immediately go out for a walk, window-shop, pick up some lunch. When you come back and have eaten, you'll be surprised what might have popped into your head – or you scientists may feel re-invigorated to tackle that list you made!

Either way allow some time for 'downtime' in your day to do administration, catch up with colleagues and update your system.

Then allocate some blocks of core work time in your day when you cannot be interrupted, unless for a real crisis (there is a fire or a placement falling out). Make outgoing calls only and return incoming ones later unless, again they are business critical (client calling with an offer, candidate calling to accept). You might choose two hours in the morning and two hours in the afternoon with a further hour for returning calls, arranging interviews, doing database searches and general service to candidates and clients that is not about driving business through. So your two hours are focused on:

- SPEQing in candidates to clients (see pp 111–13 for information on SPEQ candidates);
- resourcing roles you are recruiting for;
- taking candidate and client feedback;
- prepping candidates and clients for interview and de-briefing;
- making new business calls;
- making business development calls to existing clients;
- arranging to meet candidates and clients;
- attracting new candidates;
- taking job briefs/vacancies.

That leaves you two hours a day to do your administration and deal with unexpected things that happen: a new client rings in, in the afternoon, with four contract opportunities that he wants CVs on by tomorrow and your allotted time won't cover it; an old client drops by for a coffee; a fantastic candidate calls and wants to meet for a drink for some advice; or a candidate fails to get the job she really wanted (your client has chosen another of your candidates) and wants to talk through her career options now.

Of course many recruiters work longer hours than this; that is your choice. When you first start the job you may need to put in more time.

CASE STUDY

Richard Herring, Senior Vice-President of Volt, suggests that managing time effectively is the difference between proactive and reactive time management. Failing to organize yourself can leave you working to everyone else's agenda, running the risk of achieving little.

He suggests allocating specific periods in the day to deal with e-mails, 'You would be surprised how much of your time can be absorbed dealing with non business-critical e-mails,' he says. 'Be brutal over this.'

He suggests consultants need to manage their diaries carefully, allowing preparation time for meetings. He structures his week around meetings booked, and then writes a list of daily tasks. Advocating always leaving 'ad hoc' time in the diary for the unexpected, he also suggests you start and end your meetings on time. Last of all, communication breakdown takes a great deal of time while people re-visit what was really meant, so clear communication can be a real time saver.

Working nearest the placement

It's surprising how easy it is to become diverted by activities that may not directly lead to a placement. Of course it's also important to work on activities that will lead to a placement in the long term. If you are in a specialist niche market almost all activity will lead to a placement at some point, as there are a finite level of people and companies. If however you work in a very broad market, you need to be much more careful about dealing with candidates you can never place or companies who are using you for a shortlist to assess their internal candidate.

The activity nearest the placement is the candidate's job acceptance, then the offer management, then the interview de-briefing and so on. Time tends to kill business in this industry, so the longer you leave it between stages, the slimmer the chances of success, particularly at a lower level.

Working the recruitment cycle

You need to be working in all four areas consistently over the week. The temptation is to pick up a search or vacancy (or several) and to work on that until it is filled. Meanwhile, you ignore client acquisition. Even as an internal recruiter, if you are not out having conversations with potential clients in your business, when they come to recruit they will forget you are there and call their favourite external recruiter – they will certainly have one. The result is that you place all your roles and have nothing to work on, so need to start from scratch again.

Every week you need to devote some time to client acquisition and candidate attraction. These two activities are the engine room of the recruitment cycle. Either of them will kick off the recruitment process and move you towards a placement or a deal. So, set some time aside to undertake both of these activities each week. Think of it as £50 invested well every day in your future prosperity!

CASE STUDY

Tracy Ashton of Willow training, who now trains recruiters very successfully, when working for a leading high-street agency in a management role, would always go through with her consultants the value of their order book in terms of potential vacancies they could fill. If any of them were concerned that they did not have 'enough to do', Tracy always found that when they really paid attention to what was on their desks they could often see that they had the potential of business worth £50,000.

Running a search

If you are a search consultant and run several projects at one time, allocate a certain amount of time each day to each project. In this way, you won't come to do your status reporting to your client at the end of the week and find you have good progress on three searches but nothing on a fourth, because you've not planned your week well. If you make that mistake, don't berate your researcher; planning your activity is your responsibility! Mark Forster (2000) in *Get Everything Done and Still Have Time to Play* suggests setting an alarm timer and being ruthless about when it is time to move on.

There is an argument that the most successful recruiters are the ones who naturally do all the right activities all of the time, but within that they manage their time ruthlessly. Managing your time well – without becoming diverted on to tasks that don't lead to successful placements – is one of the hallmarks of the really top recruiters.

Task

Writing your plan

This is the last task in Part 2. In Chapter 3 you did some work on considering your strengths and how important it is to work with them. In Chapter 4 you did some work on your business plan and in this chapter we have focused on how to measure what you are doing and manage your time well.

Now it's time to put that all together by developing your own business plan. In Chapter 4 we outlined the process to develop your plan. By now you should have completed all the activities you need to put the plan together.

You know:

- your goals or target;

- the gap you need to close;

- the external environment and what is relevant to you;

- your SWOT results;

- your strategy;

- the tactics you plan to employ;

- when you will measure and re-evaluate your plan (we suggest monthly);

- your own strengths and weaknesses and how to work with the strengths;

- how you work at your optimum;

- how to manage your day.

Write your plan including all the sections above. It does not need to be anything complicated. In fact, the simpler the better, but having a clear picture of what you are trying to achieve and how you plan to do so will really focus you on what you need to do on a daily basis. Once you have completed your plan, you may wish to share it with your manager or your partner – or pin it up on your wall if you are a sole operator working from home. Keep it in your mind the whole time; it can be a powerful motivator to see how far you have come.

This section has all been about planning and preparation for what to do in your role as a recruiter. It has enabled you to explore your business more strategically and think about how to take your business forward to achieve what you want in your job. All of the extremely successful people in this book started in recruitment with a desk or a patch or a few people to recruit internally, and have built their businesses or employer brand from very little. The opportunity is there for you to do exactly the same. The next section goes on to look at implementing the recruitment cycle so you can deliver great results as a recruiter.

PART THREE
How to deliver excellence in recruitment practice

Introduction

This section is the 'how-to' guide. Covering each of the four key areas of recruitment practice, it explains in detail not only what to do but also how to do it. The quality of what you do, coupled with how much you do, makes the difference between modest capability and significant success as a recruiter, in-house or external. There is a direct correlation in this business between effort and attainment – assuming a reasonable level of competence.

You'll learn the differentiators between an average and a great recruiter. Each market will have its own particular needs so you'll also need to overlay tools and techniques with this knowledge. This section is peppered with tips from successful recruiters or business owners who have built their (often large) businesses from scratch. You may recognize some of the tools from the previous section that we use in a different way here.

As you already know, you can start anywhere in the recruitment cycle, depending upon your market needs. If you have dipped into the book here you can use Figure III.1 below as a guide on 'what to do' under your current market conditions.

FIGURE III.1   The recruitment cycle starting point

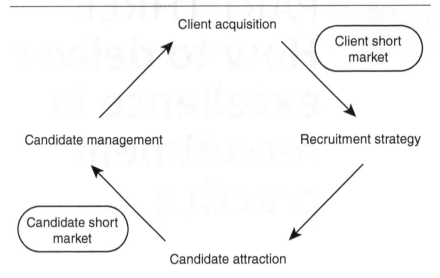

Your success as an all-round recruiter, whether working on the high street in a regional office or as a successful senior search practitioner, will depend upon working regularly in each of the four areas of the cycle appropriate to your personal business situation on a weekly basis at least. Chapter 5 on KPIs will have helped you scope out your levels of activity.

Part Three can be used as an *aide-mémoire* for when you are about to make some calls or go to a networking event, or as inspiration when you are not sure what to do next. You will almost certainly need to change the language used to suit your own style and your sector. But do use the ideas and tools at the end, as they can be translated to any situation or any business area – the most important thing is to keep thinking about what is working and what you need to develop. Evaluating for yourself your own work (and continuously developing it) is the behaviour of a successful recruiter, wherever you work and in whatever way. The next four chapters cover in detail the cornerstones:

- candidate management;
- client acquisition;
- client strategy;
- candidate attraction.

If you do 80 per cent of the activities you will be successful; do 100 per cent and you will be in the top 20 per cent of the industry, like the people profiled and quoted in this book.

Candidate management

06

This chapter deals with how to manage your candidates. Ensuring you give a great service to your candidates is as important as managing your clients. Candidates remember the recruiter who gives a great service, spends time with them, cares about them and above all finds them the jobs they want. Looking after candidates therefore means you will make successful placements, gain referrals to other candidates and develop your personal and agency brand, as well as gaining a significant amount of job satisfaction.

The candidate management process may vary in its starting point, but is always, candidate driven. In this chapter we pick up candidate management from its earliest point: an awareness of you as a recruiter – or of your company or consultancy – by your candidate. The resources include a range of tools to support the candidate management process. There are tools to analyse CVs against a specific role for example, checklists for qualifying strong candidates, techniques on interviewing and templates on writing candidate notes, along with other tools and perhaps most importantly a flow chart detailing the candidate management process.

The chapter looks at the employer or recruiter brand, and the proposition you offer as part of that brand. It examines the candidate management process in detail, starting with evaluating candidates, qualifying them, interviewing them and deciding how to help them find their new jobs. We look at whether a particular candidate fits an existing role specification you are recruiting for a client, or is someone whose skills a range of clients in your area, sector or business would be interested in learning more about. We look at how best to market your candidate to secure the greatest chance of an interview, and then how to manage the placement opportunity through the rest of the process from briefing and de-briefing in interviews through to offer management and closing the placement down. An important theme running through this whole process is that of managing expectations; whilst this is one of the most important aspects of successful recruitment consultancy, it is never more so than when managing your candidates.

The components of the recruiter's brand

Candidate management plays an important role in the development of your brand. It maintains or diminishes the brand, or keeps it in a steady state. All are possible outcomes of the ways you manage your candidates.

Managing the brand is about managing expectations and then exceeding them wherever possible by doing the best you can with all of your candidates.

CASE STUDY

Di Martyn, ex-CEO of Randstad's UK staffing business, the second largest global recruitment and HR services business, sees the 'brand' of Randstad very clearly. She says that she asks all her people to come to work and remember what Randstad is there to do: it's there to find jobs for people and people for jobs. She asks consultants to interview people and to 'become obsessed' with finding them a job. For Di Martyn it's a matter of pride that no one is interviewed in her business without a very serious commitment to find them a job.

For either an employer or a recruitment consultancy, the brand proposition (and for temps and contractors their recruitment consultancy is as much of a brand as other employers) has to be clear and is all-important, so we consider it from all angles.

Your brand is communicated through:

- how clear you are on the roles you offer for your clients;
- what the career progression path and the company's view on succession planning are;
- how many people you promote internally;
- what your policy and offering is in learning and development;
- what your benefits package says about you;
- how good the leadership in your organization is;
- what your market position in your sector is;
- how much work you can offer and whether the candidates need to register with a range of agencies;
- how often you pay your freelancers;
- what your unique selling points (USPs) are and why someone would want to work for you.

Candidates can learn an enormous amount about a recruiter or employer (but particularly the latter) not just by what they are told at their interviews, but rather what they are not told.

From an employer brand perspective, what will the candidates learn about you in the following areas?

- What is reception – and the receptionists – like?
- How flexible are you for interview times?
- How much do you treat applicants as individuals rather than as one of the crowd?
- How long do you keep candidates waiting when they arrive for interview?
- How friendly are you as interviewers?
- What sort of interview do you use? Competency-based? Behavioural? Biographical? Unstructured chat?
- How good do you make your candidates feel during and at interview? How much emphasis do you place on maintaining their self-esteem?
- What tone is set by your communications with them between interviews? Does this match your culture?
- How much does your overall culture reflect your interview process and vice versa? So, if you are a young think-tank ideas organization with some key clients and you are looking for brains above anything, and your offices are full of beanbags and pool tables, how does your interview process and communication style in between interviews, along with your attraction strategy, communicate your intentions?
- Do you contact them when you say you will and in the way you say you will?
- Do people seem to be smiling and enjoying themselves at this place or does it seem a bit miserable?
- What does the layout of the business say about you? Is it open plan or do some people sit in corner goldfish bowl offices and survey others out on the floor?
- What does your salary and benefits package say about you? Are the benefits flexible, making them work for everyone, not just the average white middle-class male?
- How diverse are you are as a business?

CASE STUDY

One firm in London, listed in the *Sunday Times'* 'Top 100 employers to work for', pays a £350 leisure allowance every year to indicate the importance it places on work–life balance. This allowance can be exchanged for week or weekend holiday-cottage rental, flights overseas for a weekend break, personal training sessions with the personal trainer in the gym or anything else related to leisure.

Branding and the employer proposition is a matter of being clear about your company brand and then fulfilling that through the interview process. This will not only reduce an organization's labour turnover but also ensures you have a good match in the first place, recruiting the people you want and finding that they stay.

It's worth analysing the percentage of rejections-to-offer that you get and tracking that over a period. It's hard to give a guideline of acceptability as you may be in a very candidate-short market with all the candidates you offer having three to four other options to consider, which will by necessity reduce your percentage. However, if you are not getting 80 per cent (as an external recruiter – some companies or internal recruiters will look for 95 per cent), then you probably need to re-consider your brand and/or your recruitment process to see how you are managing your candidates.

CASE STUDY

L'Oreal hire some 200 experienced staff a year and some 30 graduates. The company wanted to increase the retention rate of new staff by improving the on-boarding in the business, linking it even more closely to learning and development to ensure a seamless transfer from hire to induction.

They developed a programme called FIT (Full Integration Track), which kicks off before new recruits join the business. The Recruitment Manager stays with them through induction, providing a 'fuzzy line' between recruitment and when they start. Alex Snelling, who at the time was L'Oreal's Recruitment Director, and now heads up HR for the Body Shop, says that managing candidates effectively has always been a cornerstone of his beliefs. The result has been a certainty that if staff do leave after a few months (which is increasingly rare), they are leaving for the right reasons. 'We are not always going to get it absolutely right. We have a very strong culture here at L'Oreal that most of us love, but occasionally does not suit people. At least now we know we have given new joiners every possible assistance into the business,' says Snelling.

It is particularly important, then, to look after your candidates in the first three to six months of their time in new jobs. This is the time when they can be the most vulnerable. Onboarding then, and the employer brand are important components of managing the candidate through after their start with the business.

The key to candidate management

Using the flowchart shown in Figure 6.1 we are going to work our way through the recruitment process from the start of candidate management to the start of client acquisition.

FIGURE 6.1   The candidate management process

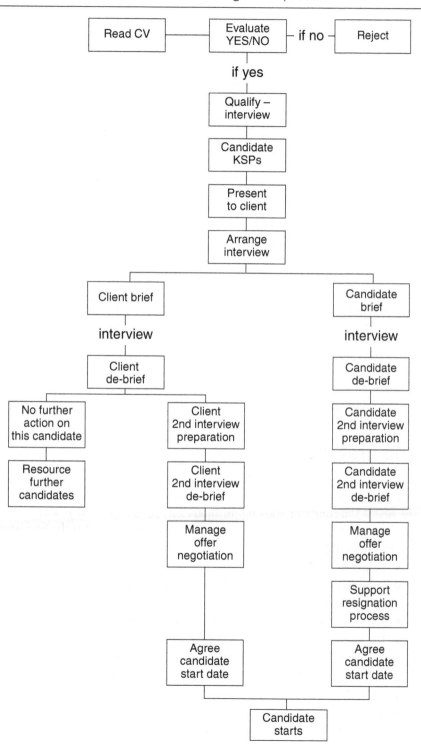

The role of the recruiter is to manage the candidate proactively and control the process.

Recruitment is about successful project management. If you manage candidates effectively the outcome for both you and them will be positive – even if they don't get the job. If you do not manage the people well, relationships can be damaged and opportunities missed. So, if candidates go for job interviews where the jobs in question bear little resemblance to that which you briefed them on, they will be disappointed, the clients will be perplexed and you will not have made a placement. Equally if a candidate is one of three contenders for a really desirable job who all interview well, the client is spoilt for choice and could potentially hire all of them. She hires one, however, and if you manage the two candidates who didn't get the job well, you may gain two new clients as well as two great candidates you can place elsewhere.

As candidates and clients can be inter-changeable it is important to manage both parties' expectations. Setting the scene and managing expectations are the most important things you do every day. This starts right at the beginning, with the evaluation process. Right away you have an opportunity to do well or badly in managing your candidates. You either have to reject or progress them. There is an art to doing both well.

Your evaluation process may start with a CV. In this case a screening tool may be useful both to help you and to ensure there is no unconscious bias in your assessment of candidates' CVs. An example is shown in Table 6.1.

Alternatively, your evaluation process may equally start with you having some direct contact with candidates. They may have spoken to your receptionist or not, they may have called in directly in response to a job advertisement. This is your opportunity to evaluate them and the first chance to start building the relationship.

The first contact

Greeting your candidate is a basic aspect of the process. First impressions count for a lot. Just as you have an instinctive reaction to a candidate within the first 15 seconds of starting an interview, so the candidate will form a similar impression of you upon meeting or speaking to you for the first time.

How should you aim to come across?

- Be professional, but warm.
- Show you are credible – let the candidate see you know your sector and business.
- Use the right pace for the candidate (match theirs).
- Use open, clear questions to get the candidate talking.
- Ask how to spell the candidate's name if you don't know.
- Build rapport through questioning or finding common ground.
- Listen – giving the candidate your full attention.
- Take overall control of the call.
- End with commitment or action.

TABLE 6.1   CV screening tool

Job title:

	Yes	No	Notes
Essential skills eg			
1: Skilled Java programmer			
2: Managed a team of six for two years			
3: Experienced at organizing travel arrangements			
Desirable skills			
1: Managed a P&L business			
2: Overseas trade negotiating experience			
Qualifications: 2:1 numerate degree			
Location: 1-hour drive from office or less			
Travelling in role: 2–3 days per month			
Current driving licence			
UK passport			

Salary: Minimum acceptable   £

Desired salary   £

Current benefits

....

Evaluating the candidate

Candidates need to be evaluated either during or directly after the attraction process. If you were searching for such candidates, or they had phoned in, you may have rejected them before you acquired their CVs. However once you do acquire a candidate's CV, or he or she is sitting in front of you, having walked in off the street, you need to evaluate that person against a range of criteria that you need to set on the basis of what your market requires. Figure 6.2 shows potential evaluation outcomes.

FIGURE 6.2　CV evaluation

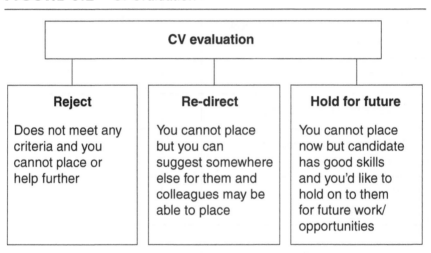

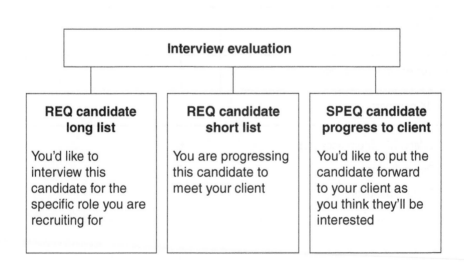

How you handle each of these outcomes has a strong impact on developing your brand with the candidate. At any point your brand can be improved or impaired and it is particularly when rejecting a candidate (see the section on headhunting in Chapter 9 on 'Candidate attraction') that there is opportunity to upset. Below we look at professional ways of dealing with each of the evaluation outcomes.

Reject

'I'm really sorry but I don't think we will be able to help you. Your skills are excellent but they are very different from the ones our clients ask us to help them recruit for. I'd like to say we'll hold on to your details but I would not wish to mis-manage your expectations at this point. You might find a more general recruitment agency in your area more able to help you.'

Reject and re-direct

'I'm really sorry but I don't think I will be able to help you. However, my colleague Barbara deals with contract and freelance staff in your sector and I am sure she can help you. Let me have her give a call back within the next half hour. What's the best number for her to get you on?'

Or

'I'm really sorry but I don't think I will be able to help you. Have you tried posting your CV on a job board/looking in the paper/contacting X agency who deals specifically in the medical sector?'

Hold for the future (candidate-rich market)

'I don't believe I have any clients with live opportunities that might suit you currently. However, you do have exactly the type of skills my clients seek and I am sure it will not be long before a suitable role comes up. I'd like to keep your details on our database so that when something does come up we can contact you straight away to discuss it. Is that OK?'

Potential progress to clients

'Your skills are exactly what my clients are looking for at the moment so you have chosen a good time to make a move. I'd like to consider approaching a range of my clients on your behalf – we'll agree which ones between us – and set up some meetings so you can explore all the best opportunities on the market. Now, here's whom I suggest...'

Potential short-list

'I'd like to explore what you are looking for and your skills in more detail, and if we agree that it makes sense I'll arrange for you to meet with my client. Now, what would make a move attractive for you?'

Notice here, you need to be clear about what they want as although you have already decided to short-list them from their CV you need to understand about what will attract them. Then you can present the role you have to them appropriately or re-direct them. You will also need to qualify them further before progressing, which we'll come on to shortly.

Potential long-list

'Thank you so much, Sarah, for sending in your CV for the role of XXX following our advertisement/your conversation with our research team. I'd really like to meet you/catch up for a coffee to discuss the role further. When's good for you – Monday next week or Thursday evening?'

The next stage, having decided it will potentially be possible to work with particular candidates, is to qualify them.

Qualifying the candidate

This differs from evaluating and goes one step further – it is identifying whether this is definitely a candidate to work with now or progress to your client. Some sectors will have more flexibility on qualification than others. In some sectors you will be able to find a role for the vast majority of candidates who approach you so long as they have some skills and qualities. In others you will need to qualify them very hard before deciding whether you should work hard on their behalf.

CASE STUDY

A consultant secured an offer for her candidate at a highly regarded employer. He turned it down in favour of a counter-offer. This was the third time he had turned down a role that she had secured him and the third counter-offer he had accepted.

You might imagine that this recruiter was quite naïve in working with this candidate, who needless to say was a very good candidate (in some ways!) but in actual fact she is one of the highest revenue generators in her successful recruitment consultancy. She felt she had done all she could to qualify her candidate each time, but it is an indication of how important the qualifying process can be. Even the best recruiters never cover every single eventuality. The important thing here is to be sure you have done everything you can to ensure your candidate takes your job offer – if they then do not you can at least be clear that this was not due to lack of effort on your part or lack of direction from you to your client.

Two activities can take up a recruiter's time and not yield results; one is working on unqualified candidates and the other is working on unqualified jobs.

Categorizing your candidate

There are two types of candidates you will want to qualify in, regardless of whether you are candidate or client driven: REQ candidates and SPEQ candidates (see Figure 6.3).

FIGURE 6.3   REQ or SPEQ

REQ	SPEQ
Candidates who suit client requirements you currently have	Candidates in demand from your clients but without a specific brief
R – Ready to move **E** – Experience fits the client need **Q** – Qualifies in against CV checklist	**S** – Scarce skill **P** – Personality/cultural fit **E** – Experience fits the client need **Q** – Qualified candidate

You will want to be working with both types of candidates but if you are working with candidates who do not fit either category – and also do not meet any of your networking needs – you need to ask yourself what you plan to gain.

Qualifying a candidate in

This will vary from requirement to requirement and you will need to develop your own list but here are some key pointers:

- clear they want to make a move;
- interviewing elsewhere in last six months (demonstrates commitment) although not an important criterion for a search candidate;

- discussed their thoughts about a new role with other people in the family, if relevant;
- considered how they will deal with a counter-offer;
- keen to come and meet you;
- have not been interviewing with every other recruiter or employer in town;
- are realistic about what they want;
- have few constraints around location or the working week.

In short, to the best of your assessment, are these candidates who will work with you in partnership to find their next move? Ideally you'll want to ask them to agree to use you exclusively as their recruitment advisor. So long as you feel you have a good range of options for them and you are genuinely prepared to put a lot of work into finding them the right role, then this is a win–win for both you and them. It is particularly useful to take this approach with SPEQ candidates.

SPEQ candidates are a top priority if you are deciding where to spend your time. If you work in anything other than a purely client-retained environment, as an external recruiter you will find SPEQ candidates, in the right market, offer not only opportunities to place them – and make fees – but also your best opportunity to deliver credibility and open doors to new potential clients you are not currently dealing with.

CASE STUDY

Damien Stork, Director at The Buzz, part of Ochre House, a leading recruiter in the UK and Middle East for the leisure, retail and call centre markets, recently introduced a high-value candidate to a completely new client by making exactly the right match. He says that placing a candidate 'off PSL' relies on one thing critically: knowing your candidate inside out.

'Engage them early and get to know the person, know they are high-performing and be confident that their achievements stand up under close examination.'

Damian had been nursing the seeds of a relationship with a leading organic skin-care brand, but been excluded from senior roles, when a candidate became available that had previously been a client.

Culturally he was exactly what the prospective client needed for MD. When I called the candidate about the role he was immediately engaged, so I knew the 'sales job' I had in front of me was only with the client. His CV would have landed him almost any senior commercial role in just about any retailer, but this client is a passionately organic and ethical retailer and his background just didn't fit their ethos. Once I had relayed the organic and ethical credentials of the person rather than the CV, the HR

Director needed little persuasion to meet him over coffee as the retained search firm had drawn a blank at short list.

She then took up the role of 'Champion' within the business to ensure that the second interview with the Chairman and Chief Exec went well. He is now the proud new MD of the client.

Of course SPEQ candidates can fulfil both the SPEC and REQ criteria as the chances of them also fitting one of the roles you are recruiting for currently are also high.

Task

Decide whether any of the candidates you are dealing with currently are REQ (you'll know if you have a role for them) or SPEQ candidates in your market. What still seems unconfirmed that you might wish to qualify further?

If you have simply qualified your candidate as someone you want to work with then the next stage will be to interview him or her. An interview can take a range of forms. It can mean registering a candidate who walks in off the street in a regional agency, checking the skill set of a contract consultant whom you are unlikely to meet before you recruit him or her, or setting up a whole interview and assessment process for graduates or senior hires that you are running. We will cover a basic interview, with some evidence-based hiring techniques.

Interviewing your candidate

An area where recruiters can add real value to their clients is in thoroughly interviewing and assessing their candidates against the role and person specification in order to provide a great match. Although at one level this is perceived to be a 'given' to clients it is uncommon enough to consistently provide an excellent match to differentiate you from your competitors, especially if this is coupled with some useful market intelligence.

It does not matter whether the interview is face to face or over the telephone, it is important to follow a process. This is particularly important if you are interviewing a range of consultants as part of a selection process, because structured interviews, being the same for all candidates, deliver a higher degree of interview validity.

The objectives of an interview

You will want to develop a good relationship with your candidate; the interview is a great opportunity to do that, as well as establish how you plan to work together. It is also important to understand your candidate's motivations and aspirations so you can find roles and organizations that will meet those needs. The interview will also give you clear evidence on how the candidate performs at interview, and this will help you in preparing him or her for interviews with your client; one of the most valuable services a consultant can offer their candidate.

If you are an in-house recruiter you may not wish to brief the candidate so fully, as you may wish to see how much homework he or she has done on the company. Your key objective will be to assess whether this candidate has the capability and cultural fit to join the business you work for. There is a slightly different feel to an in-house interview. It is most closely aligned to an interview during a selection process where the objective is to see if the candidate can do the job.

It may be necessary to write detailed notes on a candidate after the interview to progress them through to your client as part of a short-list or if you particularly need to convince the client to see the candidate and cannot persuade them to do so over the phone. You may find the template below helpful if you are uncertain how to set these out. It also helps to have the notes in mind before you start the interview as it really speeds the process of writing them up when you have a picture of how they need to look before the interview itself. See Figure 6.4 for a simple outline example.

Design your interview with the rest of the recruitment or assessment process in mind so that you and colleagues are all assessing a range of competencies or behaviours. If you are interviewing after psychometric testing there may be areas of the test results you wish to explore further at interview. All of these need factoring in to the interview design.

The contingency interviewer will, of course, be concerned with a candidate's motivations and determination to move. Most recruiters are measured on the revenue they deliver so they would be less able to spend a significant amount of time on a candidate who is just securing an internal rise by way of an external job offer. All recruiters will be happy to help with information on the market, market rates and salaries when they know where a candidate's real motivations lie.

Interviewers also need to manage the candidate's self-esteem. It is important that the candidate leaves the interview feeling challenged perhaps, but not interrogated. A simple way of doing this is to manage the time element of the interview – suggesting an interview will take an hour and then finishing in 20 minutes clearly suggests you had better things to do. However, taking an hour to interview a candidate if you have established within 20 minutes that this will not be someone you can work with is also a poor use of your time. So allow for about 40 minutes on average.

Lastly, an interview provides a real opportunity to manage the candidate's expectations about possible roles, opportunities and remuneration.

FIGURE 6.4 Candidate notes template

Overview of Candidate
• Ability to build rapport – if relevant to role • Personality — extrovert, introvert, friendly, reserved • Interpersonal skills — eye contact, asking questions, relaxed, smiling • Motivations — what the candidate is looking for; why this is important to them
Capacity to fulfil a role
• Skills and experience • Achievements • Benefits of achievements and how they can be transferred to a new environment – 'What the candidate can do for you' • Areas to be explored further at next interview
Personal details
• Salary • Location • Ability to meet specific demands of the job (eg travelling hours)

Preparing for and conducting an interview

There are numerous interview plans and structures. It does not really matter which one you choose, so long as you choose one and cover all bases. A simple one is WIGGS as outlined in Figure 6.5.

FIGURE 6.5 Candidate interview structure

W	Welcome and rapport
I	Introduction
G	Gathering Information
G	Giving Information
S	Selling and Closing

Welcome and rapport

Introduce yourself. Put candidates at their ease – offer drinks etc. Make some 'small talk' to start the interview off. You will get more from your candidates if you are friendly but professional. Say how long the interview will last and what you plan to cover. If you are planning to use any evidence-based (competency or behavioural) questions it will be useful to let them know that now. Reassure them they will have a chance to ask lots of questions about either the role or the way in which you suggest you both work together at the end of the session. Check the timing works for them. Say that notes will be taken. Check they are happy with that and are ready to start.

Introduction

Tell them a brief couple of sentences about the company you are working for or the business you are representing. This is just to further relax the candidate but is also a mini 'sales-pitch' to remind them of why you are both meeting and what the benefit might be to them. Resist the temptation here to tell them 'all about' the job (or your company if you are in-house); you don't want to tell them everything so they can successfully sell it back to you. You will have plenty of opportunity to sell back later.

Gathering information

This is the largest section of the interview. Here you need to collect the following:

- *Housekeeping*: Location, salary/pay rate and benefits/expenses, their minimum and what they want, willingness to re-locate (if relevant) and criteria for doing so, working hours, any personal circumstances that affect their work. Show-stoppers – eg they are getting married in five weeks and need a month off for their honeymoon.

- *Career highlights and reasons for moving on*: A broad biographical sketch of their career history and why they have taken the roles that they have and then moved on. If they work for a company you are interested in exploring as a client, without taking up the entire interview by asking questions about it, it is a good opportunity to ask the candidate about the firm and perhaps source some names to contact. Or you might ask them: 'I gather there's quite a bit of recruitment going in your firm at the moment. What do you know about all that?'

- *Motivations and aspirations*: What is important to them, and crucially why: why they want a new role now, their career aspirations for the future. This will help you when you come to match your candidates to a role and understand whether it is likely to work for them. Crucially here you'll want to understand their reasons for looking for a new role. If permanent candidates are only interested in moving for money, they will always be open to counter-offers from their existing employer or another agency. You'll need to develop a relationship with your temp or contractor so they are not vulnerable to other financially better offers.

- *KSPs (Key selling points)*: This is one of the most important parts of the interview process. Unless you clearly identify the candidates' KSPs it will be harder to market them most effectively. Bear in mind that KSPs may be different for different clients. Here you are matching the needs of the clients with the attributes of the candidates. These could range hugely from – 'They are available now and have an up-to-date HGV licence and are willing to work over Christmas,' through 'They have managed a range of accounts and sold from cold into Sainsbury's' to 'They have a good understanding of US GAAP regulations.'

Task

Key selling points

Choose four of your current candidates. What are their KSPs? How will you present them to a client, whether they are REQ or SPEC?

CASE STUDY

A wonderful example of using KSPs to great advantage, which also serves to indicate again the fabulous breadth of this terrific industry, was overheard at a Bond St recruitment agency some few years ago. The consultant was presenting a long-term temp to a client (this agency supplied all the up market shops and society offices in the area as well as one of the best-known households in the capital) and said: 'Oh no please don't worry, she has all her own jewellery, I'd say she's a Tiffany kind of girl. Yes, I know the last one wasn't quite right, I completely agree I should have told her not to wear her diamonds during the day, but then equally one might have hoped her mother would have told her that don't you think?'

So it really doesn't matter what those selling points are, so long as they are relevant to the client. You need to gather the key information you can sell on to your client.

Competency or behavioural interviewing section

You may offer this service as part of a search or selection process or it may be a normal part of your interview process in-house. You ask open and probing questions against a range of competencies, capabilities or behaviours in this section. Tell the interviewee that you are about to change over to competency-based questions – perhaps after you have had them take you through their CV in brief over, say, 10 minutes.

At the end of the behavioural section you should have enough information about whether the candidate meets your role criteria (REQ) or how to market them out to a range of clients as a SPEQ candidate. It may also be that candidates are temps and you cannot use them immediately, but you can also see that you can use them in the future and therefore they are a very useful addition to your database; or again, some candidate, who has come in to register at your high-street office, could be very useful at XYZ company at their contact centre when they have a vacancy.

If you are using competency-based interviewing Figure 6.6 may be useful. When you are asking your candidate questions it's easier to gather evidence by framing them in this way. Each question has four distinct parts and the idea is to get an answer to each part.

FIGURE 6.6   Interviewing a STAR candidate

For each competency, capability or behaviour you are assessing, this is a useful framework for gathering answers.

S	**Situation**	What was the situation?
T	**Task**	What did you want to achieve?
A	**Action**	What did you do?
R	**Result**	What happened as a result?

If you do not have a full STAR and cannot achieve one through more probing, then it is unlikely the candidate can meet that competency, capability or behaviour.

Candidate status

The last piece of information gathering is designed to understand what candidates have done so far in relation to their job search. This sits in the qualification section and you may have already covered this before inviting the candidate to interview, but even so now is a good time, having developed the relationship further, to probe this a little more fully. The probing will establish what other options candidates are looking at and where they are with them. They may also give you some clues as to the type of companies and roles they are looking at already so you can see if this is in line with your thoughts and options. For example, if they say they are looking at temp roles but tell you they have been interviewing for several permanent roles, you can know that this is also in their minds.

The key skills you need to demonstrate here are asking questions and listening. It may sound ridiculously obvious but it's all too easy to miss them out, which means you miss an opportunity either to match candidates to something you had not thought of before or to understand why they will buy. Listening is a skill that will also gain trust between you and the candidate, and you may learn things that will help you. This next case study is contributed by Colin Etheridge, now CEO at K2 Partnering Solutions, one of the largest specialist IT recruiters, from his time in accountancy recruitment in the 1991 recession.

CASE STUDY

I was approached by a candidate who was an IPA (registered insolvency practitioner). He was also a recovering alcoholic just out of a treatment centre as a result of stress. Everyone wanted IPAs, as liquidations were the only business that was thriving!

He had been rejected by all of my competitors, the major names in my market, as they felt his background and recent experiences would cause them problems.

I felt that, as long as we were honest and he was honest with potential employers, then I could help him. I took a very straight approach with all of the potential clients and told them exactly what the situation was and what my thoughts were on the candidate.

We ended up with offers from all the 'Big Eight' at the time as well as others. He chose a smaller specialist firm that felt like the right move for him then. As far as I know he lived and worked happily ever after.

Working with this candidate opened some new doors to senior partners for me – they appreciated the way the candidate and I had approached the situation so ethically and professionally. It also meant that I validated having the courage of my convictions. It is possible to see both a human being and a possible placement and for both to please all three parties. My competitors looked at my candidate and saw a problem – I saw an opportunity, and it's a mindset that has been helpful to me throughout my career.

Table 6.2 is a resource to explore the kinds of questions you should use under which circumstances.

TABLE 6.2   Questioning techniques

Question type	Purpose and when to use	Example and how to use
Open questions Where the other person talks more than you	To get someone talking	How, Why, What, Who, When: 'How did you come to take your current role?'
Demand open questions As open questions	To take control or assert authority	Tell me, Take me through, Explain to me, Show me, Talk to me about: 'Take me through your current role.'
Probing questions Allow you to find more information on a topic	To develop the conversation further	'Say more about that...' 'Can you give me an example of that?' 'Go on...'
Reflective questions Alternative to a probe – reflect back someone's answers and keep the person talking	In client meetings When you want to find out more about someone or something When you want to help someone talk	'You're not happy with the current service then?' 'You're looking for a longer-term option you say?'
Direct questions Ask for information	To elicit specific information	'What's your base salary/ hourly/daily rate?' 'What's your current journey time to work?' 'How many people report to you?'
Closed questions Person answers yes or no only	To gain confirmation To take control of the conversation To change the subject	'You'd be happy with Birmingham then?' 'Do you feel you could work with the team?'
Evidence-based questions (competency, behaviour or capability questions) To uncover evidence of particular capability Also use probing and direct questions	When conducting competency-based or behavioural interviews If running a selection or search	'Can you think of a time when you were able to persuade someone to change their minds?' 'What was the situation?' (S) 'What did you want to achieve?' (T) 'What did you do?' (A) 'What was the outcome?' (R)

TABLE 6.2 *Continued*

Question type	Purpose and when to use	Example and how to use
Hypothetical questions Asking what someone would do, if...	Rarely; this will not tell you what someone would do, only what they like to think they would do	'If you took this role what would you do first?'
Leading questions Tell the listener what you want to hear	If a candidate needs relaxing or reassuring, but not if you want to find something out. Dangerous if used with clients as it is easy to make false assumptions	'I'm sure you'll agree our website is great.' 'I think drawing up a balance sheet is the easy part, isn't it?'
Multiple questions Asking more than one question at once	Never	'Did you enjoy your interview, how long did the journey take and did they ask you back for a second?'

Giving information

You may wish to by-pass this section or use it fully. You may have decided that you will not progress your candidate to short-list and therefore will not be giving detailed information on your client – although some brief information would also be appropriate. If you can only re-direct the candidate there is little point in speaking at length about how your agency works. Much fairer for the candidate to have five minutes help with where else they can look. However, if you do want to work with or progress this candidate, this is the time to go into advice or sales mode.

Selling and closing

Here you may agree the job opportunities open to the candidate, you may tell your candidate much more about your client and the role, you may agree a list of companies to approach on their behalf, and you may give them some advice on their career direction or some information on the market for jobs in their sector at the moment and the rates and salaries being paid.

This may also be the point at which you present to a candidate a role that you are recruiting for, or this may come after the interview as a role becomes available. In the client strategy stage you will have developed a client role proposition, which you will use to attract your candidate. Understanding therefore what's important for your candidates and what they want will enable you to both match the attributes of the role closely but also to explain clearly how the role you have chosen to progress them for matches their motivations and aspirations.

You will also, at this point, agree how you will work together, what the next steps and timescales are. It may be helpful to outline how the process works for people who have never worked with a consultancy or an agency before. Perhaps take them through a typical recruitment process and what you would need them to do as their part in that process; ensure they attend interviews, do some of their own research on the organization, let you know if they become unavailable for work at any point.

Before you part company it is a great idea to ask them if there is anything you have not discussed with them that might affect you working together or them taking up any job offers. Agree when you will next speak.

You want your candidates leaving your interviews feeling good about themselves, and positive about your company and your capacity to help them. You want them to go out and be ambassadors for your business.

Placement strategies

Assuming you are working with your candidate after evaluation, qualification and interview you now have four choices around what you will do with them, ensuring you are working within both legal and ethical boundaries. In reality you can choose a blend of all four for each candidate or one or two. These are outlined below. Your strategy will depend on whether they are a REQ or a SPEQ candidate. The four broad choices are outlined in the diagram (Figure 6.7).

FIGURE 6.7   REQ and SPEQ marketing strategies

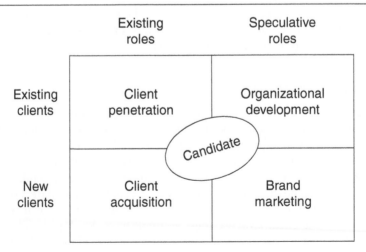

Client penetration

Submit your candidate to an existing client who has an existing role spec. This may be the only option available to internal recruiters, but there should be consideration about which internal clients this candidate is suitable for. In some firms there may be up to 15 or 20 clients to introduce the candidate to. Whilst there is a need for internal recruiters to add value in terms of screening, there is an equal danger in making too many assumptions and limiting the options for the candidate and the business as a whole. Client penetration is a good strategy for the candidates as they are not required to attend a speculative interview, and good for the client as they get a qualified candidate for their role and, if the matching is good, a placement. Doing this in isolation however means that your candidate has fewer choices and you have no means of extending your market.

Client acquisition

Introduce your candidates to a new client that you are aware has a specific role that is suitable for them. You are aware of the role through market intelligence or perhaps you have seen the client advertising the role as well. This is a great method as you know there is a role, the client can see a candidate whom it might not have been aware of, and you have an opportunity to introduce yourself and begin to develop a relationship with a new client.

Organizational development

Present your SPEQ candidate to your client where you are not aware of a specific role but you would like to introduce the candidate as you feel there could be some synergy and a role could be created. These situations are often best in revenue-generating roles or where you know the business has plans to recruit someone in such roles in the future. It does have disadvantages in that both your client and your candidate need to invest some time and effort (as do you!) into the meeting. However, it can be a great way of really cementing a relationship with a client and adding value over and above 'filling live jobs', as it shows you understand the clients' business and you think of them from a business partnership perspective.

Take care not to use this strategy if you don't have a really good relationship with the client, ideally the potential hiring manager and you are not clear where and how your candidate could add real value. Many organizations receive too many unsolicited CVs with no regard for a good match. This devalues the candidates who are submitted to add value after careful consideration.

Brand marketing

Although this last option is clearly not just about brand marketing, it is a great way of contributing to your brand's worth and perceived value in the market. In the same way that shotgun scattering of CVs into the market hoping some will hit does not help your brand, a targeted campaign for a key candidate can develop strong credibility in new markets. Clearly this is the highest risk in terms of managing your time, and your own desk development strategy would be unwise to include a high proportion of this option, but it is a great way of offering value to all – your candidate, your client and you. Again, make sure this is really well targeted and born out of good knowledge rather than sketchy hope.

With the best REQ and SPEQ candidates of course you may choose to use all four options to broaden your market reach and 'cover' your market with your candidate. This last point is important from a candidate perspective, as if you do not introduce candidates to a wide enough range of options then they may very well consider looking elsewhere, either via another agency or under their own steam. Achieving a balance of enough opportunities without overwhelming the candidate needs careful consideration.

Once you have chosen your strategy, the question of how you take these candidates to 'market' then needs to be addressed.

Marketing SPEQ candidates

The first question to ask yourself is who are your potential clients. They make up your 'market'.

Market

What/who is your market?
Who will want to buy?

Then consider developing your tactics based on the classic marketeer's four Ps (as seen in Chapter 4, page 80 and Figure 4.4). They stand for:

- *Product*: what the key selling points of the product are.
- *Place*: how the product will be distributed.
- *Promotion*: how the product is promoted.
- *Price*: the right price – the market rate for a candidate, in our case.

This may be a tool you also find helpful to suggest that candidates who come to you for advice on a career change or move may wish to complete. For candidates who are making a major career change and with whom you are likely to spend a lot of time – they may be working with you exclusively for example – you could ask them to complete a SWOT (see Chapter 4) analysis on themselves and then develop their career planning under the four P headings.

Experienced recruiters will be carrying out the next part of the process in their heads as they interview someone, but if you are starting out this is not a bad process to work with when developing how you will take your candidates to market.

Developing your process

1 *Market*: Draw up a list of organizations or people you think would be interested to learn that this candidate is on the market. Agree this list with your candidate and ensure that s/he has not already started talking to these organizations, or is not being put forward by another consultancy. Discuss with the candidate the types of role you will agree between you to focus on. Focus on those organizations you have a good relationship with and understand well so best to position your candidate. If there are some others you do not know so well do your research before introducing your candidate so you have a better chance of presenting them to the right person in the right way.

2 *Product*: Decide on the candidates' KSPs; if they have worked for a key competitor this may be a KSP to a particular client. When interviewing the candidates, make sure that you have established some of the great results that they have achieved during their careers and particularly in their last role, but also what the fit of each candidate is. You'll have seen from the case study on the 'off PSL' placement that the key was knowing the candidate really well, not just that person's skills. In that case it was the capacity to understand what was important to both candidate and client. Both of these aspects will help you work out what a candidate may be able to offer an employer to increase your chances of getting this person an interview.

3 *Price*: Agree with your candidates the parameters of their required package or fees/rate and the variables that affect this. Consider this with them in light of the market rate and what you think your clients will pay. You may need to manage candidates' expectations about what is realistic in market conditions. The 'price' you can achieve also of course depends upon how quickly various candidates want to find work and how close a match they require to what they want. The more exacting they are on price and role the harder they may be to place.

4 *Promotion/Place*: Decide on the best approach to each of the organizations you have on your list. What is their normal recruiting modus operandi? Whom should you contact? How? Should you send an introductory e-mail or a CV with it? Many of these decisions are based on personal choice but you may want to consider sending an introductory e-mail or making an introductory phone call to explore whether there would be some interest in learning more about your candidate. Certainly if you want to stand out and have a meaningful discussion the telephone will always be the best option. E-mail is best for confirming arrangements and agreements.

Interview arrangements

Let's assume as a result of this activity that you now have a range of interviews for your candidate. Clearly you need to arrange the interview. This in itself can be a challenging affair. It is one of the tasks that is most tempting to delegate, but think of it as a great opportunity to build relationships each time, if not directly with the decision-makers then with their PAs, and with your candidate. Sometimes it requires a level of assertiveness that will be hard for someone else to achieve. Whilst arranging the interview you will also be able to prepare both parties for their meeting so it all runs smoothly. Your preparation at each stage will depend upon the number of stages your candidate is likely to need to go through.

Interview preparation

This is a vital part of the interview process, and setting the scene for both candidates and interviewers will set them up for a fruitful meeting. You'll need to tell your client about your candidate and what they can do for their business or organization and your candidate all about your client and what the organization can potentially do for them. If both parties are meeting with a view to being interested and impressed by each other than they stand a much better chance of a successful meeting. Make a point of talking, if at all possible, directly with your candidate's interviewer as this both builds the relationship with you the supplier, and enables them to hear first hand about your candidate.

However, where this is not possible you may want to brief the internal recruiter or HRM so they can pass the briefing on. Your candidate may be being interviewed over a day by a range of people on a panel so, at the very least, most internal organizers or RPOs should be provided with a cover sheet that you can use to brief in writing or you can attach notes to the CV.

This is what you should cover with your candidate and client, using a preparatory checklist:

- Your candidate:
  - The company – present a balanced perspective.
  - The role – same.
  - The interviewer – background, values and personality.
  - Commonality between the candidate and the interviewer.
  - Interview tips and techniques if useful, perhaps feedback from your own interview with them.
  - Housekeeping – interview time, location, travel time from candidate's start point, any dress code.
  - Pre-closing – depending upon the process, you may want to check what the candidates' thoughts would be about accepting a satisfactory offer, if they like what they see and hear.
  - Check they will catch up with you after the interview.
- Your client:
  - The candidate – career history, job motivations and aspirations.
  - Issues you have concerns about that you feel the client should explore further (senior/retained roles only in depth).
  - Candidate status – are they active or passive and how, therefore should the client behave with them (is this an 'interview' or 'an exploratory chat'?); what other opportunities is the candidate looking at?
  - Arrange a time to de-brief with them after interview.

After the interview

Fast follow-up here is really important – potential placements can be lost because a recruiter has not managed to keep a level of interest and urgency alive in all parties. Try to take response and feedback from your candidate first, and as soon after their interview as possible. This means you can get their true 'first impressions' rather than considered ones after long conversations with other people. Then call your client and say you'd like to give them your candidate's feedback on them and the role. Most clients are keen to get feedback on themselves and are more likely to want to take one call where they can both give and receive feedback than they are two, one with their own and then another with candidate feedback.

These are the post-interview questions you need to ask your candidate and client:

- Your candidate:
  - How did the interview go?
  - How did you find the interviewer/the panel?

- Was the role as described?
- How well can the role satisfy your XXX (motivations and aspirations – short and long term)?
- What was the journey like/the offices/the panel (or any other area of possible concern)?
- What information might you still need?
- How interested are you?
- How does it compare with the other interviews you have been on this week?
- Are there any issues that concern you?

● Your client:
- How did the interview go?
- What were your impressions of the candidate?
- What were their key strengths?
- How well could they do the job?
- How would they fit in to the team?
- What did you think about the areas I had some concerns about (if needed)?
- How did they compare with the other candidates? Who would be your first and second choices at this stage?
- What is the next stage?
- What further information do you need?
- Will anyone else need to be involved in the decision?
- Is there anything else I should be aware of like internal candidates or a possible spec. change?
- Is there anything else you need from me at this point?
- If you were to move ahead, are you confident you could offer a good increase on my candidate's current package?

In-house processes can also win here by taking care about how they stand out from the crowd if a candidate has had a range of second interviews. In a candidate-short market your candidate is likely to have a range of options to choose from, hopefully through you an external recruiter but keep checking what else they have going on. If you don't it's not likely they will venture the information. Every piece of communication you have with your candidate will have an impact on them – make sure it's one which will improve the relationship.

CASE STUDY

The Boston advertising agency Mullen has devised a different way of both keeping in contact with its candidates after interview and continuing the brand development. **http://mullen.com/thanks** is an e-mail sent to all their candidates after interview. It is a designed mailer that also provides click-through to a favourite recipe for choc-chip cookies and a link to some photos of Mullen's people amongst other things, all brought alive with clever use of a pencil and sight of an iPod. As Jim Stroud, the US recruitment blogger who drew attention to this, stated: 'You see a lot of companies putting a lot of effort into attracting candidates, but less making an effort to say "thank you for your time".'

At second interview you will cover some of the same questions, but you will be moving towards trial closing both your candidate and your client.
Questions to ask:

- If you were to consider making an offer, are you confident you could offer a good increase on my candidate's current package?
- If you were to be made an offer you are happy with from my client, what might that offer look like/be?
- Say my client made you an offer you are happy to accept and when you resign your current company offer you more money, what might you do? Suppose they offered you a promotion? Or a £5,000 salary increase?
- Are there any other considerations we have not discussed that I need to be aware of as we move towards an offer?
- What other roles are you looking at, at this point? Are there any others? Is there anything we have not discussed?
- How are you feeling about an offer?
- How does this candidate compare with the other candidates you have seen?
- What other steps do you need to take in the business to enable you to move towards an offer?
- Is there anything that could stop you making an offer to my candidate?
- Are there any concerns about my candidate?
- Are there any concerns about taking the role?
- What are going to be the decision-making criteria for you to choose to take this role?

If this feels like endless questions to your candidate through the process and is uncomfortable, either think about the level of discomfort both you and your client will feel if your candidate takes another job you are unaware of or signpost to them why you are asking; 'my client and I will want to be aware of other things you are looking at and how you see them so we can tailor any potential offer and the timing of it to your situation'.

After all the interviews you will either be moving towards an offer or a rejection of your candidate.

Managing a rejection

The objective of a rejection is always to try and manage the candidate's self-esteem, to allow them to complete the process while still holding the recruiting organization in high regard, and perhaps having learned something to their benefit – at the very least having found the process an interesting and good experience.

The best companies will not promise progression or make offers to candidates they have no interest in hiring and will give comprehensive feedback. Occasionally you will have inexperienced junior hiring managers who say to the candidate they would like to put him/her through to the next stage but then change their minds, and you are left to deal with an enthusiastic candidate whom you have to let down. Sometimes you will have no feedback to pass on. There is not space here to cover all eventualities but there are a few general guidelines that you might find helpful, not least of which is 'do as you would be done by':

- Don't reject immediately after interview. We'd all prefer to think the rejection took at least some level of consideration.
- Tell the truth, but judiciously. If there was a better candidate, say so, and why. If the one being rejected was bottom of four, there's no need to point that out.
- If you have a relationship with the candidate always make the rejection over the phone.
- Don't leave a cheery-sounding message only for them to call back to bad news. Let them know in your tone this is not great news.
- If the rejection is for an interpersonal skills reason, you may not wish to be the one to deliver this feedback. Your feedback is unlikely to occasion a change, and worrying about one person's opinion is likely to do more harm than good. You can however say that their lack of practice at interviewing skills may have let them down and suggest they get some coaching for next time.

This is one of the more challenging parts of the recruiter's role, particularly with candidates who go through a long process, really want the role and fall at the final interview stage, as some invariably will. If you are an internal recruiter it's good to have a standard form of interview feedback and policy on this so you can become practised at delivering it to all candidates. External recruiters will have to work with a range of differing client practices.

A more satisfactory part of the recruitment process is managing the offer. Often, the success factors in such cases are already determined by your early management of those 'show-stoppers' discussed in the section on 'Qualifying the candidate' earlier in this chapter. Actually making an offer should be 'like a hot knife through butter', and below we deal with how to make it so.

Managing the offer

Any job offer will comprise a range of factors:

- job content;
- prospects for progression, learning and development;
- boss and/or co-workers;
- working environment;
- location and travelling times/travel;
- pay.

The objective is to create a win–win situation so that your client and candidate are both happy with the outcome. The way to do this is to manage expectations from the outset.

As part of your interview you will have established what is important to your candidate out of the above list, and so the rest of the offer should be clear enough. The last thing to be negotiated usually is the pay, which can be a make or break part of the process. As you will have put a huge amount of work into getting this potential placement to this point, you do not want to fall at the last hurdle.

However, it is also important that all other possible areas for negotiation are discussed first. Otherwise you can spend a lot of time negotiating a salary that your candidate is happy with, only for him or her to say 'there's just one more thing' – a dreaded few words that no recruiter wants to hear as it shows the job has not been done as effectively as it might! To avoid this follow the checklists on qualification to ensure you have covered all bases.

You can add huge value as a recruiter in negotiating salaries, terms and conditions to help achieve the win–win you are looking for. This is likely to mean getting the candidate a little more money or better benefits than they were hoping for – which, if you have managed their expectations appropriately, will be a little less than the client was expecting to have to pay or offer. In this section we focus on pay. As there are so many variables to add to this offer mix (booked holiday, time off in lieu, bonus rates, guarantees of pay, start and finish times, weekly hours worked etc), there is not enough space to cover those areas here, but you can use the same techniques to manage any aspect of the offer.

Find space in the 'magic circle'

Figure 6.8 shows the most common pattern of salary or rate negotiations. Candidates will have a minimum they will accept to take a role and a further figure they would like; clients will have an amount they would like to pay and a maximum they would pay if they really had to. Ideally you will find a space where both meet in the middle. The greater the size of the circle, the easier the task.

FIGURE 6.8   The negotiating space

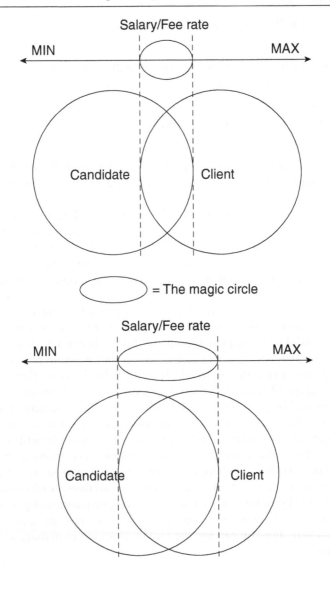

Both your candidate and client will have some salary and pay constraints they have to keep within. A wide range of things can affect this. From the client side it might be pay grades, comparative team salaries, the rate they have always paid for the role, what the role is worth to them, how much they like the candidate, the set rate for the role, the last hire in their project budget needing to fall into a certain band, and so on. From the candidates' side it might be a determination to have an increase on their current earnings, they may need compensation for a longer journey, or the rewards have to be more than in other roles they have been offered; conversely, they may accept a decrease if the role offers them something else like flexible hours, career change, public sector experience; the offer has to be at a certain level to cover their out-goings, or be good enough to prompt a move if they are a passive candidate. It's useful to find out what those constraints are and the reason behind them as sometimes constraints can be moved and sometimes they cannot.

- Don't:
  - Tell the candidate the maximum salary or rate right at the beginning.
  - Tell the client the candidate's minimum package at the beginning.
  - Tell either of them the band you have identified from both that they want to work within.
  - Go to your client for more money for your candidate without trial closing them on whether they will accept.
  - Carry on regardless if the bracket they both need to be in has no 'magic circle' at all.
  - Hope that the salary will be less of an issue once they have met (this can work in very senior roles where the client boundaries are less set, but you still need to know you are in the right 'ballpark').
  - Assume the client will pay more as the candidate is so great.
  - Assume that the candidate will accept less than their minimum (however little less) as the job is so great.
  - Make any assumptions!
- Do:
  - Give broad brush guidelines as to what people can expect to pay/earn ('Hmmm, this role's paying quite a bit more than that,' when headhunting; 'Hmmm, you might need to pay rather more than that to attract that type of candidate,' when taking the brief). Set the scene early here.
  - Discuss salary ranges early on in the discussion so as to conserve time and effort on both parts.
  - Tell the client the candidate's desired pay bracket and suggest that s/he would accept a figure somewhere in the middle of this that you know is what the candidate would definitely accept – but only if you have trial-closed them on it.

- Tell the candidate what the client is expecting to pay – but make sure it is in the low-to-middle part of their scale and not at the top.
- Explore salary minimums and maximums in detail at the appropriate point (this depends upon the interview process, but before reaching offer stage).
- Re-discuss salary with your candidate in the light of every role. At interview they may have given you broad guidelines; for one opportunity they may alter it (higher for a less exciting role) and again for another (lower for a more desirable, career-enhancing aspirational company with lower pay rates).
- Trial close with both candidate and client before making an offer.
- Ask your candidate to commit to taking a certain package if you go to the client to achieve it – and check there is nothing else you need discuss before you do so!
- Take care to give the whole negotiation process a light touch, but be thorough at the same time.

Closing the deal

If you do need to 'close' the deal there are a variety of 'closes' available of course. You can be assumptive – offering alternative start dates, simply asking whether they are taking the role, though if you have pre-closed them none of this should be necessary. Sometimes however you might need something more sophisticated.

The Benjamin Franklin close (see case study below), also known as the Balance Sheet close is, according to internet folklore, the method Benjamin Franklin would use when having to make a decision. It's best to be careful with this as it can seem a little too sales-oriented but when used in the right way, in a spirit of service to the candidate, it works well. A further way to use something similar is to suggest to the candidate that they think about walking down a road, with offices to their left and right. Their current workplace is to their left and their new one is to their right and they are in the middle and they have to decide which way to go. Psychologically here you have moved them out of their current workplace to a neutral space that is empty and allows them to follow their instincts.

CASE STUDY

Peter Tanner, founder of Tanner Menzies, a recruitment consultancy operating across a wide range of industry sectors in Australia, uses the Benjamin Franklin close. Alongside running the business he still does the occasional piece of search, and he recently approached a senior candidate working for a private company who was interested in some public company experience with one of Peter's clients. The candidate had been with his previous company for 15 years and secured three new offers quite quickly, one of which was with a client of Peter's, and was struggling to decide which one to take.

Peter invited him in to discuss it and then took a sheet of blank paper and went through each of the roles looking at reasons to join. He also arranged for the candidate to meet with his prospective team at the client company. The candidate himself identified that the role Peter had on offer was the best opportunity, in part because he had met the team and liked them and he had only met the boards of the other companies, but also that he had talked to the client about how people had progressed through the firm, which was a really important aspect of any new role. So, the list for Peter's client was longer than for the others and it became clear on paper what he needed to do.

Managing the resignation

Once you have agreed an offer and your candidate has accepted it verbally and received the client's offer letter or contract, they'll need to resign from their current role, which can be crucial for permanent scarce-skill staff.

Counter-offers need discussing at interview before any likelihood of one occurring and a market which is experiencing a high level of counter-offers will be either very candidate-short or could be in a downturn where businesses feel they will not get replacement headcount if people leave. Some organizations are more likely to move to counter-offer than others and if you are a specialist in a particular market you'll get to know which ones they are. However, whatever the market conditions you'll need to be prepared for counter-offers. If your candidate receives one here are some thoughts to share:

- 'It is never a good time for you to leave your current role (unexpectedly) as there is unlikely to be a replacement waiting in the wings, so your employers are likely to act in one of three ways if they are more concerned for themselves than for you: make you a counter-offer and give you the corner office you have been coveting for years; love you to bits and be terribly nice in the hope you might change your mind – they may ask you to delay your start date; or make you feel very guilty and spend a great deal of time working on you 'not to let them down.'
- 'Counter-offers are not about what's good for you, they are about what's good for the company. They are generally a knee-jerk reaction to your resignation while they buy some time to consider what to do. A sticking plaster for them.'
- If a candidate is tempted to take a counter-offer, that may just be due to a little nervousness about the new role. Engage your client, the new employer, to help with this – this will work particularly well if you have pre-warned your client of this and asked them to involve

the candidate in the new business as soon as possible – show them their office/desk/ have them meet the team/go for lunch/talk about new projects to get going on straight away and other activities to mentally move them from their old employer to the new.

- 'Reasons for leaving rarely go away after a counter-offer is accepted. Nothing changes (you may be earning a little more money) except that now your boss may be actively looking for your replacement and you are much more vulnerable. You may no longer be considered part of the team.'

- Suggest your candidate makes a list of the pros and cons of their existing role and their new one and see what has changed in terms of their reason for leaving.

- Suggest they say, in response to a counter-offer, 'I'm flattered that you want to keep me but I have made my decision and I plan to leave as soon as my notice period is expired – I am working towards X date. What can I do to make the transition work best for you?'

- Explain that research has shown that after accepting a counter-offer only six out of 100 employees are still with their company after six months, as either the company makes them redundant or they still feel dissatisfied.

Generally when people leave jobs they only do so for money if they feel significantly underpaid and so undervalued. These candidates are especially vulnerable to counter-offer and need to be identified early on in the process.

You'll also have identified when your market is vulnerable to counter-offer and have paid particular attention to this early in the process. Counter-offers are most prevalent in a candidate-short, professional services market where it is hugely costly to acquire new talent, and much more effective to retain what you have. Enlightened firms are taking a much longer view of retention and not just relying on counter-offer to stem the labour turnover rate in their organizations.

Managing your candidate through to start date and beyond

You'll need to keep in touch with your candidates through to their start date and increasingly support their on-boarding process as well, particularly if their new company does not place a big emphasis on this. The risk of not managing your candidate is that they may find other opportunities.

Develop an understanding of what your candidate's plans are after accepting the offer. Are other roles now fully rejected, or is s/he still waiting to hear from that dream job in Rio? Is the candidate at home on gardening leave for three months – in which case they could be vulnerable to other approaches, going along to meetings 'just to see' or to network for the future. Your candidate's notice period or time before starting can vary hugely but in general try to keep in touch on a weekly basis and do the occasional lunch or coffee, ensuring also that your client keeps in touch and invites the candidate along to team social outings or meetings without breaking any contractual constraints. Keep in touch too during the first weeks of the new role as this can sometimes be challenging and you can provide a bridge between the old role and the new.

For contractors and temps it is as important to keep in regular touch but this is always the case and if you are running a group of contractors or temps you will have systems in place to ensure a regular telephone contact, backed up with the odd get-together on client site. If you do not have a system in place, develop a diary-based system now that enables you to speak to temps once a week and contractors once a month, or every fortnight on a shorter contract.

Of course once your candidates are placed in work they also become great people both to network with and to act as advocates in developing new client relationships. This is the next stage we explore: client acquisition.

Industry profile – Di Martyn

We mentioned Di Martyn earlier and her strong commitment to candidates in recruiting:

Profile for Di Martyn, ex-CEO of Randstad UK's staffing business
Born: Suffolk
Educated: Degree in European Finance and Accounting at Leeds with a year in Bremen at a German University

Early career: Di's first job was in the recruitment industry and she started as a consultant with Blue Arrow in Norwich, working her way up to Office Manager through Area and Regional Manager, and becoming MD of Blue Arrow in 1997. If you ask her how she became so successful Di says she had no specific intention to become MD, she simply did 'the best she could every day', and this would be her advice today to recruiters who want to develop their careers, and even those who don't but still want to do well.

In 2000 she was headhunted by Vedior, who needed someone to take over the Select Group, one of their flagship companies. Select has a range of services and Di has focused on growing the business through franchising that, she believes, enables and supports the business in staying true to its brand, which is about servicing the SME market with a model of strong relationships at a local level.

Di has just celebrated her 21st year in recruitment!

Key advice for recruiters:

- Remember what you're here for – to find jobs for people and people for jobs! Be obsessed with doing your best!

- One thing you should always do – treat your candidate and client with the utmost respect. Always follow through.

- One thing you should never do – interview someone, commit to finding them a job and then not do so.

Still to achieve: To continue to be the best that I can every day. Who knows where that will lead me – it's been a great mantra thus far.

Interests outside work: Getting into my sweatshirts and wellies on Friday nights and spending time on my 14-acre farm in Suffolk over the weekends. My briefcase and suits stay firmly in the car and my weekday flat!

Di is a woman who really lives by her values and her career has shown that a belief in the simplicity of what you do in recruitment will move you forward. Her mantra of doing the best you can with the talents you have (also used by JK Rowling) is great advice to anyone in the industry.

Industry profile – Jack Gratton

Profile for Jack Gratton, Founder and CEO of Major Players
Born: In the Lake District
Educated: First class honours degree in Mineral Engineering from Leeds University

Early career: Jack joined Mobil Oil on their graduate scheme and sold petrol as a first role. He moved on into the agency world and from there started Major Players (with a range of other ventures along the way some of which he sold) which, when he wasn't racing motorbikes (which he did semi-professionally), he built into a successful business – the largest still of those who serve the creative industries. He sold it five or so years ago but has continued to run it since then.

Key advice for recruiters: Do all the right things; give great service, get to know understand your market and put lots of clients and candidates together then the money will follow – although it doesn't hurt to keep an eye on this too.

One thing recruiters should always do: Always stay true to your word – you'll build trust and loyalty with your clients that way.

One thing recruiters should never do: Over-promise and under-deliver. Also remember that recruitment is a people business so I've always focused on making Major Players a great place to work.

Still to achieve: Too many things to do and not enough time to do them; the list is long!

Interests outside work: Rather too many children and slightly expensive hobbies.

Jack is one of a relatively small number of people within the industry to have built a successful business and sold it at the right time. There are great rewards to be had in recruitment and Jack leads the field in entrepreneurial success. He also manages to be a thoroughly decent bloke!

Client acquisition

07

Introduction

In the recruitment cycle, client acquisition follows on from client management. This chapter provides an outline to the more sales-oriented elements of the recruiter's role. We will look at the buying process from a client perspective, and then consider how to source, approach, qualify, win and develop your client base. Although this material may not seem immediately relevant to in-house recruiters, it does provide an insight into how external suppliers offer their services. Some of the ideas are also relevant to creating successful, valued relationships with your internal client base. For professional recruitment consultants, winning the opportunity to supply is arguably the major factor in differentiating this role from that of an in-house provider.

The phrase 'winning the opportunity to supply' is used intentionally. There can be too much self-congratulation in the staffing industry when a new client is 'won', even though at that point no actual revenue may be generated. Remember, clients, except in retained assignments, are only invoiced upon a successful placement. However important candidates are to the process it is the client that pays the bill, which can leave recruiters desperate for a relationship at all costs – a potentially hazardous place to be. It is worth considering first how this impacts the business relationships we build.

The power in communication

When communicating, people emanate a level of power perceived by the other person. The balance of power creates a 'rulebook' for the communication, and indeed relationship, created between the two parties. Most of us would agree that a bit of extra power rarely goes amiss when developing either a consultant/client or a candidate/consultant relationship.

Perceived power boosters are:

- *Seniority*: hence corporate job titles.
- *Financial status*: wealth equals power.
- *Age*: recently up to about 55, however this is changing and power is becoming more evenly distributed with both younger and older people achieving and retaining power.
- *Gender*: males perceived to be more powerful although again, this is changing.
- *Knowledge*: especially if it's something others want to know.
- *Intellect*: judged by the questions asked.
- *Vocabulary*: that's what a private education does!
- *Physical size*: tall, athletic – think broad shoulders, high heels.
- *Efficiency*: does what it says on the tin.
- *Price*: must be worth more if more expensive.

There is also a strong personality element, generally along two further lines:

- *Authoritative*: do as I say because I know best.
- *Popularity*: do as I say because I am a well liked person.

Without re-engineering yourself you can add value to your own personal power base, either by boosting the elements that you already have or by diminishing the focus of those you do not.

CASE STUDY

A consultant who started in the 1980s in the recruitment industry aged 22, lacked seniority, age and financial wealth! She decided to develop her own personal power by dressing rather as Margaret Thatcher did in strong coloured suits and sensible court shoes, and by carrying a low-key but reassuringly expensive bag with proper pens etc (going out straight from work with friends was not an option!). This approach enabled her to work with people who might otherwise have dismissed her. As she grew older and became more successful, accumulating a level of knowledge, seniority and even a modicum of financial security, she was able to become also more relaxed with her wardrobe as personal power became more evident.

Consider further the personality element:

- With candidates we use mainly authoritative communication: 'Call me directly after the interview,' 'Don't forget to prepare questions to ask', 'Have you googled the company?'

- With clients we use mainly personality-based communication: 'I will work extremely hard to find the right candidate', 'Could you possibly go a little higher on the salary?', 'Thank you for the opportunity to work on this assignment.'

However, if we use an authoritative approach, an intimidated candidate may avoid us and not trust us, not give us the full picture and not return our calls. Equally a too popularity-hungry approach means respect can be lost with both candidates and clients. It is important to achieve a balance between authoritative and personality-based communication so you see both as tools to use when appropriate. A balance means that the old adage 'people buy from people' is not lost completely (particularly at individual candidate and line-manager level), but equally respect is won by being authoritative and negotiating effectively to win for our clients, our candidates and ourselves.

Task

Ask a range of people you work with, and whom you trust, to tell you where your own power lies and what communication style you most often adopt. Ask your manager or a good colleague to attend a client meeting with you and give you feedback on how you come across to the client. This person's role in the meeting is not to help you as a colleague but to observe closely the interaction between you and the client and give constructive feedback on how to develop your own personal power and communication style.

Much of success in sales, consultancy and relationship building with clients is around developing your own self-awareness and honing your own skills in presentation and client development. Your awareness of your personal impact is a strong part of that but it's equally important to understand the process needed to acquire a new client. Rather as with the recruitment cycle, success can be determined by how well you follow each of the steps in the process.

Acquiring a new client

Before we look at what you need to do to acquire a new client, it's worth bearing in mind what clients report they don't like!

Top five 'pet hates' of clients:

- consultants who know nothing about them;
- arrogant consultants who tell us what is wrong with them as an employer without being asked;

- consultants who send irrelevant unsolicited CVs;
- consultants who mailshot without considering their client's specific needs;
- consultants who over-promise (especially at a face to face meeting) and then under-deliver.

(Sourced from a range of clients and internal recruiters)

We'll look now at the steps you need to take to acquire new clients effectively.

Steps in client acquisition

- Identify the types of clients you are good at working with.
- Generate a list of target accounts.
- Do your research on each account.
- Identify the right person or decision-making group member to approach.
- In light of that, choose your approach strategy.
- Implement your approach.

Identifying types of clients

Part Two provides information on how to identify new market segments or types of clients to approach. The ones you are currently successfully working with will give you a good clue to which sorts of organizations you prefer to work with (large or small, well-known or growing). It's clearly a good plan to work with organizations you can get enthusiastic about or roles you feel you can market successfully, whether because they are large employers in the area, pay well, have great training schemes or because no one else is recruiting for them. It's also useful to have a blend of organizations, which spreads your risk of clients of one type stopping recruiting at any point.

Many recruiters fail to do this and work with only one type of client, often the well-known successful ones where all other recruiters have targeted their efforts as well. The top 20 per cent of employers want the top 20 per cent of candidates. Yet the other 80 per cent of clients and candidates all successfully get jobs as well. A blend of top accounts, middling accounts, and lesser accounts enables you to place a much wider range of candidate capability. So when you are identifying accounts to work with, make sure you have a range both to spread your risk of accounts suddenly stopping recruiting and to be able to place almost all qualified candidates. In recessions recruiters who focus on a few accounts are highly vulnerable.

You will have decided from Part Two also whether you are an artistic or scientific recruiter, which will have a bearing on how you might choose your next client. Artistic types will want to be inspired by their potential clients while scientific types will want them to fit a pattern and a mould; knowing which you are helps you decide the best approach for you.

Generating a list of target accounts

You may already have a database in the business from which you can choose accounts to work on, or you may have been given a list of target accounts to develop. Here are some other ways of generating accounts; many are not dissimilar from some of the methods used in attracting candidates.

- Attend trade exhibitions; choose the stands you like but be sure to visit a range – you want small and large clients, well-known and less so.
- Network: go to trade or sector events and meetings where your clients go. Steer clear of recruitment – show your knowledge of the clients' sector.
- Read the press and find out what companies are doing.
- Check out which companies are advertising roles.
- Ask your candidates whom they rate in your sector.
- Directories: sector and geographical if you are based in one area.
- Internet – although beware of untargeted surfing as it will cost you time.
- Colleagues.

CASE STUDY

David Hay, a specialist recruiter, works almost exclusively with US clients planning to set up in the UK. He has recently worked with a California-based software business, five years old and very successful in its domestic market though hitherto unknown in the UK, that he identified through a range of approaches:

- He built a network of contacts in other, non-competing businesses in the UK seeking to work with similar companies, such as bankers, accountants and employee-benefits consultants.
- He made his services known to the overseas, inward investment offices of the DTI (UKTI).
- He undertook direct research of growing overseas companies (especially the United States/Canada).
- He made personal visits/business development trips to the United States.

He first spoke with the HR Director in San Francisco at the end of one year. Over the next few months, via e-mail and telephone contact he provided him with 'free' advice regarding sources of technical and sales skills in the UK, suitable locations to set up base, salaries and benefits. Throughout this period he was conducting research and reading to enhance his understanding of the company's niche area.

Some six months later he was asked to recruit a UK sales manager and a senior software engineer. Both candidates joined the company in November, travelling to San Francisco for induction and training.

An important element of the success of David's story is that he made sure he could add value by becoming knowledgeable in the client's area.

Do your research

Do not underestimate the importance of knowledge about your prospective clients before you approach them. That is not to say you need to spend weeks researching them, but with the wealth of information available at the touch of a button few clients will be impressed by consultants whose opening line is: 'Tell me a little about your business.'

Task

Try to identify from this case study what this consultant should have done differently.

CASE STUDY

Jazz's boss had told her she didn't seem to have enough requirements to work on and that was why she didn't seem to be generating enough revenue at the moment. Jazz decided she needed to generate some more requirements and thought she'd spend the morning phoning some clients to do so.

She went on to the database and started casting through it, looking for a company she'd not worked with before or ideally never heard of as she fancied working on something new. Eventually she found one. They sounded different she thought and dialled their number. She asked to be put through to the person in charge of recruiting and someone said 'Hello'. Jazz said Hello and asked whom she was speaking to; 'Pete Ryan' came back the reply. 'Great,' said Jazz. She explained which recruitment company she was from and asked: 'Do you have any briefs I could help you with filling?'

There was quite a long silence and Pete asked Jazz what she knew about his business. Jazz stuttered out that she didn't really know anything but she quite liked the name. Peter told her that he was one of the founders and that the company had unexpectedly lost two key accounts last week. He said he was deciding whom to make redundant. Jazz went rather red, said she was really sorry to have called and got off the phone as quickly as she could.

What Jazz should have done differently

The critical errors here were not conducting any research before the approach, or identifying a strong approach. An artistic recruiter might well be inspired by the name of the company but still needs to do some research and choose an approach.

- Before the call:
  - She needed to think harder and more constructively about the briefs she did have. The vast majority of jobs do get filled and it's too tempting to cast about for the 'perfect' job to work on. Options: look at the brief from another angle or with fresh eyes, ask colleagues for their view on it (new angle perhaps), re-negotiate the brief with the client.
  - If new briefs are really needed, think about the sort of companies you might have candidates for rather than randomly calling from the database. If you do turn to the database, don't discard 20 clients you don't like the look of – someone will place in them next week. Be systematic.
  - Take a different perspective on sourcing new clients. Read the trade press for information about new bids won, expansion and awards, and approach companies who may have some likelihood of needing new staff.
  - Take a candidate you know you can place and think about which new clients you could market the candidate to. Once you have agreed the list of clients with your candidate (which you need to do before approaching them), this is a great way of gaining credibility with new clients as they'll see you work with quality candidates. If the candidate is not suitable for a role that prospective clients currently have, it is likely they will brief you on other roles instead.
  - Research! It helps you choose your approach plan and angle. What to say...
- During the call:
  - Jazz should have found out the name and the role of the person she was planning to speak to, calling twice if necessary so she was not left wondering who she was speaking to.
  - Once she was speaking to the person, she needed to have established that he was the right person to speak to before involving him in a long conversation about something that might not have been his responsibility.
  - Jazz needed to consider what her opening line might be – the one in the case study is probably the worst opener for new clients. They have no reason to imagine you might have any capability.

Try and find something out about the person you are calling – are they on the database, what comes up when you google them? Use this to help you craft an opening line. Ask an open question. How, what, where, when, who... 'I noticed you won an award last week – that must have been great – and it looked like there was some stiff competition – how was the party afterwards?'

- Jazz also needed to consider how she would present her company if this becomes appropriate, or whether she would try and make an appointment to visit the client. Set an objective before making the call – this doesn't need to be hard and fast, just some thoughts on what you might want to get out of a call.

- Consider how her use of questioning and listening skills will help take and negotiate a brief. For more help with this read Chapter 8 on 'Client strategy'.

- Use 'matching' on the phone to match both the pace of speech of the client and the sort of language s/he uses. The best recruiters are also chameleons and can adapt themselves to everyone they meet. People like people whom they recognize to be like themselves – it's self-affirming!

Sources for information about your prospective client

- Internet: company website.
- Other consultants in your company: who also works with this client?
- Articles.
- Trade press.
- LinkedIn: names of people who work there plus company information.
- Your database: as above.
- General internet search.

All of these will offer you an opportunity to demonstrate some knowledge when you do call your clients so you can show you are sufficiently interested in them.

Research, however, applies equally well to the internal recruiter: it is just as important for you to arm yourself with information about a client's business division before a meeting to discuss their recruitment needs. Clients will buy from both people who deliver and whom they also like. So to put yourself in the best possible supplier position with your clients it is important to work in a way that enables you to both deliver placements and build great relationships.

With this in mind, and once you have conducted your research, you need to identify who to approach in your client.

Identifying the right person or group to approach

This in itself may be another research topic and will vary hugely between organization to organization. In a small company it may be that the line manager or even the MD is the right person. Bear in mind it is harder to 'work up' the chain than 'work down'. So if you call the MD it is easier to then call the Sales Director, but if you start with the Sales Director it is then quite tricky to call the MD.

In a larger organization a good first port of call may also be a line manager as they often have the recruiting need – but they may also not hold the recruiting budget or have authorization to hire through any supplier. The scale of the need for the types of candidates you supply, coupled with the size and formality of the business, may indicate how much more flexible this may be. Either way, the line managers are a great source of information as they will be able to tell you what their needs are and what the recruitment process is, and can advise you who to speak to next.

In large organizations your next point of call may be procurement, in which case the section below will be helpful, or it may be HR, which is increasingly a dedicated internal resourcing team, either outsourced to a recruitment provider but located in-house or employed directly by the client. Normally you will need to agree terms with them. Often, you may need to supply and invoice them as well. It is important not to feel too frustrated by this sort of organizational hurdle and to recognize that the internal teams have the same sorts of targets that you do and are equally under pressure to deliver. The smart ones recognize that you and they make a good partnership and both need each other to be successful, especially if you can provide a great service level with a stress-free supply of excellent candidates and they can provide a ready supply of appealing vacancies! Either way, your contact, or the decision-making group needs to have all of the attributes outlined in Table 7.1.

Too often in any sales situation it is easy to neglect the qualification of a client in this way. You may spend any amount of time marketing your services to the wrong person, or to someone with no need of your services or no budget signed off. Do bear in mind that many internal recruiters and outsourcers will try and fill the roles themselves first so you may end up working on roles which are 'hard to fill'. Increasingly the role of the external recruiter is to augment the organization's own resourcing strategies. This means external recruiters need to have a range of great candidates at their fingertips who also have scarce skills.

TABLE 7.1 Qualifying your prospective clients

- Money
- Authority
- Need

You'll need to ask questions to establish all of the three qualifiers. Here are some of the questions you need to ask:

- Has a budget been allocated?
- What is involved in the hiring process?
- How may temps do they typically use?
- Is the role 'live' now?
- When do they need this person to start?
- How many new staff have been hired over the last six months?
- Where are you in the procurement process?
- How will the procurement decision be made – what are the buying criteria?

Build this in to your approach to check out that your chosen contacts have the capacity to work with you and that you want to work with them.

The approach strategy

At this point then you have reached the next key step – choosing your approach strategy. Before considering this in more detail it's worth understanding exactly how clients actually buy recruitment services.

How clients buy

If we understand the buying psychology and the decision-making processes behind the procurement of our services we are better placed to gear the sales process towards a successful outcome. The extent of the arrangement, the time frame of the project and the scale of the expenditure will have an impact on how formal and lengthy the buying process will actually be. A line manager or individual will often decide upon individual placements made within small organizations. Medium and large-sized clients will usually have budgeted for increased permanent headcount or a strategic use of flexible resources, with decision making falling to HR and line management as to which individuals to hire or which recruitment companies to receive details from. As one looks at a growing acceptance of a PSL with some level of exclusivity of supply or large-scale staffing opportunities, the decision-making group and the buying process can become both quite large and lengthy.

Decision-making groups

Understanding where your buyer sits in the client corporate structure provides an insight into the deemed value of the process they are planning to implement. The higher up the corporate structure the decision-makers, the more important the project. This also provides a better understanding of the individual buyer's motivations and decision-making criteria.

If a team has been created to implement and manage the buying process, it is also worth looking at the team with the users of the service (eg line managers).

It's important to consider:

- What are the dynamics of the relationship?
- How well established is it?
- How good is the understanding of the key issues facing the sponsors?
- Is this team locally, nationally or even globally based?

Corporate politics and internal conflict have a huge impact on the buying process and potentially endanger your opportunity to win business. Business process re-engineering, strategic changes, mergers, buy-outs or changes in personnel all affect the buyer process. Internal conflict can be created from shifts such as power struggles, the movement of goal posts, conflicts of interest and personality clashes. This can produce fractured buying teams, disillusionment and sometimes panic. If significant issues of conflict or politics become apparent during the buying phase, it is imperative that you do not allow yourself to be dragged in or used as a scapegoat in any way. Remain neutral at all times, in case you back the proverbial 'wrong horse'. In a meeting offer to step outside if discussions between decision-makers become heated!

Formal roles in the buying process

Evaluator

This person will be responsible for designing an invitation to tender (ITT) with input from others, and analysing your proposal, pitch or tender to compare it with pre-defined criteria. In large projects procurement or a committee may undertake this role.

Decision maker

The decision maker has responsibility and accountability for accomplishing the set objectives of choosing a supplier or group of suppliers. It is the decision-maker who will listen to the evaluation results and recommendations and push forward to make the agreement happen. This person is often the overall sponsor of the staffing project.

Approver

This is the most senior person who retains the right to review, approve or veto the lower-level decisions. Decisions by credible subordinates with a proven track record are routinely approved. The size of the organization and the scale and financial implications for the staffing project dictate the level of this individual.

User

Often a senior line manager or departmental head who will have direct use of the service and own the relationship with the providers. This person may get involved on other roles too.

As you go into a formal sales process, chart which position each of your decision-making group is taking. This will help you determine their relative importance (although in truth they are all important), and how you should best deal with them given where their buying interests lie.

Group buying orientation

Both their job title and personality drivers affect the buying orientation of any individual. If you have an understanding of what focus someone will have, you can make sure that you have provided them with the right information in order for them to choose your service. There will be a range of interests, as outlined below.

Business

The CEO or senior executive of the organization will usually have a view of the 'big picture'. Their interest will be in how your proposal will affect their company's present and future. Their vision will often extend beyond their company to include their customers, their competition and sometimes their community. Articulating business versus service value and sharing industry knowledge, along with clarity about what is important to this level of individual, are crucial to successful selling here.

Financial

The Finance Director, COO and procurement department (in a smaller business this could still be a CEO) will have a primary focus on price, cost and economics. While your service offering must be viable, numbers and negotiation will be the key buying orientations. These will be some of the most frustrating buyers as it can seem as if they have no understanding of – or indeed interest in – your key differentiators. There has been a growth of the power-base of the finance team in recent times and you'll need to be careful not to negotiate a non-viable, or profitless arrangement that you will live to regret.

Many recruitment businesses have fallen foul of 'buying' a position on PSL's agreeing such low rates that the business cannot be delivered profitably. As the old saying goes 'turnover is vanity, profit is sanity'. There was a fond belief that being able to supply blue-chip large clients with staff at a low rate would somehow be beneficial. There is no doubt that there has been, and is likely to continue to be, a downward pressure on rates within some sectors, particularly generalist ones, but in areas of scarce skills like mobile development, SEO, Search, social media, ecommerce where demand outstrips supply fair rates will still be achievable so it's important to understand the dynamics of your market when negotiating.

If you are negotiating on behalf of a larger group take care of agreeing an overall average rate for a range of market sectors. Clients are increasingly appointing specialist PSL's with different ones for digital, account handling and marketing, for example. Rates should be negotiated to suit each specialist market as otherwise business areas will be unable or unwilling to deliver at lower rates than they can command elsewhere. This is particularly the case given the likelihood that roles will be 'hard to fill'.

Technical

This individual's primary focus will be on how the process will work and whether the infrastructure is in place to back up your service claims. Technical personnel will often be detail-oriented and analytical regarding proof of all your service and delivery claims. External consultants and line managers often fall into this buying orientation.

Relationships

This refers to individuals who believe that they are forming a business partnership and whose buying focus is the supplier company, its ethos and the people that will be serving their organization. Whilst your solution must be viable, support, trust, effort and responsiveness will be key. Recruitment professionals often prefer to sell to this type of buyer. The difficulties in creating clear differentiation between recruitment businesses prompt recruiters to sell themselves as the 'unique selling point' of their companies. As the business platform elevates, the ability to close deals on this basis, other than at an individual level, has diminished. Although of major importance to certain individuals it is by no means enough to be 'nice people to do business with'.

Status

With any decision-making group there will be differing views on your company, services or solution. Some individuals will not have preconceived ideas about any of the suppliers, but more usually most will have a view. It is important to create a positive impression with as many members of the decision-making group as you can, and to be acutely aware of their standpoint and how to influence it. Once you have identified the formal role each individual plays in the process, be aware that many may take up an informal role as well.

There are five main informal roles that participants in the decision-making process can have, independent of their formal role.

Mentors or sponsors

Mentors believe that your success is critical to their company or to them personally. They will work to help you win by giving guidance, competitive information, political insight or regular feedback. Mentors will proactively sell on your behalf and tie their own success to yours. Developing sponsors in key clients is the best way of being able to supply across business.

CASE STUDY

An RPO provider had completed a three-year contract with a client and was negotiating a further three years when there was a significant shift in personnel in the business; a new recruitment director took over responsibility for the RPO team and its possible new contract. This individual could have taken up any informal role within the upcoming decision-making group of which they were part. The senior team in the RPO company identified the new recruitment director as a key influencer in their negotiations and decided to turn them into their mentor. Their success in signing the new contract some two months later confirmed that this had been a smart move.

Supporters
These people prefer your solution and think that you should win. A supporter will help when asked and provide positive references if questioned, but may not be proactive or particularly vocal in their support.

Neutrals
The neutrals have no preference (yet!). They may be undecided or feel that they have not had sufficient information to make a decision.

Non-supporters
These are people who believe that yours is not the right solution, either because they prefer an alternative (and indeed may be a supporter of another supplier), a completely internal solution or no solution at all. It could also be someone who has had a poor experience of, or heard negative comments about, your company or service.

Enemies
These people believe that your success will damage them or their company. They may have a special interest or be mentors for a competitive organization. They will create opportunities to show you or your company or your proposal in a poor light and cast doubt on your suitability to fulfil the brief.

It's important to identify the positions that each individual involved in the buying process is likely to take up. It's equally important to be aware that there may be things you don't know you don't know! So, if you don't ask the right questions of your mentor or sponsor – 'Who else is acting as a mentor for one of my competitors?', 'Who might have an interest in someone other than us winning the tender?' and 'How might we change X's mind about suppliers?' for example – you may sail along blithely assuming everything is going well just because you and your mentor have a great relationship, without realizing there is an enemy out there, or another supplier with a more corporately powerful mentor. So asking the right questions here is crucial and so is not making assumptions – not a bad mantra for any sales situation.

You also need to have a clear understanding of how your prospective client or organization goes about its procurement process. This will vary depending upon whether you are intending to supply one candidate (perhaps initially in a one-off situation) or whether you wish to supply a whole service across a range of candidates. It may be that you choose to use supplying one candidate as a useful initial 'door-opener' to a new client. You may be part of a corporate recruitment sales team whose remit it is to open and develop new client relationships through a blend of one-to-one sales skills and tender submissions, in which case the sections below on 'The procurement process' and 'The procurement plan' will be of value. If you are an individual recruiter with a view to developing a new account or developing new relationships within existing accounts the next sections will be useful.

Choose your approach strategy

There are broadly two choices when making an initial approach. You can either choose to approach a client with a candidate you wish to introduce, or to approach a client offering your services. Initial research should indicate which service might be of interest. This means you'll choose between:

- a candidate-led approach;
- a service-led approach.

Once you have chosen, you'll need then to identify how to best make your approach. The methods below will apply to either strategy. There are a few (non-exhaustive) choices:

- letter/or e-mail – building your capability or with specific information;
- web-based – an indirect approach to build your brand and show your interest and knowledge in a particular area to draw people to you rather than you approaching them directly. All client approach strategies should have an element of this activity in them;
- telephone – a direct approach with a candidate or service in mind;
- face to face – networking events or exhibitions;
- social media;
- blogs and newsletters;
- video based.

Equally you may choose each of these in a structured campaign to develop a relationship with your clients over a period of time. You may start off with following a business on LinkedIn or Twitter to get a feel for it. You might then send them a letter or an e-mail to introduce yourself, perhaps with an invitation to receive interesting content from you, which you'd follow up with a phone call and then aim to develop a relationship with a visit.

We know clients like market information. External recruiters particularly, but internal recruiters too, are uniquely placed to give a wide perspective on their market places, which their clients are not as they will view things very much from their own internal reality. So the provision of relevant market intelligence and data will be very valuable.

Whichever method(s) you choose, it's important to find a way to demonstrate your credibility at the beginning of the call, or approach, so that you make a compelling proposition as to why they should deal with you.

Speaking and meeting with clients is the only way to differentiate our service from another supplier's. In this way we can also increase our credibility by demonstrating the types of candidates we work with, how we manage them and therefore how we add value to the client in a range of ways.

If your candidates are exclusively working through you and you are in a candidate-short market, you can for a period get away with a transactional style of working (where the purchase is rarely an emotional decision but based on supply and demand for a particular product, and is also not a long-term supply relationship). If your market shifts to a client-led market, however, a transactional way of working will mean you are likely to be the first recruiter to be dropped from the PSL (remembering that clients will work with people they like, not just those who deliver). So a relationship-based style of working will generate longer-term rewards for you, and this means you will need to develop a relationship with your clients both on the telephone and face to face. The initial approach to reach that stage may well be via written communication however.

Letter/e-mail

Although the use of print is in decline, this can mean a letter-based approach can have more impact. E-mail is of course faster, and if you want to let someone know about 'four great candidates available today' then a letter will be too slow. Equally an e-mail may be deleted before it is read so the subject line is a crucial part of crafting the mail. A possible two-stroke approach could be adopted with a letter followed by a follow-up e-mail covering both bases.

Nothing will irritate some clients more than sloppy communication over e-mail or paper-based communication:

- In all written communication, remember the medium you are using and don't muddle them; so in e-mail don't resort to texting abbreviations. If you are writing a letter, make sure the layout rules are correct.

- Think about who you are writing to and the appropriate language and style.

- Learn the rules of e-mail approaching – e-mail etiquette, although much of it unwritten, is very important. Never use capital letters in a string for example as that suggests you are shouting, and take care not to introduce too many acronyms as they can confuse.

- Make sure you can spell and that your grammar is correct – don't just rely on a spellchecker.

- If you are not sure about your grammar and spelling or your capacity to write well, write a template for a range of e-mails you might use, get that checked over by someone and stick to it – but take care that your e-mails are not written as 'stock' e-mails – add a personal touch where you can.

Following a structured approach to crafting a piece of written communication can be helpful – we use the mnemonic AIDA here (see Table 7.2), both when crafting advertising and in considering how to approach a candidate.

The beginning of the letter is important here. You'll need to capture their attention with something of interest to them whether this be detail of a scarce candidate or an attention-grabber about managing to recruit all required staff on time and to budget or some market intelligence which will help them in business. Imagine you are a newspaper and you want to sell that news... you need to make your market communications something clients would pay for to know. Build on that interest and always end by telling them how to take the next step.

Web-based

Increasingly the use of blogs and chat forums can create a presence online, as described earlier. Following your clients on LinkedIn and Twitter shows an interest in them and is a good start as well as providing you with useful information. Blogging regularly and producing relevant video content will also help establish you as an expert in your field. Starting interest groups and getting followers again will help but do take great care that this is all thought through and targeted activity. Nothing will waste more time than

TABLE 7.2 Capturing your client's interest

A	Attention
I	Interest
D	Desire
A	Action

social networking and your Twitter feed – it needs to be a means to an end not an activity in itself. However, answering queries and taking part in chats in forums can create credibility for you, which means that you may well receive approaches from clients and candidates directly. Clearly this needs to take up a proportion of your time, and it would be easy to get too caught up in your online presence. However, this approach is more subtle than some, and means you can showcase your knowledge and expertise. Equally, take care to do that and not show your lack of knowledge as you cannot erase that once it is published!

Telephone

Many consultants will be making an initial contact over the telephone. In-house recruiters and clients are only too used to recruiters ringing up asking if there are any jobs they can help with, and it is therefore sometimes hard to get through to people on the phone in person, either because of a gatekeeper or voicemail. Experience suggests that leaving messages with new clients is ineffective. Better to try and call 'out of hours', especially in the early morning or late afternoon before or after the gatekeeper is present.

On an initial call, an approach might use the TRIC method shown in Table 7.3.

TABLE 7.3   Client call structure

T	Time out
R	Rapport
I	Introduce service or candidate
C	Confirm what happens next

Face to face

Initial face-to-face approaches will be from chance encounters at conferences, exhibitions, networking meetings – or even on the train! This is different from a planned client meeting, which we look at later but it is worth observing here that clients will buy more from people they meet regularly so long as the meetings are successful – so meeting your clients face to face under whatever circumstances must be the cornerstone of any client development strategy however logistically challenging this might be.

There is information on how to manage a networking meeting in Chapter 9 on 'Candidate attraction' and the same roles apply here, so check that out for more detail. Prospective clients will not appreciate an opening gambit of

'So, who does your recruitment then?' or 'I'm a recruitment consultant and I'd like to work with you' (although the latter is at least direct and confident). Try asking their opinion on the last speaker or the conference in general. Leave the fact you are a recruiter until towards the end of the conversation and, if you have identified that they could be a useful prospect, say you've enjoyed chatting to them, briefly ask to drop by and meet with them, and exchange business cards before moving on. Then, do not forget to follow up.

We now explore each of your options further looking specifically at both candidate and service-led methods in relation to the approach you have taken:

Candidate-led approach

In Chapter 6 on 'Candidate management' we looked at dividing qualified candidates into REQ and SPEQ candidates. You can choose to use SPEQ candidates as a great candidate-led approach to securing a new client relationship.

Some options for presenting candidates

- Telephone? Much the best if you can contact and speak to the right person, but some organizations are now so systemized that it might preclude you from putting your person forward. If you feel that telephone is the only good way of introducing this candidate keep calling the client more and more regularly until they pick up; try at 8 in the morning – senior people often get to their desk early to deal with e-mails and can be reached best then. However, waiting to get hold of someone on the phone may mean you lose competitive advantage with that candidate, especially if you do not have an exclusive arrangement with them.

- E-mail followed immediately by a follow-up call? This too is a good method as it gives the client the comfort of a CV to look at while you speak (this can be particularly useful if you have no relationship with the client) while also meaning you are following up quickly. In some ways this can be the best of both worlds but may only work if you have an e-mail address you know works.

- E-mail followed by a follow-up call at a later date? As a last resort if you cannot get through to someone. It's better to introduce someone than not, especially if you have said you would.

- E-mail with no follow-up call? In some circumstances this can work, but mainly with people you already have a good relationship with; it is more likely to be successful with line managers than corporate recruiting teams.

Placing your candidate with new clients is only one of a range of possible outcomes – you may pick up a new role or requirement or arrange to visit your client as a result of presenting a candidate. You may find some ideas below to adapt for your business.

On the phone, to a hiring manager, you might say something like

'Mr Client, I wonder if you might be able to help me? My name is Joe Smith and I work as a specialist recruiter in X field.

I have just interviewed a terrific candidate who has very sharp business development skills – he has generated over £5 million of business for his current company this year, one of your direct competitors. He and I have both agreed I will approach you to see whether you might be interested in meeting with him as he is considering a career move.

My candidate has some time booked out over the next couple of weeks for meetings and I wanted to make sure you had an opportunity to meet with him. Would Tuesday next week or the following Monday work for you?'

Or...

'Mr Client, I wonder if you might be able to help me? My name is Joe Smith and I work as a specialist temp recruiter in X field.

I have a temp with me this morning available for work with advanced PowerPoint skills. I am aware you use this package on a regular basis and wondered if you might be able to make use of her skills?'

By e-mail to an old client of your agency

'Dear or Hi (whatever suits the organization)

My name is Joe Smith. I work with XYZ a specialist recruiter in the Marketing field and I know we have worked with you before on vacancies in the past.

I am working with a candidate at the moment that I want to introduce to you as she has excellent skills for a range of roles in the business, particularly within your global team and...

- has worked for three years in a consulting capacity with ABC on large-scale projects;
- has been promoted to a managing consultant as she has developed project extensions for her firm;
- ABC want her to re-locate in the UK where they have a large project;
- however, she really wants to live in London and therefore is looking for a new role;
- prior to being here in the UK she worked in emerging markets in Eastern Europe and is happy to travel extensively.

As we have worked with you before, I have attached some details for your consideration. I am keen to tell you more about her and hear your feedback on her.

Please do call me on my direct line below, or I will call you later to catch up on your interest in her.

I look forward to speaking with you shortly.

Etc.'

To a new client

'Dear/Hi...

My name is Joe Smith. I work with XYZ a specialist recruiter in the Marketing field and whilst we have not worked with you before I am aware you are looking for someone to head up your payments team on a temporary basis.

I have just interviewed an excellent candidate, available immediately, who matches the criteria you have stipulated:

- managed a team of six for three months in accounts payable;
- part-qualified;
- experience in the legal field;
- excellent calm, unflappable personality with evidence of successful trouble-shooting;
- lives within 20 minutes of your office and is on a comparable hourly rate.

This candidate has a range of interviews this week but I would like to make sure you get to see him as I feel he would be ideal for your role.

I shall call you later to arrange a meeting, if that suits you, but enclose our firm's terms and conditions for your reference in the meantime. I will be happy to provide further details assuming this candidate is of interest.

I look forward to speaking with you shortly.

Etc.'

You will of course fashion your own approach using your own language – scripts are great for ideas but not for reading verbatim. You need to sound like yourself as that is what your clients will buy and you also need to make it pertinent for your market; avoid using management consultancy speak if you are working trades in the construction industry and equally if recruiting lawyers a cool media approach will also sound weird! Keep it short and snappy however, and make sure you sound confident – get some feedback on your style if you are unsure how you come across. Once you have made your approach then you need to manage the rest of the process, which includes being clear about fees and terms right at the beginning of the process.

Task

If you have worked through Section II you may already have completed a task similar to this – in which case skip and move on to the rest of the process.

- Draw up a profile of a SPEQ candidate in your market (see p 111 and Figure 6.3 for more information on SPEQ candidates) – you might end up with five or six bullet points of characteristics you consider to be important. Or, ideally, take a SPEQ candidate you are working with currently, or have identified.

- Decide which clients you would SPEQ this person into and prepare the KSPs in order to do that.

- Choose your approach.

- Either use the candidate you have for real and follow though the process, or resource (using some of the techniques in 'Candidate attraction' perhaps) a new SPEQ candidate using a new approach for you.

- Take this opportunity to get back on the phone if you have begun to rely a little too heavily on mail in the past.

Service-led approach

In this approach, instead of introducing a candidate you introduce your business to a potential client organization with a view to establishing an opportunity to supply.

The advantage of this is it enables you to work in a client-oriented way; you don't have to have a candidate to make the initial approach, you can simply call either to set up a meeting or to introduce your service and establish some initial contact. It will help if you have a reason to call that you can use to demonstrate your knowledge and that you have chosen to call them specifically.

Reasons to call:

- You notice an article in the trade press about the business.
- You met someone who works there at a networking event.
- You work with a competitor and want to establish credibility to supply similar candidates (although care is needed with this approach).
- You used to work with the company before.
- You notice they just raised some money.
- You notice they are advertising for staff.
- They have just recruited new senior members of staff.
- They indicate an intention to tender for supply of staff.

- You are introducing a new service or business stream, or have just opened a branch in their area.
- You have not met them in a while!
- Your consultancy's just published a new salary survey and you wonder if they'd like a copy.
- You are having an event you'd like to invite them to.
- You want to draw their attention to something in business that you think might be of interest to them.

That is not an exhaustive list; you will think of your own. You can think about following the TRIC approach here as detailed in Table 7.3 on p 156, or adapting some of the ideas outlined when discussing the candidate-led approach. Each of these also adapts well to a service-led approach.

Adapting the candidate-led approach

Instead of outlining the candidate's skills and key selling points:

- Outline the successes you have had with other clients.
- Explain why you feel the services you can offer can be of benefit to them.
- Detail how you have worked with other parts of the business and relate that to how you might help them.

If you make a successful first approach you may want to arrange to meet your client. This will really make a difference in your capacity to build a relationship with them and develop a long-term supplier partnership. One of the great reasons for the success of the outsourcing industry has been basing recruiters on site, enabling them to build close and lasting relationships with the business, both line hiring managers and buyers (typically HR).

Once you have your meeting booked it's important to plan how you are going to handle the encounter, not forgetting to do your research about the business before you go. It may sound obvious but don't forget to check all sources, including your in-house database and check with colleagues about their knowledge of the organization.

A helpful way of thinking about managing the meeting is similar to the way we suggest you run candidate interviews in the section on candidate management. You can equally successfully use the structured approach of WIGGS, outlined in Table 7.4 on overleaf page, in client meetings.

You'll notice that selling is the very last thing you do when meeting a client. The greatest mistake recruiters make in meetings is to launch into a big sales pitch about their business before trying to understand what's important to the clients. This means that what you pitch is simply guesswork as to whether this is of interest to them. The only exception to this is a 'beauty parade' where you will have been given topics to present and you are simply required to make a presentation as part of a corporate pitch.

TABLE 7.4   Client meeting structure

W	Welcome and rapport
I	Introduction
G	Gathering information
G	Giving information
S	Selling and closing

Bear in mind the information earlier on taking either a 'popular' or 'authoritative' approach. It should be possible to do both so you are seen as both authoritative and an expert in your field and as a likeable person whom people are happy to deal with. In order to take initial control of the meeting you might want to send ahead, or prepare to take with you, an agenda covering the areas you wish to discuss and your objectives. You could also communicate this on e-mail when you confirm the meeting. Confirming the meeting before travelling to it is also wise, just in case your client's plans have changed and no one else is aware of the meeting.

Whether you have sent an agenda or are taking one with you or whether you are just clear what your objectives are, the first thing you'll need to do is build some rapport in your client meeting, the first part of WIGGS.

W: Welcome and rapport

You'll often set the tone of the meeting by the way you arrive. Don't wait in reception for 20 minutes, you may get nervous and you'll look as if you have nothing to do; equally, avoid lateness. Aim to arrive five to seven minutes early for appointments.

Offer your hand to your client as you arrive or walk towards them – whether this is normal for you or not it sets a tone for the meeting and says you are a businesslike person who should be taken seriously. It is also a subtle way of taking some control of the meeting. Don't forget to smile but keep it warm and confident rather than over-excited.

Building a rapport is about finding an area of common interest, making small talk perhaps about the offices, location, something you have read about the client or the business they work for, and then seeking to find an area of mutual interest, whether that be work or social. If you launch straight into business conversation you miss an opportunity to begin to build a relationship with this client.

I: Introduction

This is an opportunity to take control subtly. It's important not to take control in a bombastic way and to exercise some good social skills.

Introduce your agenda and say what you think it might be useful to cover. Ask, of course, what they would like to cover at this point. Using positive language helps here. 'What would you like to get out of the meeting?' rather than 'Is there anything you'd like to get?'

You might say something like: 'I've brought a brief suggested agenda with me so we can make sure we both get what we need from today's meeting [hand agenda over]. What would you like to add to this?'

Then move into the next stage, which is gathering information. Here you'll need to implement your questioning and listening skills. There is a useful resource on questioning in Table 6.2 on page 120 for more information on which types of questions to use.

G: Gathering information

Whilst you don't want to bombard your clients with irrelevant questions, equally you need to understand enough about the business to present the roles effectively to your potential candidates and understand the context within which the roles will sit. Even if you are preparing to supply temps to a central resourcing pool, you need to understand what the key business drivers are and what the culture of the organization is. The business drivers will help you understand what's important to the business, which will give some important clues as to how to sell your services later in the meeting. For example, an organization in high growth mode will care less about fees and more about delivery capability. An organization in start-up may have problems paying all the fees in one go. Lastly you'll perhaps want to know what is important to them from their suppliers, but leave this set of questions until last.

There are three key areas to find out about before you move on to discussing any requirements or needs they may have at the moment, and below we list some suggested questions you might want to use under each heading. You'll need to tailor them to the particular clients you are meeting of course, and you may find it helpful to signpost the questions before you ask them.

Signposting

When you have a question that a client, or candidate for that matter, may find intrusive or surprising, or simply that you find uncomfortable to ask, use this technique to let them know the reason behind the question.

Tell them why you want to ask something:

'So I can brief any potential candidates really well about the opportunities in your business, explain to me the overall plans for growth over the next couple of years.'

'I'd like to understand what's important to you in recruitment services so we can exceed your expectations; tell me, what works particularly well with your current most successful suppliers?'

'I'd like to secure you the best offer possible, so take me through each of the components of your existing package so I can make sure we can exceed it.'

Suggested questions

- Overall business – plans and core competences:
  - What's the overall business vision and mission?
  - What are the long-term aims of the organization?
  - What are your general business plans for the business this year?
  - What are some of the key challenges of the business at the moment?
  - Who do you see as your main competitors?
  - Explain how you are structured.
  - What are the key objectives of your team this year?
  - Tell me a little about the career development opportunities for people within this team.
- Culture:
  - What sorts of values and behaviours work well here?
  - What are your core competences?
  - How do you describe your culture as a business?
  - What makes people successful here?
  - Where have some of your most successful recruits come from?
  - What made you join the business when you did?
- Recruitment process and supplier service:
  - How does your recruitment process work?
  - What do you find works especially well from your current suppliers?
  - If you could change anything about the way in which suppliers in general work, what would that be?
  - What process do you like your suppliers to follow?
  - How would you like candidates presented?

You will of course think of your own questions to add to this list depending upon your clients and the sector they operate in.

You'll then want to move on to:

- gathering specific information on any potential roles they want to recruit;
- qualifying the roles out (see page 195 in Chapter 8 'Client strategy').

Assuming you have qualified the roles at this point, you'll move into taking a brief. Again you can find more about this on page 189 in Chapter 8 on 'Client strategy'. Once you have gathered all the information move towards giving information.

G: Giving information

This is your opportunity to sell yourself as a supplier, but before you launch into a pitch about your consultancy and what you can offer, stop to consider what you have learned about your clients and what is important to them. Consider also how to tell them about your services. Starting with 'Well, the way we work is...' can be hugely off-putting to clients. It sounds as if you offer an entirely inflexible service and they need to fall in with it. Consider saying you tailor your service to their needs. If you interview all your candidates face to face, do say so but also say what that means for the clients. If you have an opportunity to 'benefit drop' during the earlier conversation, do so. This means that if the clients say they are pressured to deliver a project on time, 'drop' the fact that you have another client in a similar situation and understand the importance of having the right resource in place in time. 'Benefit dropping' is taking a throw-away approach to stating benefits, and means just referring to them in a conversational way rather than labouring a point in a heavily sales-oriented way. A benefit drop might look like this:

> Yes, Graham Jones is a good guy. He's worked for me before on more than a couple of large projects – you did really well to hire him directly. Just be a little careful as he'll try and inflate his rates during the project. When you hire people through us we guarantee the rates for the project duration regardless of market movement so it's not a problem you'd need to deal with, but Graham is a really competent manager and won't let you down.

Here the consultant demonstrates credibility through candidate knowledge, offering advice, 'benefit dropping' by letting the client know that through him he would have guaranteed rates, but moving swiftly back off the benefit without labouring it. The client will have heard it but not felt 'sold to'.

Task

Draw up a list of benefits the client may gain by using you as a supplier and consider how you can 'drop' them into conversation rather than labouring them. The best sales pitches are so subtle you do not notice you have been sold to until you have agreed to buy.

Develop your pitch

However conversational you plan to be, you'll still need to be able to deliver some succinct information about your business and its key selling points (just as when marketing a candidate) to your client, for example:

- core competence – specialist in, focused on, major supplier in ...;
- examples of previous work;
- types of candidates;
- service levels;
- delivery capability.

Have someone else critique your pitch before you deliver it, as it's easy to say what you mean and understand (after all you work there!) without communicating it clearly to others. If you can cite examples of relevant work you have done, you should do so here. Much of the reason for using a company as a supplier is that clients are convinced of its capacity to deliver, on time and within budget – but most importantly deliver.

Above all this should be the shortest part of the piece. Relevant and succinct are the keywords. Your questions and demeanour will be as important a part of the sales process as your 'pitch'.

This brings you to the last part of the process.

S: Selling and closing

Use this section to sum up, to cover any points you have not covered already and to gain commitment to move forward, checking there is authorization to do so.

A good meeting will cement you in the minds of your clients and is an opportunity to showcase your capabilities. Clearly you then need to be able to follow through and deliver on your promises.

Agreeing fees/terms and conditions

These need to be agreed before you do any business with a client. By terms and conditions we mean the entire conditions under which you will agree service – not just the fee levels although these are an integral part of the terms. Typically also this means any potential rebate period (the time within which you would agree to refund all or part of the fee if the candidate leaves) and any circumstances under which that might become void – say if the client has not paid within the agreed timescale – plus the time period within which you have ownership of the candidate, along with a range of other points.

Some recruiters may agree margins for contractors or temps on a 'deal by deal' basis; others will put margins in place at the start of a contract, and those margins will be based on volume and market. Often a candidate guarantee will be based on compliance with the payment terms, and this is also important to clarify with your clients as it is an incentive for them to pay you on time!

It can be tempting to reduce your fees to win a new client but this is usually a false economy for both candidate and client. Fee reduction not only cheapens the value of your service but also means you may not put the same degree of effort into a client who is paying you 12.5 per cent as into one who is paying you 20 per cent. So reducing your fees is in the interests of neither you nor your client. There may be circumstances under which you are prepared to offer a small fee reduction in return for an exclusive series of recruitment contracts or volume hires as you can re-coup the reduction by a lower cost of sale. It may therefore not be a case of 'never' reducing your fees, but essentially clients will pay for value-for-money and if that is what you can offer you need not reduce your fees.

Transparency or margins on either contractors or temps will also engender a feeling of trust between you and your client. Clients recognize there is a real and significant cost in employing a contractor, particularly as this often means factoring to run a weekly payroll service, so they are unlikely to be unrealistic but will equally not wish to be charged a huge margin just 'because you can'. Huge margins will erode your reputation in the market and hinder your chances of being in the business for the long haul.

If you are sending a candidate to a new client speculatively, it is crucial you include terms and conditions in your approach e-mail/note. It is good practice to do so each time with existing clients so there can be no confusion. In a corporate contract, which will be negotiated as part of the PSL, terms will be agreed at the outset and potentially reviewed at different periods and sending them each time will be unnecessary.

When you are meeting a client you have not dealt with before, agree the terms and conditions on the spot if possible. You might want to highlight the key areas on the document and verbally take the client through them so they are clear about the main elements: fees, rebate, payment terms, candidate ownership. There is no need to be frightened of fee discussion or fee negotiation. All professions charge fees and a professional recruitment service is no different.

If you are writing contracts you will want to get these looked at by a contract lawyer, but most of the bigger agencies will have an in-house team of contract managers or lawyers on hand to do this. This of course becomes more challenging as the range of clients become larger or you are dealing with a range of overseas countries. There are specialist lawyers who focus in the recruitment industry, such as Blake Lapthorn Tarlo Lyons.

Up to now our focus has been on the individual practitioner acquiring a new client to work with. If you are supplying outsourced recruitment services or volume recruitment under contract the next section will be of value.

The procurement process for large-scale supply of staffing services

There are obviously marked differences between accepting business terms for a one-off candidate placement and undertaking a large-scale procurement process. As we have looked at the types of buyers involved in decision-making groups, it is worth looking at the steps that an organization is likely to undertake in order to choose a large-scale supplier of staff. The following is a guide – there will be subtle differences in each organization.

Often in large client organizations, strategic sourcing is undertaken by purchasing professionals in order to satisfy the business's need to source and select the suppliers with the objective of delivering solutions to meet predetermined organizational requirements. The purchasing department and anyone else involved in the decision-making group must have a clear view of the specific needs of the organization before starting the procurement. Once this position has been reached the position then looks like the following.

Steps in the process

Analysis of existing purchasing procedures

Who is buying what, from which suppliers, at what volume, how often and on what terms? The objective is to identify the buying patterns and trends, and to take a clear note of what contracts and agreements are already in place, their terms and expiry dates.

Process and competence analysis

Who are the internal stake holders, their positions and relationships to any supplier? What is their perception of how the process works at the moment?

Spend analysis

How much is being spent, what is the average cost per hire, which suppliers are providing what fees, what value is this providing and how is the spend controlled?

Supply base analysis

Here the buyer looks at supplier performance, portfolio analysis (can they supply an extended requirement?), supplier and customer performance mapping (do we like doing business with them?), value analysis (are there value-added services that we use or need that we do not wish to lose?).

Supply and value stream mapping

A matrix is created in order to collate the information gathered and a SWOT is developed to enable an analysis of the strengths and opportunities in the existing model.

Proactive demand management

This is the process of the purchasing department working with internal customers to ascertain the organization's requirements over a given future period (often three years) and deriving from the business's resource plan. Then procurement works with the business to explore the best sourcing options that have been generated from the previous sourcing analysis.

Creation of a buying group made up of the key stakeholders

- *The sponsor*: usually a very senior player who owns the budget of the recruitment – initiates the request and owns responsibility for the success of the tender process.
- *The business*: areas of the existing services and proposed solution – often line management.
- *Procurement*: responsible for the scoping of the requirement, creation and management of the bid process; it is the negotiator of the terms and conditions and manager of the contractual obligations and service level agreements (SLAs).
- *Human resources*: various levels of involvement, depending upon where the operational aspects of the existing process are sited. HR ensures that the process adheres to current legislation and corporate culture.
- *Legal*: often involved from the early stages of the process, responsible for drafting and finalizing terms and conditions; participates in the negotiation process.

Slightly different things will motivate each party involved in the tender process. The sponsor will be interested in creating a process that adds business value, reduces costs and streamlines the process. The business will want a service that provides the best possible candidates in the most efficient way, saving them time and ensuring they have the capacity to get resources in place, on time and to budget. Procurement is targeted on reducing costs and ensuring supplier agreements are workable. Human resources is interested in creating a process that attracts good candidates whilst limiting liability and exposure. The legal team will ensure that the process is operationally feasible and contractually sound.

Procurement plan

After the cross-functional project team has been established, it will agree the sourcing options, devise the procurement plan and ensure that it's carried out.

Marketplace salutation

This is the process of communicating the requirement to the recruitment marketplace. Advertisements may be placed in appropriate journals, papers and websites, and well-respected suppliers may be contacted and invited to consider tendering. ITTs (invitations to tender) will be provided. ITTs are often lengthy questionnaires detailing the scope of the requirement and then asking for supplier information that should aid the evaluation of their credentials against predetermined needs.

Supplier appraisals

The purchasing department will assess the responses to the ITTs, with an agreed weighting given to the most important areas, and will generally complete an evaluation form. Whole project-life costings will be undertaken with cost analysis and modelling along with risk evaluation.

Presentations

Most large procurement projects will include a presentation opportunity. A 'beauty parade' of recruitment companies will present their solutions and answer questions from the panel of decision-makers.

Bid clarification and post-tender negotiations

This is where the final financial arrangements will be negotiated. This stage is often combined with the confirmation of the terms and conditions of the contract, service levels and schedules. Once the terms have been negotiated the project will be implemented.

De-briefing

In a well-run purchasing project the unsuccessful suppliers will be given a full de-briefing as to why they did not win the business. All of the records are retained.

Post-contract assessment

Once the contract is signed, it will be communicated to the internal service users, the winning company (or companies) will be introduced and the assignment will commence. The client agreement will have created key performance indicators and there should be regular performance reviews to monitor success and look for opportunities for continuous improvements.

Often in recruitment this is only the start of the hard work to make the most of the opportunity provided. As we said at the beginning of the book the only thing which has been won is the opportunity to supply. Many organizations go to great effort getting themselves on the PSL of a business, either at low margins so little or no profit can be made, or simply to then ignore the client thinking the hard work has been done.

Every client and their way of working will be different. Often inclusion on the PSL simply means that the competitive landscape has been reduced with the possible inclusion of competitors with the in-house resourcing team alongside. Relationships still need building and clients need meeting and their needs understood and delivered against.

It makes no sense for agencies or clients to appoint to the PSL and then waste all the effort by not servicing the account and worse still thereby gaining a reputation for non-delivery which will either impact your division's chances of re-bidding or impact a different part of your business.

So before you start considering your response to an ITT, consider the return on this time investment as the next paragraph suggests.

Your response to an invitation to tender

In order to get to the presentation or beauty parade stage you'll need to develop the art of tender writing. Here we suggest some key criteria for having your tender stand out from the crowd.

There are three key questions to consider before you spend a lot of time and effort on tendering: Do you actually want this business? Can you deliver this business? Do you have any chance of winning it? You should qualify yourself out of the process if any of the answers to these questions are less than 100 per cent positive.

First impressions are substantially more important than you think. Have your document checked and double-checked for all the grammar and spelling details – they'll need to be just right. Even small imperfections in the presentation of your documentation can have an adverse effect on the credibility of your offering. Most of your competitors will have someone focused on completing all their tenders brilliantly.

- Break the documentation into sections with a full index and appendices to make it easy for the procurement team to read through in their chosen order.
- Always answer every question and include everything that has been asked for. If, for any reason, you are unable to, explain why.
- Provide your response in multiple media: e-mailed, hard copy and a CD or memory stick.
- Confirm how many copies they require and provide exactly that amount.
- Keep it concise and not overly 'salesy'. Professionalism is key.
- Be 100 per cent honest. The details will be checked. Site visits may be requested to confirm details – even to your clients.

The document is likely to be assessed by the purchasing department and only sometimes will it be read by the other individuals within the decision-making group.

E-auctions

An e-auction or reverse electronic auction can be part of a traditional purchasing process, often slotting in at the negotiation stage. In some circumstances the client organization will actually use this to replace the presentation stage of the process, preferring not to bother meeting or getting a feel for the supplier companies, relying on qualification using the tender documentation and closing the 'deal' using the internet.

Potential suppliers become bidders, placing online bids of decreasing value (ie the reverse of a traditional auction). The bidders know the best offer through the process, although not the identity of the bidders. Although cost savings can be made by the client when bulk-buying commodities from a densely populated supplier base, staffing services cannot be specified well enough to make this a long-term success for clients. It is worth client companies remembering that the e-auction dynamic can lead to naïve staffing suppliers bidding as low as they can for business, with unattractive or even unworkable margins or placement fees. The result of this is that the suppliers will have other clients who pay better and realistically receive a better service with the higher quality candidates offered to them.

A number of staffing businesses decide that they will not participate in e-auctions but others do, and some recruitment firms even feel that it has provided some worthwhile business opportunities.

Performing successfully at e-auctions

If you or your company decide to participate you must do some detailed preparation.

- Before the auction:
  - Get a clear outline of the selection criteria and weightings.
  - Seek to amend the lots structure to suit your offering.
  - Accept any training given on the software.
  - Gain an understanding of the bidding format and constraints.
  - Assess the likelihood of post-auction negotiation.
  - Check who to contact if there is a technology problem.
  - Agree your bidding plan.
  - Assign roles for your bidding team.
  - Adopt a positive role about the process.
- During the auction:
  - Observe and record all of the bidding.
  - Bid to be noticed!
  - Stick to your agreed bidding plan.
- After the auction:
  - Capture any data.
  - Review your performance.
  - Assess the required skills and knowledge for future opportunities.

Developing your client

However you acquire your client initially, continued success will be found through developing that client relationship until they become an advocate of your service throughout their business and in general.

Consider your CRM (customer relationship management) strategy. This focuses on developing the relationship between you and your customer and clearly points to a partnership approach. Tesco have developed the art of a relationship with their customers and their CRM strategy through the use of their Clubcard. Their strategy has added millions to the value of their business. It's interesting to consider what they have delivered to their customers, from the four Ps perspective again:

- *Price/value for money*: regardless of who you are – a customer struggling to make ends meet using their Value range or a customer looking to use high-quality products at home using the Finest range.

- *Product*: wide range of branded and own brands.

- *Place*: a strong property strategy enabling them to service most households, coupled with Tesco Direct, means everyone can use Tesco with ease.

- *Promotion*: Every Little Helps!

To emulate them you'll need to identify what you and your client might wish to gain from the relationship, develop rapport with that client and convince them of your capacity to supply benefit and to deliver, which will produce a great perception of you. Then you'll need to keep delivering and developing your service.

The capacity to do that, and perhaps to extend your service offering to meet new identified needs, will move you up their value chain.

Client development pathway

Initially when you first supply a client you demonstrate you can supply. They then have a perception that you 'can do'.

The next stage is when you consistently deliver over a period of time. Your client will develop a perception that you are 'reliable'. You keep your promises and always do what you say you will. Your client can trust you.

Gradually they will come to rely on you to supply, but may also begin to develop a reliance and respect for your advice and knowledge. They will have a perception that you can 'add value'. You perhaps are doing a particularly great job of marketing them to your candidates, leaving them very little to do except choose the best one.

The next stage is where they become reluctant to use anyone else and may begin to phase other suppliers out – you are 'ring fencing' your client and at this point they are your advocate. Hey, maybe your supporter as discussed in the section on buying roles!

At about this point they will then potentially tell other people about your service and how valuable they find it. They have become your mentor or sponsor and as such will provide both internal and external referrals for your services.

The challenge is to keep your clients in the mentor space and continue to add value, which means you need to grow with them, always keeping one step ahead and continuing to add value to the relationship. As we have seen before, most client relationships falter due to lack of interest on the part of the supplier. The opportunity to grow and develop your clients is entirely down to you.

Industry profile – Brian Wilkinson

A strong believer in the value of developing your clients is Brian Wilkinson, who is a member of the Executive Board of Randstad Holdings (the second-largest staffing provider worldwide) and responsible for their operations in the UK, Australia and the Pacific, Asia and the United Emirates. We profile him here as an inspiration.

Born: A Geordie!

Educated: Degree in English literature and language

Early career: First job with Mars (Brian wanted a car!) as a field sales rep, where the training was brilliant. Wishing to get ahead quickly Brian joined the recruitment industry, working at an early stage with Keith Austin, who went on to run Austin Benn at a consultancy called SOS. Brian stayed with this company for 20 years whilst it underwent a range of takeovers and change, with his last role as MD. During the 1990 recession his capacity to spot an opportunity in adding value in the food safety market enabled the business to grow and by the mid-1990s the business was acquired again, at which point Brian decided it was time for a new challenge. After a spell in venture capital (which gave him really good experience in M & A) Brian joined Select, acquired by Vedior and most recently acquired by Randstad; he moved into his current role in 2008.

Brian says the recruitment industry has been a fantastic career – he has never once dreaded going to work and he has learned a huge amount.

Key advice for recruiters:

- Make more calls than anyone else!

One thing you should always do: Prepare and research before you make calls or visit your clients, and when you do, make sure you ask lots of really good open questions.

One thing you should never do: Tell anything other than the truth.

Still to achieve: Always more to achieve in life!

Interests outside work: Keeping fit at the gym, theatre and great restaurants, DIY in two barn conversions.

Brian is a great example of how you can get ahead in this business by being a thoroughly nice chap: unassuming, fair, thoughtful and with the courage of your convictions. The industry is about being strong but treating others as you would be treated by them. It is not always the loudest person with strong charisma.

Industry profile – Becky Gloyne

Becky is Global Talent Acquisition Manager for the Marketing and Communications teams in Nokia. She is also part of the global project team on employer branding with colleagues from Finland and New York and a sought-after speaker on social media and its role in talent acquisition.

Born: Kent
Educated: 'A' Level

Early career: Becky fell straight into recruitment after school and loved it. She worked agency-side for eight years specializing in the digital market culminating in working for Major Players, the market leader recruiter in the creative industries, and so was quick to see the opportunity for talent acquisition through digital channels. She was head hunted by Nokia directly into her current role two years ago.

Key advice for recruiters:

- Get to grips with all the talent sources available to you; don't just rely on one route as it won't find you the very best talent. Candidates themselves are a great source of knowledge and market information.

- Build relationships and trust with people and identify where both of you can add value to each other.

One thing you should always do: Use social media as a listening platform; have a conversation with people through it.

One thing you should never do: Use social media as a broadcasting tool.

Still to achieve: playing a key role in Nokia's global transformation – the biggest transformation in the technology market right now.

Interests outside work: I've just got married so we like nothing better than going home at weekends to chill out with family and friends and I'm a bit of a gym fanatic too!

Becky is a leading new thinker in the talent acquisition space. Quick to identify and harness the possibilities of social media, she is way ahead of the curve. She also credits her meteoric rise to support and help from her mentor Matthew Jeffrey from EA. She'd like more leaders to understand the possibilities of digital sourcing and get involved themselves.

08

Client strategy

In the recruitment cycle, client strategy follows on from client acquisition. Acquiring a client is not an end in itself; it is the start of the recruitment process. Once your client is acquired, you need to decide how to deliver a service to meet their needs. The same process holds true whether you are just starting a job with a company as Head of Resourcing, a recruiter with a retained search brief, or a temp controller.

This chapter covers the development of a delivery strategy, exploring the alternatives from whole-company strategies through deciding on a recruitment method for one role. Although the chapter will not provide all the options, certainly for the former, it will provide a framework to consider the factors and what's important. Alongside this, and running in parallel with managing your candidates, is of course managing your clients through the development of the right strategy for them and the relationship you are building with them.

The range of methods to attract candidates can be divided broadly into two types. The first type is 'direct', involving acquiring a candidate directly for your role, database potential, temp pool or as a useful contact for the future. Examples might be job-specific advertising or headhunting. The second type is 'indirect', this makes it easier to acquire candidates, widen your candidate base or support their acquisition through the direct methods. Examples would be running events, attending networking gatherings, corporate advertising or branding in general.

If you are working in-house it is important to understand the motivations of the agencies and consultancy suppliers working with you, and how best to manage them. This chapter also offers some advice on this important topic. Arguably this is an area that has not yet found its equilibrium and needs considerable work if both parties are to leverage maximum value for their clients and employers. At the end we consider the impact some of the indirect methods can have on your overall recruitment success.

Devising an 'out-of-the-box' client strategy can really gain you a competitive advantage, both for managed service providers (MSPs) and at the individual desk level. Providing a new and innovative solution to a client's problem will ensure you rise to the top of the supplier list and will win more business with clients or win praise and promotion with your employer. Many RPO solutions are about delivering financial value. This will clearly remain a key driver for many organizations but those looking to talent management to deliver them competitive advantage in their own markets will be looking for suppliers, or themselves, to be a step ahead in the game and first to market with new resourcing solutions. Equally some of the most successful temp controllers say long-term success comes from fulfilling roles for a client outside their area, which means that the client gets excellent service and the consultant prevents their client from going to the competition, thus gaining competitive advantage.

Paradoxically, not only is it important to deliver a competitive strategy but it's also important that the strategy should be based both around relationships and at the same time independent of them. This is a people business and it is all too easy to forget that people are at the heart of what we do, but people also change and we need to be prepared for that too. In other words the delivery strategy and results need to transcend changes of stakeholder or decision-maker in the recruitment process, even though our opportunity to supply will have been built to some degree on those relationships.

CASE STUDY

Jonathan Barber, a senior interim IT executive, uses specialist provider Highams Recruitment for his top team recruitment. His consultant there, Denise Morris who runs the interim practice, really understands the industry and his needs. He recruits both technical and change teams. He believes strongly that for technical roles a good job specification is needed to ensure technical expertise. For change roles, however, a fluid perspective on how his team might be built is really helpful.

Before even considering a strategy there is a range of considerations. First, you need to identify what you are trying to achieve and within which business or organizational context.

Decide your objective

Sourcing volume candidates will require a different approach from finding one to three candidates to fulfil one client requirement. A senior strategic hire for a business will need a different approach from a junior programmer – and the implication to the business of not hiring that individual will also be very different.

The senior strategic hire, for example, may need to be recruited from a blend of passive and active candidates. The junior programmer would simply need to be short-listed from available active candidates.

Attracting permanent or temporary candidates or contractors can require some of the same techniques, but it is unlikely to be appropriate to 'search' for an IT contractor or a junior health locum for example. It may well be worth your while however to network amongst existing candidates (contractors and temps) for new candidates. You may find they are working with someone from another agency and that person is unhappy – they may feel they would like to recommend their colleague to you at some point.

CASE STUDY

Matt Hobson of Pioneer Consulting, the IT recruiter, works in a niche software market and conducts much of the contract recruitment in this sector within his firm. Through a referral from an existing contractor a new candidate contacted him, whom he then placed at one of the leading equity investment firms. This candidate then introduced him to a further candidate and, although Matt did not place him, he took the trouble to travel out from London to Swindon to meet him one day, some four years ago. This effort paid off: recently this particular candidate was appointed Head of Financial Systems at a FTSE 50 company and called Matt to be his sole supplier for a range of roles he needed recruiting. Within two weeks Matt had written £75,000 worth of business.

Cost of candidate acquisition

Some external consultants will be more concerned with this than others – internal recruiters, recruitment consultants, business owners and sole practitioners will be very concerned about it. As with any other business, recruitment is not just about the revenue you bring in, it is also about the costs that you incur in order to deliver that revenue. Some markets will be 'candidate-rich' and others 'candidate-poor'. Anyone in recruitment who has lived through one of the recessions will understand how it is possible to go from eight replies to a series of good, well-designed job board ads for senior salespeople to 500 over a space of six months. So, in a candidate-poor market the cost of attracting your candidates also becomes something to focus on.

For internal recruiters this cost is often a KPI against which they are closely measured. An organization in high growth wanting to take advantage of market conditions will care less about the cost of acquisition and more about filling the roles – the opportunity cost of not doing so being too high – but a business in steady market state or carefully managing costs will have some clear objectives around this, which of course then play out to the external suppliers as well.

The key to success is to use a range of techniques to deliver candidates in the best-value way possible. Any candidate attraction strategy will employ all the techniques detailed below to ensure that it is covering its entire market and enabling the cost of candidate attraction to be kept at a value for money level. Any strong strategy will also be looking at the attraction of both active and passive candidates and the development of a strong brand to generate candidates.

Active and passive candidates

An active candidate is actively on the job market and looking for a role. Passive candidates are not actively looking for their next role. Arguably that is every other candidate you might come across. Within these categories there will be huge variations in candidates' motivations.

Some apparently active candidates may appear active by having loaded their details on a job board for example, but may only be looking around to see whether they are being paid enough or to make them feel wanted by a range of presenting opportunities.

Some passive candidates may be seriously considering a job move but have not yet started looking and your contact comes at an opportune time.

Accessing passive candidates is appropriate and desirable when the role is of great importance to the business and it wants to ensure it is interviewing the best people with the right skills in the market, or when the role is hard to fill and there are few active candidates available. Increasingly, in the war for talent passive candidate recruitment and relationship building for a future hire at some point will be the key to an organization's recruitment success. The capacity of a business's recruiters to attract people to their brand and then to gain feedback from them and hold conversations until a point at which the candidate becomes interested in a move will dramatically shift an organization's capacity to get the best people into the right jobs. Recruiting solely from an active candidate base is a good strategy when there are multiple roles, a range of available candidates with the right background and skill sets, and the role is not of strategic importance to the business. This is also likely to be particularly the case in times of high unemployment meaning organizations are well placed to deliver a cost-effective strategy as well as build skills and goodwill for the future. As this second edition comes out we are likely to see long-term unemployment amongst young people as well as tougher times for everyone. The active candidate pool is large but scarce skills will still be hard to track down; people with skills in energy, oil and gas, engineering, digital and e-commerce capability will still require a highly tactical approach on an individual basis to acquire.

The most important element of any strategy is that it reflects the market for skills and is developed from the outside in; with a view to external events and market movements, not just the internal landscape.

Chris Sale, Director of Prism Executive Recruitment, is clear that when a management consultancy or IT services client has won a project that they have tendered for, they need good staff on site to deadline. This means recruiting and attracting candidates from an active candidate database in the main, through advertising and some highly specific targeted search. Clients take the pragmatic approach of recruiting the best available person to do the job today rather than combing the market for 'Mr Perfect', a strategy that could lead them to under-delivery – just not an option for the key players in this sector.

Upstream and downstream recruitment

Increasingly internal recruitment teams are focusing on both upstream and downstream recruitment in workforce planning. Upstream is all about building talent banks and developing CRM campaigns with candidates over long periods, with a view to succession planning and building candidate pipelines for the future. Downstream is about recruiting for jobs that are here today. The focus of a good recruiter, specifically perhaps within niche markets, is always to keep in touch with a wide range of candidates who may not be placed for a period of years but who might often turn into clients. Passive candidates of course are primary targets for talent banking.

Here is an example of how good candidate management of a downstream project both built brand and paid off in the medium term for Richard Fisher and his team at Square One Resources, the IT recruiter. Richard now applies the same sorts of approaches at his new business: Skill search.

> We were working with a candidate to place them as a project manager in Central London. At the last minute the project was stopped, but through regular updates with the candidate throughout the interview process we had built a good rapport and asked the candidate to consider us when they moved to their next role. That role turned out to involve a £5 million project budget and recruitment responsibilities so it worked out pretty well. They also recommended us to represent their personal partner, a business analyst whom we have also placed.

Upstream recruitment can also contribute to the building of an employer brand. Done poorly it will adversely impact on the brand but done well it can build a brand most effectively, a topic that we consider more closely at the end of the chapter.

Whole-company solutions

First, however, to develop a client strategy we look at whole-company solutions. If you are an in-house, RPO on-site, or external recruiter tasked with recruiting all of the role for a particular client you are likely to need to develop an overall attraction strategy that is likely to include a whole range of the activities below plus a few more. Here are some of the options.

In-house strategy options

As stated in the introduction, recruitment becomes increasingly strategically important to any business in the knowledge economy. In the early part of this century a small percentage of roles needed knowledge – now it's 60 per cent and rising. The capture, development and retention of talent is now a specialization, rather than just a part of anyone's human resources remit. This book confines itself to the consideration of talent acquisition, although without a firm link between development and retention the acquisition of talent is made that much more challenging. If potential candidates cannot see how they fulfil their ambitions or develop themselves and their careers personally whilst feeling what they are engaged in is worthwhile, then they are less likely to join, or indeed stay!

Organizations are increasingly using marketing tools and techniques to deliver their recruiting numbers ever more efficiently, at lower cost per hire and in a more targeted fashion, adopting a wide range of promotional marketing techniques to help them.

With this in mind as a backdrop, organizations have a wide range of choices in handling their recruitment. The factors they need to consider are:

- number of hires;
- locations;
- level and discipline;
- competitive market;
- candidate supply chain;
- candidate-short or candidate-rich;
- candidate proposition;
- employer brand;
- attrition rate;
- other factors affecting attrition – internal mobility of labour for example;

- job offer to acceptance rate;
- number of applications required to fill all roles;
- appetite and competence of the business to hire.

The choices for strategy vary from outsourcing it all to one provider through bringing it all in-house. Outsourcing itself has a range of guises, which can vary from a short-term internal upskilling, through the transfer of knowledge from the outsourcer to the client, to a long-term solution. There are a myriad of variations in between these two, a wide range of which are detailed below with the advantages and disadvantages of each.

Strategy options

Manage all the recruitment in-house through HR manager/s or business partners

This keeps all of the control and the accountability in the business. HR managers will be much closer potentially to the needs of the business and they can see recruitment within its wider context, advising on a range of issues. This is a good solution if the number of hires required each year is small and manageable.

CASE STUDY

Sally Scutt, Deputy Chief Executive of the British Bankers Association, occasionally uses press directly but more often these days her HR team uses two or three agencies with consultants whom they really feel understand the type of people they need; consultants with very strong intellect, an excellent understanding of their markets and good facilitation skills. Increasingly she finds advertisements she runs bring a huge filtering and screening effort for her HR team with no real cost benefit, and she can rely on the good agencies to deliver the right people at the right time.

Outsourcing to one provider

Outsource it entirely to one provider. Negotiate a set fee per grade of hire (excluding any internal referral scheme), with a set of KPIs in place to ensure delivery.

This locates the delivery under one accountable provider, whilst also allowing the business to focus on its core competence of delivering its own service or products to its own clients or customers. It should result in good cost savings. The supplier takes on the risk of success around candidate attraction and invests in programmes to that end.

Have the outsourcer manage agencies, your internal referral programme and specialist searches for senior hires, and drive down fees by negotiating well with tier-one agencies who are specialists in their own fields and will in turn use a range of smaller tier-two suppliers to deliver in to them – in other words specify how the delivery is to be achieved. The delivery team is usually based onsite.

This is a similar model to the previous one except that you are now outsourcing all of your recruitment but at the same time specifying how that recruitment will be delivered, in agreement with your outsourcer. This requires in many ways more of a partnership approach and ensures you abdicate less responsibility. Primary research by Jill Walters, who runs CIPD courses, shows that success in outsourcing in small to medium-sized companies depends quite strongly on identifying similar values when choosing an outsource partner and a strong relationship. Enabling the partner to develop a good cultural understanding of the business – by being based on-site perhaps – makes a real difference to the project outcomes.

Partial outsourcing

Outsource parts of your recruitment – perhaps the more challenging parts – to specialist providers. This could be IT recruitment perhaps, or senior recruitment.

This means you can keep the less crucial parts of the business, perhaps the less mission-critical aspects where recruitment is all about process and volume, rather than the attraction of scarce resource. Cost savings can be made so long as the business has expertise and strong process in-house.

This works well for specific technically specialist projects or if you have a steady-state set of recruitment needs across the business all year but a heavy demand of recruitment projects from time to time.

A full-service approach for senior appointments has the benefit of also buying in expertise on assessment and resource to facilitate the whole recruitment process if required.

CASE STUDY

Tracey Richardson, in a previous role as managing consultant at specialist public sector recruiter, is called in by local authorities to recruit senior staff. She recently recruited the CE of one of the most exciting authorities in the UK. Her expertise is relied on right through the process, from advising on the attraction strategy (in this case she chose a combined advertising and search approach using advertisements with strong graphics, a departure from the normal 'safer' route), the assessment process, right through to facilitating the process itself, including guiding elected members in process and decision-making. Tracey is now Principal Resource Specialist at Vodafone Group, having taken all of her expertise in-house.

In this case there is real benefit derived from outsourcing critical or specialist hires to a skilled provider who really knows the market and can both advise on and facilitate the whole recruitment process.

Outsource the strategy and in-source the operational aspects

The advantage of this is you can gain some help and leading-edge thinking on client strategy, or elements of your recruitment that are causing problems, but you can still implement these internally.

Develop the strategy and outsource the back office

If you have the strategic expertise located in-house, and you know your market better than anyone, are abreast of all the new methodologies and are an innovation business as a core competence, this may be a great strategy for you as it means you can reduce costs on process management.

In-house with external support

Bring it all in-house, delivering the bulk of the recruitment in-house and using external agencies to source additional staff where needed. This model has a high degree of flexibility in that it can turn additional agency resources on and off as and when needed. The disadvantage of this is there is less capacity to reduce costs quickly.

CASE STUDY

David Mason, now Head of Resourcing, UK and Europe, Royal Bank of Scotland, formerly worked at AXA where he developed an internal strategy which took the percentage of recruitment delivered directly from 25 per cent to nearly 80 per cent over four years. Recruiting 3,500 people each year he ran four teams in the business: a delivery team made up of recruitment consultants and co-coordinators, a team of strategic account managers who worked closely with senior managers in the business advising on client strategy, a team of internally based executive search recruiters recruiting directly their mid-management roles (David still contracted out highly specialist or specific senior roles to a search firm) and a brand advertising team. Alongside this he developed the use of a profiling tool, used in areas of the business with a high recruitment need, in order to target more effectively the people he needed to reach, and drove up the internal promotions and re-deployments of staff from 40 per cent (of roles) to 71 per cent.

Operate a shared services model across a range of businesses

This can be a useful model if you are working in a larger business and recruitment is not a core part of the business strategy, either outsourced or run by in-house personnel. However, if the model is too far removed from the needs of the business it can falter where it becomes a process rather than being driven.

Locate recruitment internally in specialist teams all reporting through to the HRD

The advantage of this is that the recruiter sits within the business and can therefore develop close relationships with the line managers and hiring managers. The closer that recruitment sits to the business and the more motivated they are, the more effective they can be at managing the process.

CASE STUDY

Penny Davis, whilst Head of HR for T-Mobile and responsible for approximately 3,500 hires a year, operated this model although she did outsource her contractor and temp management to an MSP under a range of SLAs (service level agreements). As well as that, she had teams recruiting professional head-office-based staff using a proactive direct sourcing model and a team working on HR marketing, and decided to bring back in-house an initial response centre. Penny is now the Divisional HR Director for Balfour Beatty Support Services.

Locate recruitment internally within local business partners in the HR teams but with a central application process online and through a recruitment advertising or response agency

This solution has the advantage of embedding the recruitment process in the overall human resources policy and operation. The disadvantage is that often the human resources team do not enjoy 'on-the-ground' recruitment, seeing it as necessary to support the business, but not something they enjoy spending much time on.

There are of, course, any number of variations on any of the above strategies, with hybrid solutions tailored to the needs of the individual business providing the bulk of the solutions. Typically, making these choices will be determined by the importance of recruitment to the business, balanced with the cost of hiring and the philosophy of the board around talent management.

For many knowledge-based organizations talent is on the board agenda at all times, for without it many businesses are unable to deliver what their clients need. Yet at the same time if the cost of acquiring and retaining that talent becomes uncompetitive margins on delivery are erased.

So there is a triangular balance to be achieved (Figure 8.1).

FIGURE 8.1   The balancing act

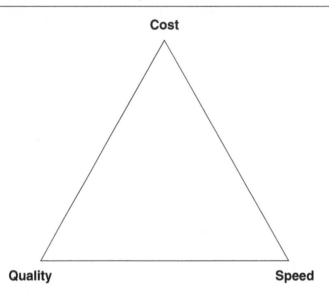

If costs are not considered an issue then it is always possible to recruit good candidates. The strategy needs to deliver to meet the corporate business objectives and provide a good enough balance between cost, quality of hire and speed of delivery. It is likely to demand a range of recruitment methods for an in-house strategy. For an in-house recruiter the skill lies in managing the needs of both the internal stakeholders and the suppliers and for an external recruiter it's all about managing your clients, not to mention your own employer.

Client management

Managing your client through the recruitment process is strongly akin to managing your candidate. Indeed many of the client management processes and touch-points (the points in the process when the candidate touches base with the recruiter) are outlined in the candidate management section, particularly where following through the recruitment process is concerned. As a recruiter you may need to take an assertive stance with your clients to ensure the process works well and flows in the appropriate timeframe.

How to manage clients assertively

In-house recruiters who get the most out of their suppliers do so because they have a forward view of partnership supplier management. Equally, line managers who get the most out of their in-house recruiters or RPO team share that view. The old adage of 'getting back what you put in' applies not only to IT systems but also systems and processes, which include human interaction.

It is logical to conclude that if you put a lot of time and effort into developing and managing your supplier relationships, you will get a lot more from them. External recruiters (and many in-house recruiters will know this as they have moved from agency-side to client-side) are keen to do a great job and work hard on behalf of a client – so long as that client ensures it makes business sense for the recruiter to do so.

The recruiter and client relationship is really very symbiotic. Both need one another. Supplier management in all areas of business has developed a long way in the last 20 years and partnership relationships are demonstrably best practice as they will deliver superior results.

Briefing suppliers well, and extensively, and holding agency briefings for clusters of roles, will help the agencies determine the appropriate client strategy for you and develop the most robust candidate attraction strategy. Treating any supplier with anything other than respect, fairness and a partnership approach is a false economy. When we come to motivation theory towards the end of the chapter, consider how it can help you manage your suppliers and clients equally as well as your potential candidates. One of the key elements, often forgotten, is recognition. It may be worth asking yourself how often you tell your suppliers they are doing a great job for you?

Ways to be assertive

This works for both internal and external recruiters:

- Be prepared to offer advice contrary to the client's wishes, if you feel their preferred strategy will not work.
- Negotiate timescales; 'If I can finish the role specification for you by tomorrow and brief the agencies, can I have your assurance you will have reviewed the CVs within 72 hours of receipt?'
- Be upfront about problems and present solutions at the same time. Develop a 'can-do' attitude.
- Steer clear of apologizing profusely but take responsibility when it is your fault.
- Don't take a 'No' personally – this is business, not a marriage.
- Avoid saying 'I can't'. Stick to positive responses and make refusals in the third person.
- Think about what you want to achieve and say before a client meeting and prepare your first sentence.

- Manage your body language to reflect back the way in which you want to be perceived and how you are speaking.
- Above all, try and get to meet clients face to face whatever that might take. Take a CV in personally, drop a time sheet by, visit your contractors and your temps, and arrange a spur of the moment coffee.

Managing client meetings

Recruiters are likely to attend many meetings where they have to both persuade a client of their point of view and also confirm in the client's mind that using their service or buying from them is the right thing to do. Chapter 7 on 'Client acquisition' will have given you some useful thoughts on how best to manage meetings but this case study is an example of where good consulting helped get a client a better result.

CASE STUDY

Matthew Eames, of the eponymous Eames Consulting Group, worked with a client, a FTSE100 global banking client with locations all across the UK. Following a restructure the client identified four new senior IT positions with salaries of £100–120,000.

The client felt a retained search was the right approach but our view was that the options on recruiting people in various locations – Scotland, London or the South West plus the number of roles – meant that an advertised campaign would work well.

We worked with the profile and demographics of *The Sunday Times* readers to demonstrate our market reach. It also became clear to our client that an advertising campaign would also add value to their employer brand, marketing their brand positively and updating the market with a recent restructure. As such a proposal was written and signed off.

You may be in a role where you work purely over the phone. Any contact you have with a client works to the same principles. Whether you are an internal or external recruiter, clients always have a choice. It's important that, whatever meeting, conference call or video conference you attend, you prepare fully for it and set clear goals. As far as client strategy is concerned you are likely to be meeting people for the following reasons:

- to take a brief or a role/person spec;
- to present your thoughts on solving their recruitment problem.

We'll look at both of these in turn. It's likely you will have an outline role specification before presenting your thoughts so we'll look at this first. You may not choose to take a full specification but an outline one at first, to evaluate (as you evaluate candidates in candidate management) whether this is a role you can help with or wish to take on.

Taking a job spec or brief

You'll need both a role specification and a person specification. The role specification is a description of the job and what it entails, often referred to as a brief, a job specification or job description. A person spec will either be a separate document or combined with the role spec as one document. Often your client will have a role and person spec to give you to work from but if not, you could base it on the examples in Tables 8.1–8.3: separate job and person specifications or a joint job and person specification.

There is a wide range of resources available to help you develop a good role and person specification if you need to do so. Success in placing candidates often depends, as we see in other chapters, upon success in four key factors:

- taking a good workable job and person spec;
- developing a good relationship with the hiring manager;
- your capacity to deliver good-quality candidates through your chosen client strategy to fulfil the spec;
- managing the process through to successful conclusion.

The consequences of not taking a good brief are many, and one of them may be that you cannot make a placement.

CASE STUDY

Keith Evans, Director at leading search firm Grosvenor Clive and Stokes, believes that taking a full and clear job spec and developing a strong candidate profile are crucial to the outcome of a project. He has some specific advice to offer.

> The effort that is put into developing the criteria for the specification and under-standing the true needs of the client is well worth it at the beginning of the project as deep understanding of the business you are recruiting for creates a greater chance of success at the end. In fact without a good brief, you may be spending time on attracting entirely the wrong profile of candidates.
>
> To ensure we get a good brief we always ask the client the following key questions:
>
> - Where do you envisage your ideal candidate is currently working, and in what sort of role?
> - If he/she has a successful first six months with you, what do you expect to be the impact(s) of the appointment? How will your business have changed or improved?
> - What will be key performance measures in the first year?
> - Are particular personal attributes more important than specific experience in the appointee to this role?

TABLE 8.1   Sample job specification

Company name

JOB SPECIFICATION

JOB TITLE:	Marketing Services Manager
LOCATION	
REPORTING TO:	Marketing Manager
BASIC FUNCTION: (Summary of job)	To plan, manage and implement marketing services to include direct marketing, telemarketing and field marketing programmes to support the development of the product groups and to support marketing programmes in line with the Marketing Plan
PRINCIPAL AREAS OF ACTIVITY (up to 12)	1. Plan, co-ordinate and implement customer retention and up- and cross-selling programmes to increase direct sales and customer loyalty 2. Plan, co-ordinate and implement direct marketing, telemarketing and field marketing programmes in conjunction with Sales and Marketing to support specific channel and account requirements 3. Manage the design and production of all materials to support the direct marketing, telemarketing and field marketing programmes 4. Deliver all activities on time and on budget 5. Liaise between internal departments regarding the implementation of all marketing programmes 6. Liaise with external agencies 7. Promote positively all the Company brands in all marketing services programmes
KEY MEASUREMENTS	1. Performance against targets and objectives 2. Ability to deliver effective database/direct marketing, telemarketing and field marketing programmes against agreed key dates and budgets 3. Ability to provide required marketing services support to Sales and Marketing 4. Effectiveness and quality of communications and interpersonal skills to achieve objectives

TABLE 8.1 *Continued*

DIRECT SUBORDINATES (job titles)	None
TOTAL IN LINE CONTROL	None
OTHER RELEVANT RESPONSIBILITY INDICATORS (Annual Sales Value, Production Value, Quality/ Assets Controlled, Budgets etc)	

Signed by ....   Line Mgr

Date:...............................

Signed by..   Employee

Date...............................

TABLE 8.2 Sample person specification

Company name

PERSON SPECIFICATION

JOB TITLE:	Marketing Services Manager
LOCATION	
REPORTING TO:	Marketing Manager
BASIC FUNCTION: (Summary of job)	To plan, manage and implement a change programme in marketing services to include direct marketing, telemarketing and field marketing programmes to support the development of the product groups and to support marketing programmes in line with the Marketing Plan

TABLE 8.2 *Continued*

KEY EXPERIENCE AND QUALIFICATIONS	Essential 1. Sound business-to-business marketing or experience of working with a recognized business brand instigating and leading on a range of brand-development activities. 2. Market planning experience. 3. Demonstrable results in running campaigns. 4. Ability to work with both technical and sales teams – bridging the gap. 5. Excellent analytical and research skills. 6. Good first degree, 2:1 minimum. Desirable 7. CIM qualification or MRS membership. 8. Business degree with marketing as a specialization or MBA. 9. Run project teams to deliver programmes. 10. Agency and supplier development and management. 11. Demonstrable knowledge of common database application.
PERSONAL SKILLS	Essential 1. Influencing and communications skills. 2. Presentational skills. 3. Team working and interpersonal skills. 4. Personally charismatic with good leadership skills.
CANDIDATE'S MOTIVATIONS AND ASPIRATIONS	A candidate who is motivated by change, success, making a difference and moving a business forward. Creative and an ideas person. Someone with good agency contacts who can deliver.
OTHER RELEVANT RESPONSIBILITY INDICATORS (Annual Sales Value, Production Value, Quality/ Assets Controlled, Budgets etc)	

Signed by ....   Line Mgr

Date:................................

TABLE 8.3   Sample joint job and person specification

JOB AND PERSON SPECIFICATION

1. Role details:	
Role Title:	*Region/Department/Team:*
Reports to:	*Location:*

2. Organigram: (To show the role, its peer roles and subordinate roles – titles)
Illustrate the role's formal relationship to other jobs within the organization.

3. Purpose of role:
One or two sentences at the most, stating why the job exists in the organization and what it is there to achieve.

4. Key Results/ Accountabilities expected from role
    a.
    b.
    c.
    d.
    e.

5. Key challenges faced on the role (in relation to Section 4 above)
Highlight any particular challenges faced in delivering the role in the context of the accountabilities highlighted in Section 4 above.

6. Any other relevant information
This section can be used to outline the background to the role or the department or how the role came about.

7. Experience & expertise (typical educational qualification & experience)
    a. Educational background
    b. Experience
    c. Core competencies
    d. Technical competencies
    e. Additional skills, qualities, motivations and aspirations of candidate

8. Economic dimensions associated with role (if any)
This is to detail relevant data around budget, target revenue responsibilities, P & L etc.

9. Location, salary and benefits
Detail here where the role is based and what travel needs are associated with the role. Include an indication of salary and detail the benefits.

'Primary' accountabilities are those over which the jobholder has control. Express these accountabilities in a series of short statements. Each statement should indicate what the accountability is and how the results will be measured.

Three guidelines

There are three aspects to taking a good role specification from a candidate, internally or externally:

- Developing a list of 'essential' and 'desirable' skills to assess candidates against. What must the client have for the role and what would they like but can manage without. Getting the mix right will ensure a robust candidate proposition but a tight short-list.

- Understanding the cultural fit of the business and the hiring manager – getting 'under their skin'. The capacity of a recruiter to match the culture and chemistry of individuals is a key 'value-add' for clients. This means spending time with your clients and building up a relationship of trust and mutual understanding.

- Qualifying the role as 'live'. In order to make it a good use of time to work on a role it must be possible to recruit the right candidate as soon as he/she becomes available. If this is not the case, this is unlikely to be a 'live' role.

In taking the brief or vacancy always ask your client what the essential and desirable skills are. If you have a large number of candidates this can really help you when it comes to honing the shortlist, as it is easy to assess them in a logical fashion using this method.

Developing a good relationship and understanding the client's needs means you can sometimes circumvent the facts of the role spec yet still delight the client with creative candidate sourcing.

CASE STUDY

Danielle Asano, Director of Cherry Professional Ltd, says part of her success in placing part-qualified and qualified finance people is the capacity to both recognize the brief and the company and then match the right person to that organization, even though sometimes they may not match the brief exactly. She has particular success placing people in part-time roles, where a full-time role is specified but, because she has identified someone who can add huge value to the organization and her client agrees with her after meeting the candidate, the client then re-allocates the demands of the role to suit the candidate.

It may seem a contradiction to suggest you work both within the confines of the role and outside it, but perhaps this is where the great skill of managing your clients really bears fruit. Failing to develop a good relationship with your candidates and clients, or to really understand their drivers, can mean you will miss opportunities to add value to their business because you are working too literally to the paper-based brief. Sometimes clients will move on factual issues like hours of work or location because you have found them the essence of the candidate they really want.

Equally there is a danger of recruiters behaving as hiring decision-makers, qualifying their candidates too closely, believing that they 'know best' and as a consequence providing limited choice. The recruiter's role is to provide a range of qualified candidates, not to second-guess what the client's decision will be in advance. There is a fine line between adding value and removing choice. Too much second-guessing on the part of the recruiter can leave the client without enough options, turning to another agency for more candidates. It is not unheard of for one candidate, whom one recruiter did not believe right for the role, to be placed in the same role by another recruiter as the latter did not try and cut down the client's choice too much. However it is of course important to work on roles that you know are 'real'.

Qualifying the role

When recruiters first start the job, their most common mistake is to spend time on roles that don't really exist. Sometimes employers will tell a consultant, or an internal recruiter, about a role they are hoping to recruit for, or give a person specification for a role they may wish they had. More experienced recruiters will use their knowledge and skills to place candidates with clients where there may not be a specific role. You will find more information on this in Chapter 9 on 'Candidate attraction'. Our focus here is on working with 'live' or 'qualified' roles (just as you qualify a candidate) and on ways to ensure a role is signed-off by an organization before spending time recruiting for it.

To qualify a role it helps to establish the criteria outlined below.

Establish a genuine need

Check out with the client, when taking a spec, that this is a role they are recruiting for now and not one they are thinking about getting clearance for.

Checking needs to be done carefully. Ask perhaps how the role has come about. Not only is this useful information for briefing potential candidates, it also gives you an indication of genuine need.

Check you are not taking a role spec purely for the purposes of then advising on market rates. Recruiters will be happy to help with this but ideally not via a fully qualified, interviewed and submitted short-list!

Identify skills required

When you take a detailed spec, use the guidelines of 'essential' and 'desirable' skills suggested in the sample person spec in Table 8.2. Here you will need to use your market knowledge to guide the client on what is realistic and what is unlikely. You may well need to advise and manage expectations on this.

You may say any of the following:

- 'As you know this type of candidate is in short supply currently. From your "essential" list, if I could not resource someone with all of these skills, which of them could you live without?'

- 'We are finding these candidates are commanding particularly high rates as demand is outstripping supply. How far would you be prepared either to move on rates for this candidate or re-consider some of your skills requirements?'

Some markets are tougher than others and you do not want to leave the client with a false impression of how easy it will be to succeed in filling their requirement or brief.

Identify the unique selling points of the role

In order to develop a compelling proposition for potential candidates, you need to understand why the role, the department or section and the company are of interest to a potential new hire. This information has a different feel from the rest of the role of person spec as it is not so objective. This is about getting under the skin of this organization, or this part of it, and really understanding what the business is like to work for and what someone could experience while working there.

For some that will be working alone on an intellectually challenging piece of work; for others it will be a great group of sociable people in the office providing a 'whole life' rather than just a job; for others it will be the chance to earn very good money and achieve. For some potential candidates – temps, locums and contractors for example – it will be the capacity to always be in work at a good rate of pay and be paid on time, looked after with no hassle, be able to take time off when needed and – overriding this – the feeling that one is being looked after and valued.

You'll need to gather information on the job itself:

- What's exciting about the role? This of course needs to be wide-ranging, as different things will appeal to different candidates.
- What are the key drivers of the role? (A slightly different edge to the main responsibilities.) How is their boss going to measure them?
- How does the role contribute to the wider organization?
- Double check why the role has come about. Is the team expanding? What might that mean for the role in terms of wider opportunity?
- How might a candidate develop through doing the role – eg gain new skills and experience?
- What learning and development opportunities might be available within the role?
- What are the career progression options from the role?

And to find out about the people involved:

- What is the manager/director like? What is their background? What common experiences might they share with potential candidates?
- Why did they join the organization?
- What have they found since they joined?
- How is the rest of the team made up and what are their backgrounds?
- How long have other team members been with the business?
- What is the culture of the team or the organization?
- How well do the rest of the team work together?
- What other parts of the business does the team connect with?

It is crucial when you are taking the requirement or vacancy that you establish what the parameters of salary or rates are. In some pieces of recruitment this will be more important than others but it is all too easy to assume that there are no constraints on this.

Budget/salary confirmed

Ensure that you take details of the whole package both at this point from your client and equally when you interview your candidates. Getting a clear picture of the salary and package is also a good indicator of intent to recruit.

Questioning on salary for permanent roles will need to include:

- Base salary:
  - expected range;
  - preferred base;
  - absolute maximum.
- Commission scheme – how does this work?
- Bonus – how much, on what basis is it paid, what has been the norm for the last year or two, when is it paid, what about people who join part way through a year?
- Car or car allowance?
- Holiday allowances.
- Flexible working policies.
- Benefits:
  - All possible here, don't skimp on detail.

It's also very useful to gain an understanding of the grading system in the company – if there is one: how people are promoted and what kind of performance management system is in place. Strong knowledge about the client really develops a recruiter's credibility and will really support a developing relationship with the candidate.

Status

Gathering data on what the client has done so far to recruit for the role is a helpful indicator of how real the role is. It will also aid you in deciding whether, or when, you should work on the role.

Start date

If the client has no start date in mind this can be a signal of a non-live role. If a client says they do not mind when someone starts, test this a little by asking: 'If I found someone to start with you pretty quickly/next week/ tomorrow would you be in a position to take them on?'

A 'No' to this has obvious issues and raises concerns. Unless there is a clear start date or a candidate can start as soon as you can hire them, this is not the best-qualified role.

Fee cleared/authorized requisition

This will vary enormously from writing a proposal, which involves a retainer fee and a presentation, to making sure the client is in agreement with your terms of business for temp, perm, interim or contractor. It is important to check that your client is happy with your terms of business before you start the process.

If you agree any rate reduction with your client ensure you do so for a reason: the opportunity to supply exclusively for example. Then always confirm the rate reduction and the reason for it in writing, making it clear that should the situation change your rates will revert to their normal level. This way your client is clear what the terms of engagement are and you ensure you are not just giving away fees lightly.

Commitment gained

Gain some commitment to working together on the process. You can gain commitment to all or some of the following:

- exclusive working;
- a retainer;
- interview times and dates in the diary;
- interviews scheduled promptly after agreement to interview reached;
- commitment to go through the shortlist face to face or over the phone;
- CV turnaround time;
- agreement to interview candidates you identify with CVs to follow.

Gaining exclusivity

Explain to your client what you plan to do to help secure this person. Explain that you are keen and happy to commit yourself over the next few hours/days to assess, screen and motivate the best candidates who match the specification to prepare them for interview with your client. Say that in the light of that you'd be keen to see some commitment back from your client that they will use you on an exclusive basis with an agreed timescale. Let them know this is a good way of them getting some undivided attention in getting their role filled without having to pay a retainer.

A retainer

The client's commitment to you is clear with a retainer fee. Although many retained pieces of work only go into profit on successful placement, at least you are having your costs covered. Retainers can be gained for specialist, scarce-skills and senior roles in general terms. Alternatively you can suggest a retainer as an option to clients whom you want to commit to and who need a dedicated resource on a project.

Agreeing interview commitment at the beginning of the process

If your client has placed the role with another consultancy, but you feel you can fill the role yourself and want to try a further way of ensuring commitment, you can use a similar structure to the above. This time you can say you expect to be back with qualified CVs in an hour, by tomorrow or two weeks (whichever is your timescale). Ask when the client would plan to interview and explain you normally like to book times so you can ensure candidates keep their diaries free. Let your client know you accept that they need to be happy with your candidates to progress to interview, whether that means you phone up to discuss their details and present them in this way or send through their CVs.

If a client is unwilling to commit to interview times or seems reluctant to do this, this may be a warning signal.

Qualified role checklist

To be completely sure that you have a qualified brief and good commitment levels to work with, double check it against the checklist in Table 8.4.

Developing the client strategy

The next stage is to formulate or deliver your client strategy. It may be that you have formulated and recommended the strategy, perhaps writing a proposal, before you gain a retainer – in which case you move straight on to implementation.

In essence your strategy is a combination of the following, some of which you may be responsible for, some of which may be the responsibility of others, and some of which is predetermined:

- Decide on the candidate attraction methods.
- Identify how to present the role to candidates to best effect.

TABLE 8.4   Qualified role checklist

You have identified or gained:

- A complete job and person specification.
- Complete compensation information.
- That the salary offered is in the right area.
- How the recruiting process will work, including decision-makers.
- That the candidate exists.
- Company and departmental information.
- Fee cleared/full fee and requisition signed.
- Complete interviewing information.
- The level of urgency and a start date.
- A co-operative hiring manager who is interested in working in partnership.
- Exclusivity or agreed operational boundaries.

- Develop a candidate briefing document (or pitch).
- Develop the assessment or interview process.
- Develop the candidate experience, including the above, but also the offer paperwork, welcome pack and on-boarding details.

Our focus in this book is on the first three as typically this is where the majority of recruiters have their focus. The latter two areas are where the wider HR community is likely to be more involved but they are nevertheless part of the candidate experience and should therefore be considered if relevant.

Task

Write down what open questions will help secure this information from your client or hiring manager and develop the list into your own personal checklist for taking a requirement or brief.

Any strategy might use a range of candidate attraction methods, as detailed in the next chapter. A good candidate attraction strategy, however, needs to be fundamentally underpinned by a clear understanding of the personal skills, experience and profile of the individuals needed for a particular job. Knowledge of where your candidate base might be drawn from is also important. As David Mason formerly of AXA said: 'Recruitment has moved on hugely from just placing an advertisement in *The Sunday Times*.'

Some organizations, including David's, have moved towards a highly scientific approach in developing candidate specifications.

Candidate profiling and CRM

Use of profiling the best people in the business is becoming increasingly common to develop a sense of the ideal candidate brief. Psychometric testing assesses the candidate's view of his or her own preferred behaviours. A wide range of organizations uses both psychometric testing and ability tests to support the interview process. Psychometric profiling tools can either be used as stand-alone assessments (many of which can be done online) and matched against the demands of the role, or can be taken one step further. A very interesting development is the capacity of tools to map the behaviours and personality traits of the top performers in a particular part of the organization and then develop a model against which the potential candidate test results can be evaluated for similarity.

Prospective candidates can be segmented into skills, experience and likely background. You may know you want the top statisticians who didn't get snapped up by the investment banks on graduation but who nevertheless have great potential for your research house. You may also know that you want particular engineers from a large global employer in one country to re-locate to another for an exciting new R&D facility being built. You may even have an ongoing requirement for call centre staff in Edinburgh. The next task is to find out what your optimum staff member's profile is and then where to locate the right people.

A new website development in the United States is **www.climber.com**, which operates from both sides of the candidate and client spectrum. It enables you to identify your 'company DNA' and then have it matched by candidates visiting the site who have discovered their 'career fingerprint'. Whether this type of site becomes the 'norm' is yet to be seen but what is certain is that sophisticated matching systems will continue to be developed, both web-based and internal.

Recruitment consultants can play a vital role in providing this service or talent development, or talent backing, for their clients. Indeed this is the core competence of database and passive candidate development. In time to come we will see technology focused on developing pipelines for upstream recruitment as well as downstream.

CASE STUDY

Denise Morris of Highams Recruitment was thrilled when she placed her last candidate in a very senior strategic IT interim role. He had first been in contact with Highams 10 years before about another role, and Denise had continued to track him, developing the relationship, sharing market intelligence and keeping in touch. He turned into a client more recently but she had never placed him until now. It's hard to think of a better example of candidate 'nurturing'.

Once the candidate profile is developed it is then time to determine the candidate proposition. This delivers a compelling opportunity to the candidates, one they want to explore further at least.

Presenting role to candidates to best effect

You will decide whether you need a corporate briefing document, website, job-brief pack or a polished verbal pitch – or a combination of all of them. Your choices will depend upon the role(s) you are recruiting for. For a temp role you would not develop a pack and for an overseas family relocation a sharp verbal pitch will not suffice – not if you want the rest of the family to go anyway! Generally the bigger the role or amount of hiring, the more resources will go into producing the briefing document or web resource.

Once you have decided on your route you'll need to decide on the content. Determine the:

- key selling points of the content of the role;
- key selling points of the career opportunity;
- key selling points of the culture of the business.

This will enable you to design your candidate briefing document or pitch for implementing your candidate attraction strategy.

Preparing a candidate briefing document or pitch

Developing and producing a great briefing document on a particular role (or a brochure on an employer) is a great way to build your brand and give a real sense of who you are as an employer or what the role is as a consultancy. From a consultancy perspective, the way you deliver a job brief to a candidate will also impact on your brand as a consultancy and will make a strong contribution towards generating candidate interest. Briefing information can be a great differentiator between candidate enthusiasm and ambivalence.

The range of presentations will vary from a whole brand development programme with web sites and community builds through to a simple pitch identifying the key selling points of a job and contacting your candidate with them. We'll look at each of these in turn.

Corporate presentations

Any organization with a large range of roles to recruit for will have a range of briefing documents, ranging from a careers site on the web to a handout given at interview or a detailed role spec, particularly for senior roles. The sorts of contents of these documents and web pages may include the following:

- videos containing success stories of past candidates;
- role profiles of successful people at all levels within the business;
- available roles;
- details of campus recruitment taking place;
- invitation and mechanism to join a talent bank;
- hints and tips on completing an application;
- the company benefits;
- policies on internal learning and development opportunities and promotion options;
- information on internships;
- information on company products and services.

It's a given now that much of this information will be online. How your careers microsite is presented and the language it uses will play a big part in attraction, or otherwise, of candidates. Your presentation needs to reflect both your own definition of brand but also speak to the candidates you want to attract. Your brand reaches out to social networking as well; Nokia went from 5,000 'likes' on its Facebook page to 20,500 in eleven months – 15,000 extra potential candidates generated in less than one year with no direct costs.

Individual roles recruited through search and/or selection

These will require a briefing document or set of notes explaining more about the role and organization. The notes add specific role and departmental information to any existing careers sections on the company web page or general information found in research.

It is most likely this will be prepared by the recruiter retained to search or select the role. In this case it becomes an important sales tool for attracting candidates. Whilst recruiting some roles, particularly in the public sector, it will be part of the process to send out a detailed briefing pack. A mark of commitment in this process will be the return of the completed, often onerous, application form.

The use of application forms may occasionally mean that a highly qualified candidate is missed from the process as the application form has been made too long and challenging. An organization with an over-supply of candidates and a really top brand can afford to make the application process more challenging than one that is struggling to attract talent.

The briefing document might look like this:

- overview of client;
- why the role has arisen;
- business objectives of the organization (in the public domain);
- business culture description;
- board or team members (wherever the role fits);
- broad objectives for the role;
- job and candidate profile;
- competences required;
- potential career direction following this role;
- remuneration and benefits – this may be very broad brush or not appropriate at this stage.

This is a marketing tool and needs to give a rich picture of the company and the role and what needs to be contributed by the potential role holder. It also needs to set out the opportunity in the best possible light in order to encourage good candidates. It is best practice to get the client to sign off the briefing document.

Multiple roles for particular departments

If there is a need for a large number of roles in one place or one department or for a graduate recruitment drive, say, it is then a great idea to publish either a web page, perhaps accessed by password on successful completion of a first-stage screening process, or a specific marketing package directed entirely at the target candidates.

You need to develop information, which reassures a candidate about the move and gives valuable practical information.

Single roles with a fast hire rate

Many recruiters will be recruiting contractors, temps or permanent staff that are one-offs, and will need a good verbal pitch; if you are doing this, you still need to be clear about the selling points of the role.

The three key points highlighted earlier should form the backbone of your pitch although it may vary from candidate to candidate depending upon what you know about them. Practise it until you have a really polished pitch that you can adjust as you need to; for example:

> This is a real opportunity to make a mark in this department as they want someone to come up with some ideas for changing the existing routine.

It could lead to a team leader role if the changes work well and it's a really lively department with a great social life.

Or...

You'll be dealing with customers who ring in with problems and can sometimes be quite distressed. People I've placed there before say that helping them and reassuring them can give a real sense of job satisfaction. As it's such a big company the training is brilliant and you get an allowance to do what you want to. There's a really good flexible working scheme and you can choose your shifts to some degree to fit in with home or other activities.

Or...

It's a great company and a really busy reception role with lots of visitors coming and going so it's never dull. It's right in the centre of the City, so good for shopping at lunchtime (or maybe bad I don't know!) and there are two other girls on reception as well who are really nice and always friendly to temps.

You'll find more examples of pitching ideas in Chapter 9 on 'Candidate attraction'.

To take a wider perspective, motivation theory can help consider what might be important to candidates, both in the pitch and in the interview process.

Motivation theories applied

Three key theories can be helpful.

Maslow's hierarchy of needs

Maslow developed a body of work on values and needs (1943) that suggested an order to our needs and wants as humans (Figure 8.2).

He argues that as humans we need to ensure that each level of need is satisfied in order and in the moment. That is to say that we do not progress up the hierarchy through life but that we have all of these needs on a daily basis. As the need arises so does the urge to satisfy that need. So, if we are out with a friend but we are really cold and hungry, it is likely we are unable to give our friend our full attention until we have satisfied our hunger and warmed up. Equally, in a wider view, candidates may come to interview with a range of needs satisfied in their current role and may be motivated by the opportunity to have their next set of needs met. Perhaps they have a good job with a great bunch of people, but are not being stretched.

Herzberg's Two Factor Theory

Herzberg developed the Two Factor Theory (1959) from his research (Figure 8.3); he argued that some aspects of a role are truly motivating and they are his 'motivators', but other elements of a role are not truly motivating in themselves, but their absence is demotivating, hence the term 'dis-satisfiers'. So, if the salary is not high enough to meet people's expectations they will

FIGURE 8.2   Maslow's hierarchy of needs

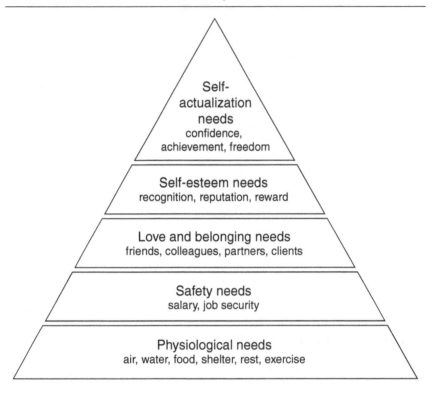

FIGURE 8.3   Herzberg's two-factor theory

Motivators	Hygiene factors
Achievement	Company policy/administration
Recognition	Supervision
Job interest	Interpersonal relations
Responsibility	Salary
Advancement	Status
	Job security
	Personal life
	Working conditions

not be keen on the role. Interestingly in this theory money is a dis-satisfier, not a motivator. Money represents achievement and success; the opportunity to earn it is a by-product of your success drive. If, however, you find you are earning less than others, then that can be very demotivating.

Glasser's Choice Theory

Glasser (1998) does not agree with the hierarchy of needs attributed to Maslow but does see a range of needs that demand satisfaction, as portrayed in Figure 8.4. In studies of Choice Theory in the 1970s, he identified five genetic needs: 'Power' is feeling in control, 'Love' is about feeling you belong somewhere, 'Freedom' is a sense of being able to make decisions at work, 'Fun' is the capacity to do something you enjoy and 'Security' is the sense that these things are not under threat.

FIGURE 8.4   Glasser's choice theory; five genetic needs

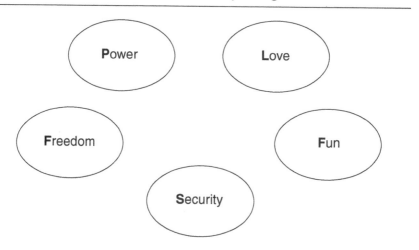

How motivation theory can help

In client strategy

- Identify which of the elements of the role align themselves with motivators and the 'five genetic needs', but also possible dis-satisfiers.
- Ensure the role design includes enough of the motivational elements. You may need to negotiate this role design with the hiring manager.
- Decide how to manage and minimize the dis-satisfiers. If the salary is not so good, decide how this might change the profile of the potential candidate and how to reach them with other benefits that mitigate needs.

In candidate attraction

- When delivering your pitch, make it punchy and ensure it contains motivators for your candidate.

- Ensure your interview process reflects the needs and motivators of the candidate group. If this is a target group of graduates make the assessment process (maybe an assessment centre) relevant to them.

- As part of your pitch consider these issues:
  - Will the role meet the candidate's security needs in terms of salary, length of contract, expenses. Will it meet the candidate's needs in work–life balance?
  - How will the role satisfy their needs for 'love' and belonging? Is this a change role where they are likely to be unpopular? There may be a loss of freedom for someone moving from self-employment to employment.
  - Ensure you detail all aspects of the job that enable learning and career development.
  - Let candidates know about the social scene at work or how people work in cross-functional teams. A sense of real belonging can be transmitted from how someone is greeted at interview through to the interview itself.

- Having so far considered direct methods of attracting candidates, we will now consider the attraction environment: the recruiter brand.

Building a brand

Nothing delivers value in a recruitment consultancy like the capacity to attract candidates and clients because of the brand. We have discussed how a brand is developed through advertising, whether client or consultancy paid, but it is also built through everything you do as a recruiter, and everything you do as a business. Many businesses have built their success on the capacity to attract the best talent when they need it, often for lower salaries than their competitors because of what they can offer as an employer brand. Microsoft is a great example of this. The same question of brand applies to your own personal brand as a recruiter. The more people who get to know you and value your service, the more they will recommend your service to their friends and colleagues, making word of mouth one of the most effective brand-building tools you can have. Equally, the more you are perceived by clients as attracting the best and most candidates, the more you will attract good clients who may not always want to work with you but who know that they need to because you will always attract the best candidates.

CASE STUDY

John Bissell of LBA specializes in advising owners to plan to exit their businesses, usually through a trade sale. John recognizes the importance of a strong brand when offering businesses for sale. He actively encourages owners to implement a programme of public relations activities to raise the profile of their businesses both in their local marketplace and in the industry as a whole.

An IT business in South London that John advises has used PR to build a brand image that gives the impression that the business is a large international group whereas in reality it operates from a single site. Brand enhancement has enabled this business to grow much more rapidly than would otherwise have been the case. John advises recruiters to use PR to develop their own brands. Anything that raises their profile in the marketplace enhances their personal brand.

According to a recent survey by jobs.ac.uk, the scientific and academic job board (**http://www.jobs.ac.uk**), a massive 86 per cent of job seekers rate an employer's brand as important when applying for jobs – only 2 per cent said it was unimportant!

Part of the brand, and the perception of the brand, is driven by what the candidate actually experiences during the selection process. Internal and external recruiters need to pay attention to both the candidate and client experience with their organization. Each of the process touch points is an opportunity to give the candidate or client either a good or bad perception.

CASE STUDY

Penny Davis, recently Head of HR for T-Mobile and now with Balfour Beatty support services, has invested considerable time and effort into commissioning a piece of work on their employer brand through an external agency. The objective was to gain greater insight into how T-mobile is perceived in their market. Penny wanted every potential recruit's experience with T-mobile to be a positive one, even if they don't join this time round.

Corporate social responsibility

Increasingly important is an organization's CSR policy. Corporate social responsibility is a growing concern, particularly for Generation Y audiences. The role your organization plays in supporting less developed countries or organizations in the third sector and addresses climate change at home with green initiatives in the office may well affect how much people want to work for you in the future. The value that your organization places on work–life balance, the capacity for people to take career breaks for whatever reason, the benefits your business pays, all speak volumes about you.

Equality and diversity

The CIPD defines diversity as 'valuing everyone as an individual and people as employees, clients and customers'.

There is a growing body of views to suggest that not only can a strongly diverse workforce increase employee well-being but also that it contributes to the bottom line. The increasingly global nature of markets and the segmentation of customers means that employing a workforce recruited from one small segment of society is unlikely to be as successful as a workforce made up of all groups in society.

On a further practical note, embracing a diverse workforce enables the recruiter to consider a far wider candidate base than might otherwise be considered. Recruitment consultants can be well placed to support organizations in this approach, many helping minority groups such as lone parents back into work in partnership with government schemes. Initiatives like the Local Employment Partnerships (LEPs) offer a range of support mechanisms to help the long-term unemployed back into work, for example. Candidates sourced through JobCentre Plus can often work a trial period while both you and the candidate assess whether you would like to work together.

The CIPD refer to the 'glass cliff' when they show that there is a stronger propensity to place women and other marginalized groups in positions where there is high chance of failure. There seems little against a positive policy on diversity and the effort involved in implementing it may be outweighed by the benefit derived from it.

The brand experience

How you, as an individual and as an organization, behave during each of those touch-points (those points at which your brand 'touches' your candidate base), plus your policies and demonstration of these policies on equal opportunities, diversity and CSR for example, will all build the brand experience. Suppose you leave a message for someone when making a headhunting call, and when they call back to speak to you the receptionist gets their name wrong or asks 'Does she know what it's about?' or 'Can I ask what it's in connection with?', then the overall brand and the candidate or client experience is not being optimized. It's important to be constantly aware of how your whole recruitment process is managed.

One way of attracting candidates is to drive traffic through to your website – and then make sure it is easy for people to navigate it and apply for opportunities. It needs to be congruent with the image you project of yourself as a brand, and the recruitment or careers section is a candidate attraction tool in its own right. Considering this section of your website as a way of building interest and candidate communities is a great place to start. Putting role specs for each job on it without much thought about how this is likely to be perceived is far too common. The better the brand name in your market sector, the greater the chances of candidates aspiring to work with you and going directly to the website. The important considerations are:

- Who is your audience?
- How does your audience like to be communicated to?
- What language will work for your audience?
- What message do you need them to understand about the benefits of working with your business?
- How can you engage with them?

Blending social brand building with a focused approach will help drive traffic through to your website. Many corporate recruiters now run virtual careers fairs on the internet and will run discussion groups or set up communities within spaces frequented by their target audience. We have seen only the tip of the iceberg of this recruiting strategy, which has made enormous strides in just the last two to three years.

Ultimately, great recruitment consultancy brands are built by placing people and delivering what you say you can to both your candidates and clients. Making sure they also have a good experience along the way means they will come back again. Building a great brand as an employer means making sure the recruitment process works really well, managing people's disappointment well and ensuring that the experience of actually working at your company is a rewarding one. A good guide to this for candidates is the 'Sunday Times 100 Best Companies to work for'. It is an inspirational space for companies to work towards.

Implementing the right strategy

Once you have 'set the scene' for candidate attraction you can move to implementing the right strategy for the circumstance you are in.

Deciding upon candidate attraction methods

Some roles will need one method of candidate attraction. For many recruiters, filling jobs will rely heavily on database search followed by some advertising as a day-to-day methodology to fulfil their requirements and vacancies.

Other recruiters, however, working in search and selection as an in-house or overall service provider to a direct employer, may wish to use a range of methods to attract candidates. A range of aspects – from how to fulfil all your corporate recruitment needs through to how to fill particular jobs – all fall under this category and we have looked in this chapter at how important it is to cover each of the elements fully: managing your client, taking a brief, qualifying the role to ensure you should be spending time on it, profiling candidates to segment your candidate market and develop a competitive proposition, preparing your candidate brief and pitch, alongside all of the indirect methods of candidate attraction such as brand and a strong diversity policy. The preparation elements of candidate attraction have therefore been covered and in the next chapter we look in detail at how to implement each of the candidate attraction methods to best effect.

Industry profile – Francesca Peters

Profile for Francesca Peters, Global HRD of dunnhumby, the brains behind Tesco Clubcard and relevance marketing

Born: In Taplow, Berkshire

Educated: A convent and then College

Early career: Interestingly Francesca's first role was as a secretarial recruitment consultant, which proved a great stepping stone into the HR space.

Moving on to the Ladbrooke Group she found herself working in OD and Management Development and took up her first HR generalist role in their hotel division. A move to Regus meant she was working in fast-growth mode, pre and post IPO – the business grew to 3,000 people across 20 countries meaning Francesca added global expertise to her skill set. After four years in advertising she joined dunnhumby in 2007 looking after 1,000 people globally with a fast growth curve internationally, beckoning.

Key advice for recruiters: See recruitment as a company-wide issue – it is part of everyone's role. Recruitment is not about one team in the business filling jobs; it's about the whole business working together to build the business for its future capability.

One thing you should always do: Treat people with respect at all times – whether you can help them now or not!

One thing you should never do: Organizations should not spend more time on recruitment than retention. Focus on hiring great leaders and great graduates, as they will be the leaders of tomorrow!

Still to achieve: 'A work/life balance!'

Interests outside work: 'Work and family – see above!'

Francesca Peters has a brilliant grasp of the 'big picture' and how recruiters contribute to the overall wellbeing, growth and profitability of a business. She completely 'gets' the value of recruiters.

Industry profile – Jerry Wright

Equally relevant to client strategy is your overall talent acquisition strategy. A clear option is RPO so this profile is of Jerry Wright, Co-Founder/MD of cph – a successful, specialist RPO provider. He also holds other roles as a Non-Executive Advisor for Grosvenor Clive & Stokes (executive search firm) and as an 'Operating Partner' (Expert Advisor) for Matrix Private Equity Partners.

Born: Wigan, Lancashire – and very proud of it!

Educated: Upholland Grammar School, near Wigan; University of Leicester – obtained a Law degree (LLB)

Early career: Jerry started as a Graduate Trainee and progressed to a Recruitment Manager in professional and executive recruitment, and then became Consultant – through to Consulting Manager HR – in PwC management consultants.

As a Divisional MD for Michael Page Group he ran the Sales and Marketing; Technology and Management Consulting businesses. For the last 2–3 years there he set up and ran their separately branded executive search firm, Questor International.

Since 1997 he has co-founded, funded and run three recruiting firms – Prism; Grosvenor Wright and, since 2005, cph, a successful, specialist RPO firm.

Key advice for recruiters: Work hard and in a structured, focused way – the results will follow.

One thing recruiters should always do: Always deliver what you say you are going to deliver – be it for clients or candidates.

One thing recruiters should never do: Fail to do what you say you will do.

Still to achieve:

- Professionally, to build cph into a leading and highly regarded player in the RPO market.

- Personally, having been on the last two British Lions tours (New Zealand & South Africa), want to complete the set by going to Australia in 2013.

Interests outside work:

- Sport and outdoor activities – play tennis regularly, go running, and do a lot of long distance hiking. Avid follower of rugby union and rugby league.

- National hunt racing – been a successful (lucky!) owner, having had three Cheltenham Festival winners, and still chasing the dream!

- Stock market follower/investor.

- Always enjoy a few beers with the lads (and lasses).

09 Candidate attraction

Candidate attraction is defined as any means you may use to find a candidate or a range of candidates. This chapter explores ways to deliver candidates: resourcing from the database, advertising, social networking, talent bank development, headhunting and networking, plus developing a range of attraction strategies for in-house recruiters.

Candidate attraction starts as soon as you have worked out 'what to do' and ends as soon as you have acquired the candidate CV, at which point you move on to candidate management.

Your strategy could include just one, or a range of, attraction methods. Each method begins with a definition, making it easy for you to work out if it is the right method for you to choose whether it is an ideal or a poor choice under particular circumstances. The section then goes on to tell you how you can implement the method and what to say and do.

Decide which of the methods most closely suit the situation you are in with your client and develop a strategy from there. Role by role, any of the methods in Table 9.1 might work well in isolation, or a range of methods might be needed for some roles.

Resourcing from your in-house database

Defined as: Contacting candidates whose details you already have, either on your internal company or recruiting consultancy database.

Ideal: If you have a great database with a wide range of skills on it. Great if you are in a hurry and in a competitive situation – a freelance, contract or temp role needs filling this morning for example. Cost-effective as you have already acquired the candidates, so the more you can use them the more profitable the cost of acquisition is.

Poor choice: You are searching for someone with skills that differ from your normal candidate base. You have never recruited for this role before and neither has your company. You are doing a search.

TABLE 9.1 Choosing a candidate attraction strategy

	Strategy	Active	Passive	Used for...
1	Executive search		✓	Individual senior roles.
2	Targeted national press advertising	✓	✓	Senior individuals, group roles or generic skills required.
3	Targeted trade press advertising	✓	✓	Specific sector background required. Senior to mid-level roles. Can be combined with 2 (above).
4	Local radio and press advertising	✓	✓	Senior to junior roles in a specific geographic location.
5	Headhunting		✓	Sourcing identified individuals for a specific role. Can be a tool in Exec Search or stand alone.
6	Internet job board advertising	✓	✓	Range of general roles.
7	Company intranet or notice boards	✓	✓	Internal applications.
8	Talent mapping or research-led sourcing		✓	Senior to mid-level roles in competitor or other organizations.
9	Building candidate communities through websites, blogging, content development		✓	Non-specific recruitment. Brand development and potential candidates for the future.
10	Internal employee referral programme	✓	✓	Pays a good internal fee for successful recommendations. A company in high growth with lots of new people joining will do well from this.
11	Database search	✓	✓	Either agency or internal. Often the first step for any role.
12	Data mining, internet, CV banks	✓		For individual roles or more general skill sets. For signed off roles and networking.
13	Campus recruitment: the milk round or targeted graduate advertising	✓		Volume graduate recruitment.
14	Local advertising in press and radio, notice boards, shop windows, press editorial coverage, open days	✓		Volume local employer recruitment, eg new shop or call centre.

Niche, specific and/or senior roles

↑

↓

Volume recruitment

It's easy to slip up here and assume that as the candidates are on your database they will be interested in what you have to say, pleased to hear from you, and exclusively yours! In fact, of course, they may have already taken six calls from recruiters this morning, be on all of your competitors' databases too and not too keen to hear from you. Take care not to make assumptions. One of the ways in which you can gain competitive advantage is by having a strong relationship with your top candidates. By a strong relationship we mean; you have interviewed your candidate, ideally in person, and have worked with them to try and find them a new role. You may not have succeeded but you have given them a great service and they remember you for that. You call them regularly (every three to six months) to discuss their career plans and update them on the market, creating value for you, them and your clients; this means that you are always aware of what their 'ideal' role might be and you can let them know when such roles come up. It also means that, if handled well, they see you as their career partner. Although candidates search specific roles through the internet today for their next move, under this model they are also much more likely to call you to discuss it than if they never hear from you.

Start resourcing a role after preparing your pitch, as discussed in the last chapter, and have your search list in front of you. Make sure you have access to the history of each candidate and their ideal role so you know how to frame your pitch. Ensure it is relevant to them. Be well prepared on your requirement or brief. Little destroys credibility more than a lack of basic information about your client and the role.

The type of information you need to give the candidate will of course vary depending upon the assignment; if you are recruiting a contractor to work in Azerbaijan, the candidates may not need to understand the business strategy of the company they will be potentially working for, but they will want to know the detail 'down to the letter' of the expenses arrangements. Equally a temp in the City will want to know the hours and whom they report to, whereas the business consultant will want to understand more about business goals of the clients they are likely to be working with. So ensure your knowledge is appropriate for the candidates you are calling.

Good candidates can be won and lost on the strength of your approach. Your knowledge and enthusiasm for the organization you are representing is crucial; this often depends upon a good relationship with the hiring manager, which you will have developed through the client strategy phase.

When you are pitching a job to a candidate use your planned pitch:

- Summarize your previous discussion.
- 'When we spoke before you said...'
- Think how the candidate might like the role presented, given what you know about them.
- Assume that the candidate will be interested in the opportunity, which is to say, maintain a positive state of mind about your call. After all, if you have done your work well, listened carefully and taken trouble to match well, they will be interested.

- Describe how the opportunity fits with their motivations uncovered at interview.

- Be positive about the organization you are marketing – often we do best when 'selling' the organizations we would ourselves like to work for. Don't hide the negatives but keep them in proportion. A negative for one person could be a positive for someone else.

- Check out how the candidate feels about what you have said: 'How does that sound?'

- Handle any objections as you go through and check there are no further concerns at the end.

- Gain diary availability for a meeting with the client. Check there is nothing to preclude the candidate from attending.

In client acquisition we used the acronym AIDA to structure the approach. The same method (shown again in Table 9.2) can be used here to structure the approach call to the candidate.

TABLE 9.2   Capturing your candidate's interest

A	Attention
I	Interest
D	Desire
A	Action

A/I – Attention and interest

The first thing you say has to gain the attention of the listener. It's important to sound awake and alert and even to smile – you'd be surprised how a smile can be 'heard' over the phone. If you don't sound upbeat and excited (whilst staying professional of course) your potential candidate certainly won't feel you have anything worth hearing. So, the focus here is on the delivery of this first sentence. Sounding like you have just woken up or had a heavy night, whilst it may be the truth, will not get you the results you want. You also have a maximum of 30 seconds to gain their attention before you have mentally lost them.

How you introduce yourself and your business will also have an impact on the attention you get. Using both first and second names increases your professionalism. Saying what your agency or company's specialization is (unless you are a household name like Korn Ferry or Unilever) enables the person to qualify you further as someone they should be talking to. Clearly if you've spoken to them before and have built a good relationship this matters less, although it does no harm to remind them of why you could be of value to them.

Options to gain Attention:

- 'Hi Jo, it's Tom from X Company – we spoke a while back about that fantastic job at Diageo but you were not free...'
- 'Hi Jo, it's Tom Smith from X Company. We specialize in recruiting senior execs for EMEA start-ups. I recruited Sam Jones, whom you know, into her current role and she suggested I speak with you about a new CEO role I am handling. Is now a good time?'
- 'Hi Jo, it's Tom Smith here – we agreed I'd be in touch as soon as I was briefed on something in a start-up situation...'
- 'Hi Jo, it's Tom Smith – we spoke last week and you said you were available for work today – is that still the case?'
- 'Jo, Tom Smith from X Company. We've not spoken before but I know you have dealt with colleagues in the past who have suggested I call you today as they feel your skills match very closely a profile I am recruiting for.'

OR, run both A and I in together – gain attention and then interest:

- 'Jo, this is Tom Smith, Recruitment Director at Y Company. I head up our internal recruitment team and am keen to touch base with you about a potential senior opportunity that has just arisen. When is good for you?'
- 'Hi Jo, I have your details in front of me – you spoke to my colleague Paul last week about a senior accountant role in Edinburgh... I'd like to run though an exciting further option with you... Is now a good time?'
- 'Hello there Jo, it's Tom – you said you were looking for a role nearer home when we last spoke – is that still the case? How does 10-minutes commute sound?'

Notice each introduction, where you have sought to gain their interest by offering a 'carrot' to them, is still sharp and swift and you then confirm the situation and 'close' that part of the conversation. Make sure your candidate speaks at a really early point in the conversation – remember the 30-second rule from above – so you've gained attention and interest.

D – create desire

Two pitching options:

Option one: direct pitch
If you know them well, know what they want and have spoken to them recently, pitch the role directly to them:

- 'Let me tell you about the role... It's based in central London, which means it's an easy commute from your house, paying 20 per cent more than you are currently earning and a similar tax compliance role so will be a really straightforward transition for you. How does that sound?'

- 'Great – I thought you were available – it's a lovely job actually – for at least three days from today. It's a great company that I've worked with many times before and the job's covering the MD's PA who is off sick and they don't think she'll be back for a few weeks. The MD's really nice, busy of course, and will be thrilled to see you. It's Covent Garden that I know you like. What time can you be there for this morning?'

Notice in the first pitch you link the features of the role to the benefits of the role to them; the commute from their house, the difference in their pay packet and a 'straightforward transition for you'. Even if you don't spell these things out, at least make sure you refer back to what you know they want, which of course you will have covered in interview and written down to refer back to when you go back to them. Here it's the little details that count, like having to get home by 5 pm to let the nanny go so your candidate cannot work past 4.30 pm.

Option two: match pitch

If you don't know what is important to the candidate, because you have not spoken to them before, you'll need to find out what they want or what they will 'buy' before you can present the role effectively to them.

So first, find out what they want... then pitch the role to them, assuming you can find a match.

- 'We've not spoken at length before so I'm keen to find out if the role I have might be suitable for you – tell me, what is important to you in your next role?'

- 'We clearly need to evaluate between us whether this might be the right career move for you at this point – tell me what might be the next role for you?'

- 'I need to establish whether this contract is right for you – what sort of commute are you happy with? What rate would you be looking for? And what rate are you currently on? What shifts are you working at present? How open are you to a change?'

Notice how in the above examples you are holding on to control of whether you progress the candidate for the role. You don't want to play games with them but you must retain control over whether they are likely to be a seriously qualified candidate to progress to your client at this point. You need to gain some commitment from them before you progress to the next stage.

Table 6.2 in Chapter Six is a resource on using questions. You can either ask an open question – preceded by 'who, where, what, how, why and when' – or you can ask a series of direct questions, as in the last example. Open questions allow the candidate to talk more. Using an open question allows you to build rapport and then a relationship, as well as find out more information. Direct questions, where you ask a series of questions designed to gain specific information, keep you in control and can be useful when you have very limited time, and when you know the candidate or they have worked with your firm regularly before and there is already a good relationship. Closed questions enable you to take back control of the conversation if you want to move on. A quick closed question will do that well without offending.

Questioning and listening are the most important skills for recruiters. It's easy, particularly if you feel you have a short space of time to get your point across, to spend more time talking than listening. Listening can be far more powerful however and give you valuable information. Aim for 80 per cent listening and 20 per cent talking in any conversation.

CASE STUDY

Anita Baglee, while she was with Blue Skies marketing recruitment, tells a story of one of her candidates who stipulated that she wanted to work for a small-sized marketing agency. Later on in the conversation she talked about a desire to work with big budget clients. This was a clear contradiction so it was important to question the candidate further to understand her real desire. It transpired that the only reason the candidate had said she wanted to work for a small company was because she assumed that bigger agencies were very process driven and political. Baglee says she was able to share her knowledge of the sector to overcome this misconception and got a useful insight into the type of culture the candidate wanted. She secured the candidate a number of interviews at small and large agencies, so she could make a comparison. The candidate joined a large agency to work with market-leading clients. Anita is now Director of Operations at Hogarth Worldwide Ltd.

Once you have established what the candidate wants then you are able to pitch back the role to them incorporating and highlighting the features of the role that match their needs and wants. Lastly, in the structure AIDA, you'll need to agree the next steps.

A – Action

This could range from confirming that the candidate will send in a CV in response to an advertisement, agreeing for you to put them forward for an interview to following through with a referral. Be clear with the candidate at the end of the call, meeting or e-mail what you have both agreed will take place next. This is an important part of candidate control.

Resourcing the database is often, rightly, the first port of call for any consultant. It should also be first for any internal recruiting function, but it is surprising how little attention is paid to sourcing candidates internally by internal or corporate recruiters – in terms of either present employees or previously interviewed candidates – although this is gradually changing. The opportunity cost for employers is twofold: the goodwill and loyalty generated by promoting from within, and the obvious costs of recruiting saved by not using external sources.

In-house recruiters and agencies alike will make use of targeting particular groups of candidates directly, once they have identified them as a segment they draw from for their workforce. Both parties can reach new candidates through job fairs, sponsorship and targeted relationship building.

Job fairs

Defined as: A heavily advertised event aimed at a discrete candidate base (graduates, retail, IT) where prospective employers pay to take a stand and market themselves directly.

Ideal: If you have volume recruitment needs from a range of people that it might either be hard to process or screen in the same timeframe, or expensive or difficult to reach.

Poor choice: If you are recruiting a scarce skill, senior candidates or small numbers of candidates.

There is now a wide range of job fairs available for different skills and candidates. The more junior the roles or the more regional, the better this works. Candidates can be managed and processed quickly and can come out of the job fair with a range of follow-up interviews. Large employers sometimes run their own: Nottingham City Council for example. There is a London LGBT job fair aimed at all lesbian, gay, bisexual and transgender candidates, attended by many blue-chip employers. Job fairs may be designed to target a particular diverse group, uncovering both a new range of potentially highly qualified but otherwise inaccessible candidates and also developing their diversity. Prospects, the graduate careers website, runs a wide range of fairs for different purposes: work experience fairs, volunteering fairs, graduate and post-graduate fairs, with specialist fairs such as law as well.

Targeted relationship development and sponsorship

Defined as: A strategy that recognizes the importance of certain university courses, or particular schools or colleges, for its workforce. This can range from recruiting the top graduates from Oxbridge for banks or advertising agencies through to doing talks at local schools and colleges for the local police force or supermarket recruitment. This may be linked with sponsoring certain events at that organization.

Ideal: If you have a specialist need for particular graduates who have completed a certain course at a particular group of universities, or when recruiting for a local employer with specific geographic needs and a limited pool to draw from.

Poor choice: If you need experienced people and could draw them from a range of places, and they are likely to be already working.

As part of a graduate development programme, your business or recruitment agency could develop relationships with specific universities who have courses that would be of interest to the business. Specialist graduate recruiters spend a great deal of time developing these relationships, and many are now doing joint development programmes with their chosen course organizers. Agencies specializing in placing candidates into marketing or advertising might target universities and colleges with specific advertising and marketing courses.

CASE STUDY

An award-winning scheme is the joint project developed by the City of Norwich School and construction services giant May Gurney, where hundreds of students at the school benefit each year from a highly successful link with the company. Activities ranging from outings and one-day engineering challenges to work placements and sponsorships bring the school and the locally based firm even closer together. Skills, experience, resources and knowledge flow both ways in this rewarding relationship – and, as a major employer, May Gurney gets closer to its potential workforce of the future.

Contrast this with the next case study which shows how one business is directly targeting candidates it wants to work with. This could become part of a longer-term campaign and as some skills become more and more scarce internal recruiting teams will spend much of their time identifying talent and building relationships with that talent.

CASE STUDY

The candidate, identified from his blog on the work he is doing at his current company, was sent a FedEx parcel containing a cleverly designed and wrapped box with a customized, engraved iPod shuffle in it with a message suggesting he play it. On the iPod was a message from the CEO of the company that was recruiting, suggesting they had some great opportunities and a new project they'd really like to talk to him about. He was then directed to their website with a code in the message to give him access. This then directed him to a further page with more information about what the company was doing and how to move to the next stage.

Although this candidate did not choose to progress to a meeting, as he was happy where he was, it is hard to see how this could not appeal to the right type of candidate. Although we in Western Europe might find it a little too personal, it is nonetheless a hugely creative and personalized strategy, which really tells candidates they have not just been called out of the blue. Read more about it at: **http://senzee.blogspot.com/2007/02/red-5s-pitch.html**.

The armed forces also make much use of sponsoring candidates through an exciting programme and their degree courses. Candidates are guaranteed a length of service after they have graduated and places are keenly fought for. So there is a wide range of ways to build links and candidate loyalty for the future, an important strategy in the upstream recruitment plans of today.

A simple approach works equally well.

CASE STUDY

Mohamed Ali, a corporate recruiter for Cisco Systems in the United States is tasked with recruiting software engineers. He says, 'Everyone loves coffee, especially if you are a software engineer breaking your head to debug. So I place some of my requirement flyers and my visiting cards near the cash counter at Starbucks branches near the target companies (in my case, Google, Microsoft, LSI logic, Juniper). I've had a lot of success with this'.

If Mohamed had not been successful in recruiting any of those candidates directly he could equally well have used them for networking. An often under-utilized method of recruitment in-house is networking from the people who have just joined. When recruitment is 'joined-up' to the on-boarding process there is a great opportunity to gain from the network of the person who has just joined through an internal referral scheme.

Internal recruitment referral schemes

Defined as: Reward and incentive programmes that offer financial (in most cases) incentives for staff in organizations to suggest their friends and old colleagues for jobs in their new company. Some recruitment consultancies also run these schemes for their candidate base.

Ideal: A 'must-have' scheme for all recruiters everywhere.

Poor choice: If relied on to staff the entire business. Needs to be blended with other techniques.

When someone new starts, sit them down for a coffee and ask them to draw out their last organization and identify people in their old department. This is a great way to map the market in the competitors you are hiring from and would like to hire more from, and will deliver more of a picture than simply relying on the new recruits to recommend someone or asking them who else they know. There will be people you cannot reach through your own networking, but reducing the overall cost per hire is a continual driver and if you can pick off even 25 per cent of your hires directly this will make a major difference to your business's bottom line in recruitment costs. This strategy will only fill a proportion of your roles however, so you'll need to include others alongside it.

For external recruiters ask yourself how much use do you make of referral gathering at interview. You know that your best placements will come from referral yet it's only too easy to slip into expecting people to call you directly. Whilst they will do that if you offer a great service you will also be missing out on a wide range of candidates by not asking for referrals to other great candidates.

So we'll now turn to another useful strategy, for internal and external recruiters alike.

Networking

Defined as: Establishing one or more mutually advantageous relationships either face to face at a networking type event or over the phone, or even e-mail occasionally.

Ideal: Generating candidates who are not actively looking in the market, ie passive candidates, which means you will not be competing with other agencies or companies for them at an offer stage. Often finds better-quality candidates so long as you are networking with good people to start with – good people tend to know other good people. Costs no 'real money' to acquire – although there is a time cost of course. Gets you out in the market being visible, building your own personal brand and developing your business's brand at the same time.

Poor choice: If you need someone today as it can take a lot longer, both to find candidates who match your specification and to convert them from passive to active – at least for your role. If you don't handle the networking well as it will adversely affect your brand.

Networking well

There are many books on the art of successful networking (for example, Lindenfield and Lindenfield, 2005; Timperley, 2002) so we cover the main options. Here you'll find some tips and techniques, the thinking behind networking, and some internet sites to work with – although these are changing every day and you'll need to keep up to date with them and where the latest action for your market is (several of them are mentioned at other points in the book).

The early days of executive search were based on networking skills and 'whom you know' (often from 'the old school tie') and a developing 'black book' of contacts. Successful recruiters who have been operating for many years in the industry will have started placing people at an early stage in their careers and kept in touch with them as they too progressed up the career ladder turning into clients. This still happens and it works equally well with recruiters who come into recruitment from a senior role in industry and start by placing and hiring candidates who used to be their colleagues. However to stay ahead in the market today you'll need to use a wide range of referral and networking mechanisms.

Developing your own black book

Developing a 'black book' of candidates and clients who themselves are well connected is a great idea to help you when you are searching for a particular candidate who is hard to find. A 'black book' can operate at any level: it can be compiled by someone operating at the top end of a search market, a geographically based recruiter who works in one town where everyone knows everyone, or a specialist recruiter in a specific technical field. Your black book will include sources of good candidates, not necessarily good candidates themselves – although they will of course from time to time also be that. So you may have a range of contacts in the top firms in your town or sector – people who are likely to have access to a range of people at those firms perhaps. These candidate sources may also of course be client sources, depending upon their level – they will certainly be able to tell you something about when their firm is hiring as well as who is around in it.

Developing client referrals through networking

You do not only have access to new candidates through networking; you can also develop referrals towards acquiring new clients through the same medium.

Candidates registering with you for a new role may work for organizations you'd like to work with as a supplier. They are perfectly placed to help you learn more about that organization, how it recruits and the key players to talk to. You can find out who is recruiting currently in their organization, and sometimes who is recruiting in the wider market; often this is in the public domain.

Ask, 'What can you tell me about recruitment in your company?' Or deliver a great service so you get referred on anyway.

CASE STUDY

Lucy Simpson, who was one of the top revenue earners at Major Players, the leading recruiter to the creative services industries has now started her own recruitment business and is Managing Partner of October London. She interviewed a good candidate from one of the top broadcasting companies. She had always been keen to work with them, and when she had placed her candidate with a direct competitor (the candidate was thrilled with her new role) the candidate called and asked if Lucy would like to be referred to her boss to recruit her replacement. Lucy had been considering asking for an introduction and was delighted that her delivery to this candidate had prompted an unsolicited referral.

Lucy met with the candidate's ex boss to take the brief and negotiate terms, and negotiated an exclusive opportunity to work on the brief that she then placed.

Great sources of market activity, and of market direction for internal recruiters, will be agency recruiters. Whilst they will not be a source of cost-free direct candidates, they can give you a really good picture of what the market is doing that will help you develop your strategy for specific hires.

Six degrees of separation

The mathematical theory behind networking is that we are all linked to everyone else on the planet through six other links. Check the 'small world phenomenon', The Milgram experiment (not the psychology one!) and Frigyes Karinthy for more (Travers and Milgram, 1969; Karinthy, 1929). This means we are only six steps away from anyone we might want to contact.

The best place to start networking, then, is with the people you already know and whom they know. As a recruitment consultant you also have access to a great range of candidates on your database, and whilst they will not all be people you know directly, they are people you can contact directly legitimately and ask for help in finding the person you need. You might consider running an event where you ask all your candidates to bring someone else if you are in a market which could work well.

The business networking site LinkedIn identifies everyone by how many degrees of separation there are between you and the person you have found on there whom you'd like to contact. This is a great source of names for headhunting and networking approaches and is being more and more widely used by consultants and in-house recruiters alike.

Increasingly it is not the availability of data that will distinguish you from the competition; it is how you use it. Skills in recruitment become even more important as a differentiator and to get candidates' attention we need to get much smarter to attract the best. How you go about attracting someone will be the difference between success and failure. Twenty years ago it was about knowing who to contact – the data itself was valuable, now it's all about how you contact them and what value you can add.

Trade events and industry conferences

There is no substitute for meeting people face to face, and so long as you set some objectives for attending trade events they are a great way to meet candidates and clients in a more relaxed setting. Conferences are expensive. Most people who are sent to a conference or an event by their employers are sent because the employer values them, so it is likely that the best people in your sector will be at the conference.

At a conference people are relaxed and less 'on their guard'. You can make sure you attend the breakout sessions that people with the skills and expertise you are looking for are likely to be attending. The return on investment of attending these conferences and events can be very high. They are not a place for direct selling but are ideal for making an initial contact that can be followed through after the event.

CASE STUDY

One search completed fully at a conference was for a senior distribution software salesperson for a start-up company. The start of the search coincided with a distribution software conference. The consultant spent the day at the conference talking to salespeople on the stand and finding out about all the products, whilst collecting the business cards of the people who came across really well. The search list was developed from that long day plus some additional name gathering after the event. The best-qualified candidates were contacted and interviewed, resulting in a short list of four candidates, a placement of one and a successfully completed search.

How to make an event work well

Think about who might be at the event, make sure you prepare by having your business cards with you, and with the potential attendees in mind consider what you are going to say to people. Potentially the last thing to talk about is recruiting. Decide on your approach. Most people will be there to learn from the event, to meet some new people and get some different views. If you can see two people standing at an angle to each other it's a great opportunity to go and join them and make the 'group' into a triangle. If you can see someone you know talking to a group of other people, catch their eye and wander over to greet the group and your existing contact. If you know no one, either choose someone standing on their own to join or go and catch a coffee and make conversation with the person standing next to you in the coffee queue. In some ways a successful piece of networking can be viewed as an interview; you'll start by relaxing the person you've approached – ask them a social question, even about their journey or make a remark about the venue, just as you might at an interview. Have a few minutes of social conversation then move the conversation to business:

- 'I see you work at XYZ Company – what do you do there?'
- 'What sector is XYZ in?'
- 'How is XYZ finding the markets at the moment?'

Once you have broken the ice and established a rapport you can move on by focusing on an area of common interest. Make sure you are informed about the latest developments in the news, from political to sports, and in your sector of the event you have chosen to go to today, whether that be your local Chamber of Commerce and what's happening in your local city, the City financial markets or your local NHS trust. Read the broadsheets or industry press to understand the hot topics. Frame some open questions around them. You might find these general questions useful:

- 'I read that XXXXX today – what's your view on that?'
- 'There was an interesting piece in *The Times* today on outsourcing – I don't know if you saw it... The key points were that... What are your thoughts around that?'
- 'How are you finding the conference so far?'
- 'How did you find the last speaker?'
- 'I thought the last speaker was very good – what did you think?'

Notice again that these are all open questions. You'll find asking great questions, listening well and reflecting back on people's answers – 'That's interesting', 'I didn't know that – tell me more about the project' for example – are great tools and techniques for events. You may find that people chat more easily if you give your opinion first, as in some of the examples above. Be prepared to tell someone what you do of course, and do make sure that you talk about both something they'd like to find out more about and something they can ask more questions about.

How to describe what you do

It's important to decide what you are planning to tell people and tell them confidently. Networking gurus refer to a 30-second 'elevator' speech. We said earlier that you have about 30 seconds to lose or gain someone's attention, which is about the time you spend in a lift... You may not want to say that you are a recruiter per se, but saying that you are an international or City or public sector or local headhunter, or a talent director always sparks an interest, and the phrase 'headhunter' is often an opportunity for a joke that breaks the ice and builds rapport.

In order to craft your own 'elevator' speech decide what you offer, what the benefits to the client or the candidate are (think about whom you have recently hired and what benefit they brought to the recruiting organization, or what difference it made to someone's life) and what results you generate. So, perhaps you say you find candidates the job they have always wanted and clients the ideal candidate they've been searching for. Make sure you put it in context. If you are speaking to someone at your local regional industry conference, talk about how much work you do in the region rather than how much work you do in London. This way you will hold people's interest and make them feel bonded to you. Naturally you'll need to use language you feel comfortable with and that reflects who you are.

The last technique is how to gracefully move on from someone to make sure you make as many useful contacts as you can – about 15 minutes to talk to each new person is about right. Asking for their card is a good way to signal that you are interested in them but that you are coming to the end of your time with them. You might want to say that you'd love to pick up with them later, maybe come and see them after the event, but that you are supposed to be picking up with a couple of clients and had better go and find them. Let them know that you have enjoyed talking with them and what was particularly interesting or useful and leave on the 'perhaps catch you later' line.

Task

Spend 10 minutes crafting your elevator speech in which you tell people what you do. Then practise it on a friend or colleague who will give you some good feedback. It's not just what you say, it's how you say it obviously; it's important to be confident and well paced in your voice, thinking about matching (mirroring the other person's pace of speech and energy levels) the other person you are speaking to.

You don't have to leave your desk to network nowadays. A huge growth area of networking is now online, as we have said.

Online networking

The development of both social and business networking sites has been meteoric and there is no reason to suppose this will stop, although some of the sites do raise privacy issues and many firms have banned their use in the workplace. The recruiter's role is to stay one step ahead and use the up-and-coming media. Wikipedia maintains a list of the main worldwide sites for further reference, or you can do your own research among your candidates and clients.

There are some key sites emerging for recruitment. LinkedIn, the prime business networking site has already been mentioned, although others such as Xing also have some following. Google's own social networking site, Google+ gained 40 million users within a very short while of being launched. Twitter has made huge ground since it was launched and is used by journalists, celebrities (or 'their people') and even the Queen. The site itself is a way from monetising itself but many recruiters are finding it good to brand-build for themselves, attracting candidates and clients alike. Many link their Twitter feeds to their LinkedIn accounts so updates appear to their network on both. There is a lack of clarity on the divide between social and business networking particularly on Twitter and Facebook but perhaps one of the big changes we see taking place in the world of work is the blurring of the edges between work and leisure. It will be interesting to see where that takes us. In the meantime recruiters may find advantage in the blurring of these lines.

CASE STUDY

Neil Clements, a Commercial Manager with Major Players, says: 'Most of us have a profile on Facebook that is linked back into Major Players' main website and I've been contacted by quite a range of candidates from there, many of whom I've been able to refer on internally. I placed a job ad in the "Marketplace" section a short while ago for a technical developer for one of the agencies, found a great candidate for my client and placed them – simple really and a great result all round.'

You may not work in an online-rich sector however. There is still a range of other ways of networking to consider.

Word-of-mouth networking

There are plenty of rural or urban areas for which online operating has not arrived yet as there is limited computer usage amongst the candidate base. Recruiting just off Heathrow, for example, for temps to work on the airport and in the distribution companies just outside requires a wholly different approach based very much on word-of-mouth. Candidates will bring friends and neighbours to the depot at five in the morning for a cup of tea, bacon roll and the newspaper, and recruiters will get on the phone and book all the operatives in to their clients. Candidates will then be bussed out, often carrying five or so more 'extra' candidates who will have been placed by the time they have reached the airport perimeter fence. So it goes on until the next shift change, and then it all starts over again. A very fast-paced recruitment environment but still focused on the core delivery of our industry, placing people in jobs. Networking here is working brilliantly, but in an entirely different context.

If you are a recruiter working in a geographic area, as above, but in a different, more office-oriented market space, face-to-face networking in a group situation might work well.

Networking groups

There are a myriad of networking groups available to join in every area. In one area alone over 20 general groups have been identified, including organizations like the Chamber of Commerce, CIPD local branches (Chartered Institute of Personnel Development), ICAEW (Institute of Chartered Accountants in England and Wales), CIM (Charted Institute of Marketing), BNI (Business Network International), BRE (Business Referral Exchange), local networking business groups, alumni groups for schools and universities, as well as many one-off networking groups and business exhibitions.

Many of them offer a speaker on a particular relevant topic and then a chance for networking. Some, like BRE, are formed specifically to help everyone sell for everyone else and actively promote referrals between members; others are much more low-key.

The challenge is not which one to join so much, but how to make best use of it and then not to spend so much time networking that you forget to make placements. Networking is a means to an end.

Everywhere can be networking territory of course, and having a recruiter mentality is helpful wherever you are, whatever you are doing. A recruiter mentality can be seen as an overwhelming interest in who people are and what they do.

CASE STUDY

Valerie Abl won a valuable contract for her team of four people with EMEA, a fast-expanding American software company that was moving into Europe. She then delivered an out-sourced recruitment service, some board development, the sourcing, recommendation and implementation of the new HR, and recruitment systems and interview training for all interviewers in the business. The contract was for 18 months and transitioned the business through to a new stage in its development.

Valerie met the Head of EMEA on a plane!

The message of this story is wherever you are, wherever you go, always find out something about people you meet. You never know how you may be able to help them. And, if you can't help them they will have appreciated your interest in them and will remember you.

A traditional source of candidates of course, often the least painful but equally the most expensive in terms of outgoing revenue is advertising, which we'll turn our thoughts to next.

Advertising

Defined as: Placing press, online or other media advertising to attract potential candidates to respond.

Ideal for: Large numbers of similar candidates. Brand building. Recruiting targeted groups of candidates, which a particular media reaches. High-profile roles. Roles where the applicants could come from a wide range of backgrounds. Roles that have to be made publicly available. Difficult location. Range of requirement over different departments. Gaining a broad choice of candidates. Role is urgent.

Poor choice: Scarce-skill specialist, identifiable roles better suited to a search.

Different mediums of advertising:

- Press, local, national and trade.
- Billboards (recruiter, McGregor Boyall uses billboards at Liverpool St station and law firm Halliwells uses boards in Manchester airport).
- Radio.

- Job centre advertising.
- Flyers.
- Job boards.
- Internal advertising – posters, intranet.

This is the easiest medium to throw money at, and it must be said that recruitment advertising in the print press has all but declined apart from senior roles in public sector high profile roles where the role needs to be seen to be advertised to a wide audience. If you want to brand build or attract scarce talent, it is best to work with one of the good recruitment advertising agencies to help you get your message across. Remember your core competence is recruiting, not advertising. However it may be that your advertising budget and strategy is determined for you, in which case you may still be responsible for placing your own job-board ads, or working with a client and the ad agency designing a client-paid ad.

The major growth area has been in online advertising, primarily through job boards, and that is set to continue.

CASE STUDY

The UK industry has developed from not existing before 1995 to being worth £300 million in the UK. It will continue to grow as companies adapt the way they look for employees and direct all advertising towards the recruitment area of their corporate website. There is an argument that if we see a down turn in the UK economy, it will drive more companies to save money and develop their recruitment strategies to attract candidates through the internet, as many large employers already do. PriceWaterhouseCoopers, for example, are the largest graduate employer in the UK, recruiting 1,000 graduates a year and recruiting them all via the web.

For the UK it will be another few years before employers 'en masse' have embraced recruiting online but it will happen and we have seen great strides in this area already. Candidates are becoming better educated and more sophisticated in finding and applying for jobs.

It's an industry that's barely a teenager. It's got a lot of growing to do.

David Hurst, Publisher, Onrec.com and *Online* recruitment magazine

Even when you are placing the smallest of job board ads, take trouble to consider what the key message is about your clients and how to attract your candidate. Use the AIDA idea at the beginning of this chapter and go back to what the key selling points of the role are. Consider the search terms that people might use to search the boards and make sure you incorporate them into your ad. If social workers are looking for a new job, what will they search under? If SAP BW contractors are looking for a new contract, what will they search under; and if secretaries want to work closer to home, what will they search under? SEO (Search Engine Optimization) and PPC (Pay per click) are becoming more sophisticated, and appearing in the top three of a Google, Yahoo, Bing or any other search engine's search is really important to stand out to the job seeker. Most consultancies and firms will use an SEO agency or expert to advise on how to develop content on their sites to get picked up by the search engine spiders. The more rich content and use of keywords and phrases you can build in to your site, the greater the chances of being at the top of the rankings. Most searches don't get past the first few entries and rarely past the first page.

CASE STUDY

Gerry Wyatt at graduate-jobs.com knows that the key to the success of his site is getting both the top quality and quantity of candidates onto the site to apply for the jobs they are advertising on behalf of their clients. Although not the largest of the graduate job boards, they have consistently maintained top place in the search engines through clever and enlightened use of copy on the site, and ensuring that it not only advertises jobs, it adds value through content too.

Finally, pay attention to obvious things like spelling and grammar, as you'll want not only to get the best response but also to portray your client in the best possible light. Finally, you can do no better than to follow Andrew Young, chairman of award-winning ThirtyThree, one of the leading recruitment advertising agencies, who has compiled his 10 top tips for advertisement design.

The 10 top tips for designing an advertisement

1 Identify quickly and clearly who you are trying to recruit. Different companies have different titles for the same role. Try to avoid internal company jargon and use titles or sub-headings that reflect what your ideal candidate is currently doing or aspires to be doing.

2 Include clear information on salary and location. It's what candidates most want to know. Being coy about it just suggests there is a problem, as well as wasting time with people who are not appropriate. If there are issues then why not confront them upfront and focus on other aspects of the role that make it attractive?

3 Keep it brief. The number of people who apply for jobs for which they are clearly not qualified shows that much of the detail in adverts is ignored. A job advert is only a snapshot, so concentrate on key objectives and essential requirements in the hope that they might actually sink in.

4 Avoid corporate hype. If every employer lived up to its promises, why do people move jobs so frequently? If you're going to make claims, back them up with facts and evidence that illustrate what those claims mean in day-to-day life. And don't be afraid to be honest about what's not perfect.

5 In defining candidate requirements, try to avoid generalizations that are difficult to measure. Most people think they have good 'interpersonal' skills and are 'team players'. These sorts of phrases are unlikely to stop people applying. Concentrate on the hard criteria in terms of education, experience and achievement that prove they have these qualities.

6 Use the second rather than third person, ie 'you' not 'the candidate'. Makes it sound more like you are interested in the reader as an individual.

7 Avoid long complicated sentences. People generally have short attention spans with advertising. Read what you've written out aloud. If it sounds long-winded it probably is.

8 Use a logical structure. There's nothing wrong with the traditional 'company, role, candidate' format.

9 Be clear about how you want people to respond and make sure contact details are prominent.

10 Try to reflect the personality of your company in the language you use and the design of the advert. Are you informal, creative and fun or traditional, serious and business focused? It's all about attracting the right kind of people.

Your brand will not only be communicated through how you advertise, but also through the way you deal with the response. It will not help your perception in the market if you pick off the 'good' candidates and ignore the rest. All advertising response needs to be dealt with appropriately. This is a good time to remember what it may be like to be a candidate who has perhaps spent all Sunday afternoon searching for a job and compiling a good application only to hear nothing back. Even if it is clear that your candidate has sent an application to every role in the paper at the touch of a button, at least they need a well-crafted rejection letter, thanking them for their time.

A further way job boards have developed is for more proactive candidates to place their CVs on the board with a view to being contacted by prospective employers or recruiters.

Job board CV searching

Defined as: Subscribing to the CV sections of the job boards appropriate to your business area, searching for candidates with the right skills and qualifications for your clients and contacting them directly, sometimes known as mining.

Ideal for: Roles you have now.

Poor choice: If you cannot call them quickly. If you want to stand out from the crowd it's also worth knowing that many other recruiters – including internal ones – will also be using the same route to market for active candidates. You are likely to get a better response as an internal recruiter. Agencies will need something very special and exciting to stand out, and external recruiters who want to offer a superior service and capability will not use this method much.

Your approach may be similar to finding a candidate on your database – except that as the candidate may not recognize your company name you will need to craft an introduction that provides a benefit to them from listening to you or calling you back. This is straightforward if you have a particular brief or requirement you are working on to tempt them with, but if you are generally interested in their skill set and feel that you would like to talk to them because your clients might be interested in them, say that too:

- 'My name is Joe Smith from XYZ Company – we specialize in recruiting part-qualified accountants into the oil and gas industries. I have a running brief from the top company in the field to recruit at your level to join their career development programme – their office also happens to be just down the road from you... but before I say too much more about it I'd like to find out more about you... Where are you in your search for a new role currently? What sort of role and company are you looking for?'

Or...

- 'My name is Joe Smith – I have your CV in front of me, which I have downloaded from X job board. I'd like to talk to you about an assignment I am handling at the moment – your skills and experience really caught my eye. Tell me, what you are you looking for?'

Whichever approach you choose, make sure there is a good reason for the person to speak to you or return your call. Bear in mind that at this point they are in control. Whilst you have their CV, clearly you need their agreement to do anything with it and they have not approached you for help, you have approached them.

It's also important with job board candidates you have approached (as opposed to ones who have responded to an advertisement) that you qualify them out on motivation. Bear in mind that there are a number of candidates placing their CVs on job boards who are testing the market. It involves them in little effort other than putting their CV online, and they can tell by the number of calls they get how many opportunities there might be out there for them and what the packages might be. This puts them in a stronger position with their own employers. It's a great service for candidates and there is no reason why you should not handle these candidates professionally and helpfully, as at some point of course they may well come back on to the market looking seriously for a new role. If you have been the one to take time over them and send them your contact details, it is likely they will contact you first next time – especially if you recommend they do so. However, it is equally important that you don't waste your client's time with candidates who have no intention of leaving their job and are just testing the water. Your role in candidate management is to assess that fine line between some intent and none.

Task

Choose six candidates to call from one of the job boards you subscribe to and, using your chosen approach strategy, go ahead and approach them and analyse what works for you and what doesn't, perfecting it until you get it right.

Assessing and sometimes developing motivation can be a crucial part of candidate management, and never more so than in our next strategy.

Headhunting

Definition: Identifying and approaching potential passive candidates for a client's role or for general roles within a specific client base.

Ideal for: Specialist roles where an identifiable skill or background is needed that may be rare. When a client wants to draw someone from a limited number of competitors. If the job is highly confidential. Senior roles at 'C' level. Finding passive candidates who are not in a competitive situation with other roles and consultancies. Roles guaranteed by a retainer. Clients with a poor reputation. No success with advertising or agencies.

Poor choice: For generalist roles where candidates are hard to identify, especially if non-retained. Increasingly, retainers are being used to identify generalist candidates who have a scarce skill set and who cannot be reached by other means – often a long, hard process but can be rewarding. High risk with no retainer. For low-level, non-business-critical roles, as cost is too high to justify.

It's important here to be clear what headhunting in this book means. This is not a book aimed specifically at the search sector of the recruitment industry so it is not our intention to advise in detail on how to run a fully retained executive search. However, there are some skills used by the search industry that general recruiters, whether operating in-house or externally, may find helpful. Increasingly contingent providers are using search as a key tool to differentiate themselves from their competitors. This works well if the agency works with a smaller number of clients and has a large pool of companies to search from. There is more of a challenge for a larger agency which may work with 75 per cent of its market and therefore cannot headhunt out of those companies. This section covers the development of some of the basic skills of a professional search consultant or headhunter, some of which can be woven into general recruitment consultancy skills. To be clear about the differences, we outline when you might choose to search, look at the process used to deliver it and suggest how a retained search might operate.

Headhunting skills

When you might choose to headhunt

In Chapter 8 on 'Client strategy' there are clear guidelines about when it would be a good idea to recommend a search strategy to your client and offer a retained proposal. Under certain circumstances it may be worthwhile offering a non-retained headhunting service to your client. This has to be a sound commercial decision on your part. It is not the purpose of this book to suggest that headhunting on a non-retained basis is a 'good idea'. The danger with offering a non-retained service is to devalue the search service. There are always going to be great differences in the quality of service offered by a non-retained search and a retained one. So long as clients are clear about the differences and are not promised one service and delivered another, a non-retained search may be a helpful service on occasion to a client.

It is also perfectly possible to headhunt candidates whom you may be aware of in your market, or have identified because you know you can place them. You may, as an internal recruiter, map your competitors and headhunt everyone in them, going to meet them for a chat over a coffee to begin to build relationships with them for the next time they are thinking of a move. Often the fact that you have contacted them and met up starts them thinking about the next move, assuming it's right for them. Of course you cannot make someone move jobs. It has to be their choice. What you can do is put opportunities in front of people (with whichever method works for you and your business), showing them the benefits of a potential role in a new company. They then have to make the decisions about how to progress.

CASE STUDY

Vicki Rogers was working in her first role since graduating with her 2:1 in business studies and was approached by one of the consultants at Morgan McKinley. She had not thought of moving but they said they had a range of roles that she might be interested in and why didn't she pop by for a coffee one lunchtime to discuss them. Would Tuesday or Friday suit her better this week? Vicki was intrigued and went to meet them – they outlined two roles, both of which she then decided to go to interview for. She was offered both but decided to accept a role with UBS Warburg. That role gave her a great springboard into a marketing role in the recruitment industry, which she was offered over and above 130 applicants. Vicki has moved away from marketing these days and looks after 'Class 3' in a primary school – it still brings its challenges.

Morgan McKinley's strategy of getting to know great people personally in their chosen markets without doubt paid off both for them and for their candidates. Recruitment is a service industry. If you are not letting people know about great opportunities in the market, you are not offering them a service. If you are not attracting great candidates for the clients you work with, you are not offering them a service.

Before you take on a search however it makes sense to qualify it.

Qualifying the 'searchable' role
Ensure that:

- You can identify the people who do the role.
- The role is business-critical (there will be an appreciable loss to the business if the business does not hire this person to time).
- You have an attractive proposition to put to people in their current role that offers some form of advancement.
- It's a permanent, valuable contract or interim role.
- You have an exclusive opportunity to fill the role.

CASE STUDY

Michael Hollobon is a senior search consultant with Tardis Group based in Sydney, a global executive search company specializing in the investment banking, environmental and pharmaceutical industries. He talks about a particularly gratifying search he completed:

> After the Sydney branch of a global investment bank had exhausted all local possibilities (in the Sydney market everyone knows everyone so it had not taken long), I was engaged to conduct a global search to find a head of its Equity Derivative Trading unit. We discussed the necessary skills and experience and pinpointed a number of key criteria that would be beneficial to have. My role then was to decide where such skills would be found, and who would most likely agree to relocate to Australia. Due to the heavy personal income taxes imposed on Australian residents, it was evident that the UK and USA markets would be the most fruitful. Taxation levels there are not too dissimilar, whereas the Asian market, for instance, enjoys far lower taxation. The search took some six months and I identified four suitable candidates – two from the UK, one from the United States and another surprisingly from Hong Kong.
>
> My pitch not only focused on the potential of the role – its seniority, its flexibility and the challenge; but considering it was mid-winter in the Northern Hemisphere, I also highlighted the benefits of the Australian climate, the wonderfully clean air and the family-friendly lifestyle that the candidates could enjoy. Therefore, my initial approach focused on the latter and then, once I had grabbed the candidates' attention, the benefits of the role.
>
> The approach was successful and my client interviewed all four candidates, one of whom was offered the post. Within three months he had joined the business and soon proved to be the bank's most successful hire of the year.

As Michael's case study illustrates the creativity that went into identifying where the right candidates might be located, both country and firm, was a strong contributor to the outcome of the successful search. We'll look at the process now from start to finish.

How a retained search operates

A retained search is when a client pays a retainer fee, usually a proportion of the final projected fee for the placement. This is paid at the beginning of the search process. A further proportion of the fee is then paid when an agreed number of candidates are submitted as part of a short list. The final fee is paid when the chosen candidate accepts an offer or starts. Clearly search firm's terms and *modus operandi* vary. Some firms now do not charge a short-list fee, but frontload the retainer, others progress candidates as they

FIGURE 9.1   The search process

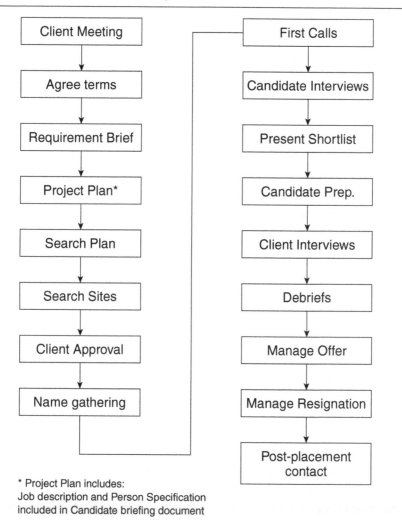

* Project Plan includes:
Job description and Person Specification
included in Candidate briefing document

find them rather than waiting to submit a short list, but in essence this is a retained search methodology.

The process (although it can vary from firm to firm and in consultation with the client) is shown in Figure 9.1.

How to conduct a search

Identifying the right people

The emergence of internet networking sites has made it easier to identify candidates but alongside this, firms themselves have made it harder with the emergence of a no-names policy. Successful knowledge management continues to be an important skill and to get a full list of potential candidates quite a bit of research will still need to be done.

The first step is to identify the companies you wish to search for people from – search sites – and the second is to gather the names of people to approach. Once you've exhausted the internet searching and networking sites here are some ideas about how to gather names:

- Read the trade press.
- Search the internet.
- Ask people you already know at the organizations you want to target.
- Ask your client.
- Ask your colleagues.
- Do a database search for people working in your search sites now or (even better) who used to work there recently and call them.
- Access an exhibition catalogue.
- Attend an event or conference.
- Ring your target companies and ask them – if the role is senior enough it will be in the public domain.
- Look on your target companies' websites – some firms have a real range of employees on there and some small firms have everyone in the business. Many companies will have directors.
- Join or access trade associations.
- Look in specific publications for your sector – *The Personnel Manager's Yearbook*, for example, and the lists of newly-qualified accountants when they are published.
- Access directories.
- Get each of your current candidates to recommend one person qualified for the role.
- And so on...

Once you have your list of target names it is time to plan your approach calls. Even the most experienced search consultants plan their calls before they make them. They also tend to choose first to contact a couple of people they are less sure about, so they don't make their first 'raw and unpractised' call to their top prospective candidate. It makes sense to block off a chunk of time to make the calls, just as it does when calling new clients. You'll get into the swing of it that way and make some progress on a project.

The best plan is to take the phone off the hook and to settle down with your plan and spend at least two hours, maybe a morning, on this particular project. It's more motivating that way as you'll both see some progress and be able to evaluate your calls as you go, making amendments where appropriate.

Planning your call

Many of the 'rules' in networking calls also apply to search. In the 30 seconds that you have to gain someone's attention, you need to deliver enough information to enable them to make a decision about speaking to you further, either now or later.

There are four stages in a search call:

1 Introduction and headline.
2 Approach.
3 Qualification of the candidate.
4 Close to move forward or gain referrals.

Retaining control in a call is all-important. Ultimately it will be your decision whether this candidate makes your interview short list. However, to get to that point you need to qualify them in or out. This will be harder to do if you lose control of the call.

Introduction and headline

This needs punch, great delivery and a compelling reason for the person to listen to you. Developing a headline works on the same principle as a newspaper or feed – you need to want to know more. Your introduction should simply be who you are – and needs to be relevant. Your introduction needs to be drawn from the role itself. Ask yourself – having asked your client – what the selling points of the role are. What is the one thing guaranteed to grab the attention of the person you are speaking to? You may need to alter this slightly depending upon who you are speaking to and how much you know about them.

Do's and Don'ts of search:

- Do...
  - Relax your voice.
  - Deliver your introduction and headline in a moderate pace with a low voice.
  - Match the pace of your delivery to theirs.
  - Use their name, but not to excess.
  - Consider standing up when making your first few calls to create energy in your voice.
  - Smile when making your calls to transmit warmth.
  - Ask lots of open questions.
  - Make it clear you are aware they are not 'on the market'.
  - Keep your client confidential until you have qualified them in or out.
- Don't...
  - Be over-familiar – ask someone how they are when you have never spoken to them before, for example.
  - Say you have the perfect role for them – even if you know them.

- Be too controlling. Do let the candidate ask questions when they want – it's a great sign of interest.
- Make calls when you have your mind on other things or you are unprepared.
- Push too hard – it may have the opposite effect. Lead rather than push.
- Miss an opportunity to close a great candidate down for a meeting.
- Forget to find out what they want before you sell back to them.
- Suggest that your prospect might be looking for a role!

Try this approach, rather as in networking:

> This is Joe Smith from XYZ. We are an international search firm/specialist ERP IT recruiter in financial markets/a finance recruiter – I work exclusively at director level/in emerging markets/with senior candidates in the care environment/in retail/in 'your market sector' [whatever that is]. Is now a good time to talk?

The key here is to sound professional – as with any call to any candidate – but here you need to stand out from the crowd. You also need to be relevant and compelling. This is not someone who needs a job remember – it's not even someone who is thinking about a job. It's also likely to be someone who is very busy and receives a range of search calls. Often the more senior people are, the more receptive they are to your calls – which may be why they are more senior!

Task

Design your approach and try it out over the phone with a colleague in the office to get some feedback before you call 'real' candidates. Get them to give you some practice handling objections as well!

Headline and approach

Deliver your headline followed smartly by your approach. This can be either a direct approach, an indirect approach or a hybrid approach.

Direct approach

You approach them directly as a potential candidate:

> I am retained by my client – a leading software company – to find an exceptional candidate to head up sales in EMEA. I'd like to tell you more about it. Does that sound like the sort of role you'd be interested in finding out more about?

> I am working on a search for a UK HR Director for a growing consultancy firm at the top of their field. Is now a good time to tell you more about the role?

- Advantages:
  - saves time;
  - establishes attitude of confidence;
  - clear about why you are calling.
- Disadvantages:
  - candidate can gain upper hand;
  - harder to probe immediately;
  - need some basic information to stay completely in control.

Indirect approach

This is when you ask for help with a role, rather than approach someone directly. It can be used in two ways: either when you do not know enough about someone to know whether they are right for, or interested in, the role; or when you genuinely want to use them as a source. If you are following the 'black book' principle outlined under the networking section, you should have a range of well-connected people in there who will act as sources for you.

This approach will sound like this:

You may remember coming to see my colleague Fred Jones about nine months ago about a senior sales role in a software house... We are now working on an assignment in XXX and wondered if we might ask your advice...

I am handling a search assignment to appoint a Head of Assessment Services. I'm wondering if you might be able to recommend some people qualified for that role that I should be speaking to – is now a good time to tell you a little about it?

- Advantages:
  - gives you a good 'get-out' clause and retains the upper hand;
  - less need to 'sell' at an early stage;
  - leaves it open for you to offer them the opportunity when qualified.
- Disadvantages:
  - can sound false if you are really making a direct approach;
  - takes longer because of softer style.

Hybrid approach

Combines the best of both potentially – or worst of both if done poorly!

I'm running a search project for a COO for a leading pharmaceutical company – I'd like to have a chat with you to see if it is something that might be of interest to you – and if not, perhaps you can point me in a different direction? My understanding is that you are Head of Operations for GlaxoSmithKline currently – is that right?

Great – how long have you been in that role?

My client is looking for someone who is interested in developing their career with a smaller firm but at a higher level – does that sound like something which may be of interest to you?

> OK good, so tell me something about the headline responsibilities in your current role...

Here you have moved on from 'telling them about the role' into asking questions about their role. It's an assumptive approach but will often work well.

When to tell the candidate whom you are recruiting for

Sometimes this will come up as a question at an early stage. And there is no right or wrong answer to this one – it depends! Some pointers:

- If the role is confidential – say the current role-holder is still in place, clearly you do not divulge until at least interview stage.
- If the role is in the public domain, so there may also be some advertising taking place and this is a multi-faceted attraction strategy, you can tell the candidate when you feel the time is right.
- Find out what they want before you reveal the company, so you can always position the company in the space that they inhabit.
- Sometimes the question, 'which company is it?' will come as an objection and you could handle that exactly as the suggestions made below for objection handling.

You'll need to see whether the candidate has potential or not; this will determine whether you want to 'acquire' the candidate this time for the role or whether you want to leave them with a return route at some point in the future.

As part of your preparation you'll have a few key qualification points, which might look like this (for more on qualifying your candidate see Chapter 6 on 'Candidate management'):

- Matches the essential skills on the person spec.
- Is at the right level in the organization.
- The role has some potential for improvement for them (role, personal circumstances, salary, career progression, company good for CV) or there is some motivation to move.
- Right salary bracket.
- Suits personal circumstances (location, travelling, unusual hours).
- Cultural fit.
- No warning bells.

You may start by signposting why you are going to ask some questions:

> Let's just explore the role a little more at this point to see whether it makes sense from both our perspectives to move the discussion to the next stage...
> The role has quite a high level of responsibility (drop a benefit, or incentive to keep listening in here)/needs a high level of qualifications/is hugely demanding/ an opportunity to really start something from the ground floor and make your own mark in the industry/is very high-profile within the group...

then move into questioning. Choose from:

- How many people report in to you currently?
- What level of P & L are you responsible for?
- What sort of package are you currently enjoying/earning?
- What sort of challenge/opportunity might tempt you to move at any point/in the future (saying 'at any point' or 'in the future' takes the pressure off someone that you're going to try and get them to move straight away)?
- A small point – but nonetheless important... How are you fixed for working in Central London?

At this stage you will need to have covered the essential skills and hiring criteria of the role and will have qualified the candidate in or out. Following the flow chart path then, you'll need to ask for a referral or 'turn them off' (reject them).

When to send a briefing document
Be discriminatory when sending a briefing document. If it only goes out to someone who has a genuine interest in the role, it is less likely to be passed around, protecting the client from direct applications or other consultancies.

A great way of being sure about this is only to send the document if a candidate shares his or her CV with you or commits to a meeting. Occasionally the request for a briefing document will be a 'fob-off', a reason to get rid of you, and will need to be handled as any other objection would be.

It may be by now that you have to reject the candidate. Wherever possible it is better to have them self-select themselves out of the process.

Turning your prospective candidate off
It's important here, as ever in recruiting, to maintain your candidate's self-esteem. Particularly as your candidate did not approach you, yet has been courteous enough to listen to you and consider an opportunity, leaving the conversation gracefully is as important as how you start it. If you cannot qualify them in for the role even though they are interested, you need to consider how you can agree between you that this is not the role for them, or the right time for a move. Ideally you will have them come to that conclusion, and there are various ways to help them to do so:

- Ask more questions that will preclude them from the role.
- Tell them where the mis-match occurs, and use the role and your client to take that decision.
- Say you have some concerns about whether this is the right role for them now... and ask them what their thoughts are. Often candidates will take the hint and agree – especially bearing in mind they are not on the market.

You could ask about the essential and desirable skills:

- Do you have an MBA from a top-five school?
- Have you taken a company to IPO?
- Have you headed up a Council before?
- or any other question that is a definite yes or no...

Suppose the answer is 'No'. You may then say:

> I'm sorry – whilst I recognize, and I'm sure you do, that it isn't always critical to success in the role, my client has been very clear they only want to see people with MBAs from top-five schools. I'm really sorry, as in all other respects you were perfect for the role. Can I come back to you at any point if my client changes that criterion or takes a different view?

This is also one of the reasons why you need to keep the identity of your client confidential at an early stage; you are able to turn your candidate off without him or her forming a negative view of your client – the candidate may be ideal for another role within the same client on another day.

You could simply take a direct approach:

> I sense that this will only be a sideways move for you at the moment, and bearing in mind you have been with your current firm less than two years it would not be my advice to think about this opportunity as your next move. I'd like to keep in touch however, as I will often have more senior roles I'd like to come back to you with – does that work for you?

If your candidate is not suitable and you have dealt well with this, it is now a good time to ask for a referral. Questions to try:

- Who else do you know who is qualified for this role?
- Who else in your market is making an impression currently?
- You said you used to work at XYZ – who was the COO there?
- Who else have you worked with in the past that you rated in this field?
- Who have you come up against recently when you've been pitching?
- What thoughts do you have about whom or where else I might try?

These questions help your candidate think; if we are asked a closed question our brains take the easiest way out – we say 'No'. If you ask someone a direct question, 'Who', it pre-supposes that they have an answer and our brains start to tackle the question. Questions also need to be assertive: if you sound like you don't much mind one way or another, people who are busy – as most of your prospective candidates will be – will take the easiest route out.

There are times when it's better not to ask for a referral – if a candidate is disappointed about not progressing for the role, it may be insensitive to immediately say, 'But whom else do you know?' There will be other occasions as well and you'll need to use your recruiter's finely tuned sense of judgement to identify these.

Handling objections

It would be optimistic to suggest that you are never going to encounter an objection from your prospective candidates or indeed clients, and this strategy can be applied to any objections you might come across. The general approach is:

1 Listen and acknowledge.

2 Discover whether this is a genuine objection.

3 Counter the objection.

4 Confirm you have done so.

For example...

Client objection: 'I'd like to see a role spec first...'
Listen and acknowledge: 'OK – sounds like you are potentially interested but you'd like to learn more about the role. Is that right?'
Counter and confirm: 'I'm very happy to send you a role spec at the point we agree it makes sense from both our viewpoints to meet up. Does that work for you?'
Or: 'I'd be very happy to exchange a role spec for your CV for example. What specific information can I give you at this point to help with your choice to move forward?' and following on... 'Does that work for you?'

Client objection: 'I'm happy where I am.'
Response: 'I absolutely respect that and it may be that at the end of our discussion we'll agree this isn't right for you and you may even point me in a different direction, but I'd welcome the opportunity to perhaps take some advice on this project – is there a better time to talk than now?

Client objection: 'I'm not sure it's enough of a package for me.'
    Here you'll need to isolate and discount the objection if possible:
    'OK – so if that were not a problem does the rest of the proposition sound of interest?'
    'Yes... OK let's look at the package...'
    'Are you happy that at this point the package need not necessarily preclude you from progressing?'
    'Yes'
    'Great – when can we get together?'

Closing for the next stage

At this point you will be closing for:

- Their CV. If asking for a CV, ask when they can get it to you. Agree you will give them a call if you have not received it to ensure it has not gone astray.

- A meeting. If you are closing for a meeting, offer two alternatives, or times, or places, or both. (If you are closing for a referral follow the practice below.)

- A referral. If you are closing for another conversation, agree a time rather than a broad-brush day/afternoon and make it clear you are diarising it.

- Another conversation. If you are closing for another conversation agree a time rather than a broad-brush day/afternoon and make it clear you are diarising to reduce the chances of missing them.

- A future contact. If closing for a future contact, let them know when you might plan to call them and send them an e-mail with your contact details on for future reference.

At the end of the conversation, make sure you end always on a good note. Be sure you have the candidate's home e-mail, personal mobile and home telephone number if possible, but a personal contact for them at least so if they move on your call has not been wasted and you can track them down another time. Remember to check you can go back to them with other roles of interest or for help with additional projects.

The last case study in this chapter encapsulates all that is possible in the world of candidate attraction and shows how a committed, combined approach of a recruiter (in this case a researcher and a consultant working as a close team) and a client can pay off big time! Rachel Riddington, at the time Head of Research at Erevena, the boutique technology search firm and now Research and Sourcing Manager at Betfair, tells how she and Director of Erevena Jon Irvine found a fantastic candidate for a regular client.

CASE STUDY

'We were retained to find a CTO to work with a pre-launch start up venture that was focused on a specific part of the entertainment industry. The client required a very particular set of skills both technologically and personally in terms of first, specific platform and mobile technical experience, second an individual who wanted to take a hands-on technical role in building a product; and finally a visionary and creative person. In reality there were probably about five individuals in EMEA that could do this role. It was important to have a fantastic brief and get the pitch perfect before approaching.

This we did, and whilst we ended up with a solid short list at interview with the client, we were still keen to get hold of an individual who was running the entertainment platform for one of the top Software Vendors globally. On paper he looked absolutely perfect. When we finally managed to touch base with this candidate it transpired that he was serving his notice, and was due to start a new role as CTO of the investment arm of a leading bank.

Clearly we could barely believe it. The timing was hideous, but the researcher still had an in-depth conversation on the basis of the individual being a useful contact – and she would never close any doors. During this conversation she also established that he was, indeed, a perfect match.

She also established his desire for a role that would enable him to really be hands on, take a product and build it in a market of interest. Knowing that the role with the investment bank would be strategic rather than hands on, Rachel convinced him it would be worth having a chat with Jon, whom he agreed to meet at a station on his way home.

The process then continued with the consultant, and then the client, both meeting with this candidate and being clear he was the ideal person for the role and streets ahead of anyone else they had identified, even though all of those were possible to recruit.

We were however unable to set up the final stages of the interview process until the candidate's first week in his new role, as the candidate, an honourable sort of chap, having started with his new firm decided that he should not pursue our opportunity and initially refused all contact. At the time this seemed a disaster, and indeed then appeared so for about a week.

All three of us chased him but then left the candidate with some space and trusted the opportunity was right enough to turn this round. Sure enough, by the end of the week he came back to us as he realized that the opportunity we were pursuing him for fitted his career aspirations far more closely than the role he had taken.

With the help of the client we were able to ensure finishing the interview process and getting an offer out to him within the week to enable him to resign in his second week. I cannot tell you how pleased we all were.'

That's a fantastic story to end this chapter on as it shows how, with a little determination it is possible to find the right candidate for your client, and the right job for your candidate but it may take more than a little effort from time to time.

There are, as we have identified, a huge range of ways to attract candidates and you'll need to decide which is right for which circumstance, which client and which role. One thing is for sure; that candidate attraction in any candidate-short market is a certain competitive advantage, and the capacity to both attract and manage candidates to best effect will mean you can deliver a great service to your clients.

An industry success story who noticed an opportunity in the market to build an impressive business is Miles Hunt.

Industry profile – Miles Hunt

Profile for Miles Hunt, Chief Executive Empresaria Group plc

Born: Sheffield

Educated: Read Law at Reading followed by the College of Law and then completed an MBA at Warwick some five years later

Early career: Trained as a solicitor but moved into commercial management which in true entrepreneurial spirit led him to spot a gap in the market for a procurement oursourcing business which he grew to 20 people and sold in 1999.

He founded Empresaria in 1996 – swiftly following on from his MBA – as a specialist staffing company with initial investment of £300,000. This initial investment achieved peak market capitalization of £70 million in 2007. He was also a founder Director of Tribal Group in early 2000, only departing when Empresaria went to IPO. Most of Empresaria's growth has been organic. Miles was an early adopter of a global model of recruitment focusing on emerging and developing staffing markets and is now operating across 18 countries, a strategy which has clearly paid dividends as the UK market continues to struggle.

Miles left Empresaria in 2011 but says he has "a few ideas in the pipeline". Whatever they are it seems likely they will be a huge success!

Key advice for recruiters:

- Take control of your career; identify what you want to achieve and work backwards from that point; ideally go against the flow and do something different.

- Look after your reputation, a good one takes hard sustained work and effort and once lost is hard to recover.

One thing you should always do: Ask yourself: what have I learned today and what can I improve tomorrow?

One thing you should never do: Never assume you know everything – this applies just as well to recruitment leaders as recruiters.

Still to achieve: I will never tire of seeing professional and financial success around me, either personally or through the people I'm working with.

Interests outside work: I love experiencing other cultures so get to do this with so much frequent travelling – I speak Spanish and have a particular interest and affinity with South America. I also study history – it's fascinating how it has a habit of repeating itself.

Miles is a great example of a strategic thinker who has been successful by analysing a market, understanding people and what makes them successful, and marrying the two to create a fabulously successful business by anyone's standards, let alone the recruitment industry's.

Industry profile – Tara Ricks

Profile for Tara Ricks – MD of Randstad Financial and Professional

Born: Essex

Educated: A Levels – Economics, English and Maths

Early career: When Tara started with Morgan Stanley there were less than 300 people in the UK. It was just after Big Bang and now there are over 10,000. She started in banking operations and then went on to the trading floor in the Japanese convertible bond department. Tara then met Hugh Joslin through a friend. Joslin Rowe (which has recently changed its name to Randstad Financial and Professional) was just six people. Hugh Joslin wanted to start growing and Tara immediately saw the opportunity with the explosion of the market. So that's where her career in recruitment all started, moving through manager then Director to MD. The business was then taken over by Vedior, then Randstad, and then took over a number of other Randstad businesses – so it has been non-stop in terms of change – a great experience. Tara sees her current role as a great opportunity to work at a senior level in a large corporate organization.

Key advice for recruiters: The things you'll need are resilience and tenacity. Landscapes in the market are changing and these key attributes are critical... and then it's relationships, relationships and relationships.

One thing you should always do: Listen to candidates and clients, and embrace technology but don't hide behind it.

One thing you should never do: Don't stop using the telephone or meeting with people – never rely on e-mail.

Still to achieve: Having come through our recent re-brand bringing five businesses together, I want us to be the true market leader in professional services recruitment in the UK.

Interests outside work: My seven year old daughter and all that goes with her and her life... seems to take up extraordinary amounts of time!

Tara is a fantastic role model for recruiters today just coming into the industry. Her career path really shows where hard work, dedication and a high level of flair can take you; to running your own business having managed a significant change programme as well. It also shows the range of opportunities available in the industry from joining a small start-up to working for one of the world's largest HR services companies, or if you're like Tara – both of the above and quite a bit along the way.

AFTERWORD

The war for talent has continued to intensify and globalize, the impact of which has been softened or slowed a little by the economic struggles of the western economies but equally buoyed up by the growth in emerging markets. The continued development of the internet and social networking has made data and access to it easy and transparent; this has conversely resulted in the actual acquisition of that talent becoming more difficult than ever. High calibre candidates, either permanent or interim, have the choice and can easily be well informed about potential employers. In order to add real value to both their client and candidates, recruiters need to be infinitely knowledgeable, superbly well resourced and very highly skilled with a real understanding and interest in the careers of both their candidates and their clients. Recruitment is shifting from a more transactional base to a highly relationship-driven and strategic one.

Whether you are new to the recruitment profession, an experienced consultant eager to maintain and improve your skills or indeed an internal corporate recruiter keen to fully understand the process and create more rounded relationships with your suppliers, we, the authors, hope that this book will continue to be your guide to best practice and success throughout your working life.

Recruitment can be a fantastic career choice for those who are intelligent, methodical and driven. Highly successful recruiters have the competencies and transferable skills that would make them effective in numerous roles, but then why would they choose anything else?

BIBLIOGRAPHY

Allen, D (2001) *Getting Things Done: The Art of Stress-free Productivity*, Piatkus Books, London

BBC (2008) *What Britain Earns*, BBC2, 9 January

Buckingham, M and Coffman, C (2001) *First, Break All the Rules: What the world's greatest managers do differently*, Simon & Schuster, London

Ciett (2007) Presentation by Ciett Managing Director Denis Pennel, London, 2 May

Covey, S (1989) *The Seven Habits of Highly Effective People*, Fireside, New York

Forster, M (2000) *Get Everything Done and Still Have Time to Play*, Hodder and Stoughton, London

Glasser, W (1998) *Choice Theory: A new psychology of personal freedom*, HarperCollins, New York

Herzberg, F (1959) *The Motivation to Work*, John Wiley, New York

Karinthy, F (1929) Chains, in *Everything is Different*, F Karinthy, Budapest (out of print)

Kolb, D and Fry, R (1975) Towards an Applied Theory of Experimental Learning, in *Theories of Group Processes*, C L Cooper (ed), John Wiley, London

Kotler, P (1980) *Marketing Management: Analysis, planning and control*, Prentice/Hall, London

Lindenfield, G and Lindenfield, S (2005) *Confident Networking for Career Success and Satisfaction*, Piatkus Books, London

Maslow, A (1943) A theory of human motivation, *Psychological Review*, 50, pp 370–96

Timperley, J (2002) *Network Your Way to Success: Discover the secrets of the world's top connectors*, Piatkus Books, London

Travers, J and Milgram, S (1969) An experimental study of the small world problem, *Sociometry*, 32 (4), pp 425–43

Warwick Institute for Employment Research (nd) *Working Futures from 2004 to 2014*, available online at http://www2.warwick.ac.uk/fac/soc/ier/research/current/wf/ (downloaded 3 September 2008)

INDEX

NB page numbers in *italics* indicate a figure or table in the text